石油科技英语系列教程

丛书主编 ◎ 吴松林　江淑娟

Economy of Oil Resource Countries

石油资源国经济

姚坤明　苏亚杰　唐俊莉　惠良虹 ◎ 编

石油工业出版社

内 容 提 要

本书是石油资源国经济相关知识的英语学习教程,遵循英语语言能力与经济背景知识相结合的原则,共分七个单元:石油与经济、石油工业的现状、石油工业的发展、石油政治经济、石油监管、石油基金、石油运输,分别介绍了石油生产国家与地区的经济发展情况、制约因素以及石油对于经济影响的相关知识。

本书适合石油相关专业的师生和石油系统员工学习石油科技英语之用。

图书在版编目(CIP)数据

石油资源国经济/姚坤明等编.
北京:石油工业出版社,2014.8
(石油科技英语系列教程)
ISBN 978 - 7 - 5183 - 0274 - 1

Ⅰ. 石…
Ⅱ. 姚…
Ⅲ. 石油经济 - 英语 - 教材
Ⅳ. H31

中国版本图书馆 CIP 数据核字(2014)第 143013 号

出版发行:石油工业出版社
　　　　(北京安定门外安华里 2 区 1 号　100011)
　　　　网　　址:http://pip.cnpc.com.cn
　　　　编辑部:(010)64523574　发行部:(010)64523620
经　　销:全国新华书店
印　　刷:北京中石油彩色印刷有限责任公司

2014 年 8 月第 1 版　2014 年 8 月第 1 次印刷
787×1092 毫米　开本:1/16　印张:18.75
字数:340 千字

定价:48.00 元
(如出现印装质量问题,我社发行部负责调换)

《石油科技英语系列教程》
编 委 会

前　言

　　全球石油资源分布、生产及消费三者间存在着严重的地区失衡,中东和亚太是失衡最严重的地区,中东地区严重供过于求,亚太地区严重供不应求。因此能源行业出现了全球化发展趋势,能源国际间的交流与合作日益密切。为保证中国能源安全,中国石油和石化行业的国际化和本土化发展势在必行。中国油气企业正在积极进行海外业务拓展,了解资源地区的文化背景、经济发展状况、能源开发政策以及掌握其石油地质结构、油气成藏条件、开发和炼制技术等,将有利于我们对资源地区的油气开发和炼制,更有力地支持中国经济的快速发展。

　　自 1993 年起,为了满足石油院校和石油职工专业英语教材的严重匮乏,丛书主编陆续出版了系列专业石油英语教科书,积累了一定的编写经验、培训经验和图书项目导向经验。20 年过去了,石油行业也发生了巨大的变化,新油气资源不断发现,开采与炼制等技术不断更新,海外合作区域也不断拓宽。为了适应新形势,我们通过不懈的技术努力,在石油工业出版社的大力支持和协调下,开始编写一套更大规模的《石油科技英语系统教程》,既包括石油上、中、下游生产技术,也包括世界主要石油资源国的经济、贸易和文化等,目的是为读者奠定走向世界石油领域的语言基础。

　　我们深感责任重大,从中国石油大学、东北大学、东北石油大学、西安石油大学及各油田石油地质研究院、设计院等单位聘请有关专家学者,确定编写体例,搜集资料。在选材上,注重内容的系统性,争取覆盖本领域主要内容;语言方面,注意遴选突出科技英语语言特点的语段和篇章,并对语言使用方法作详尽解释,以英语基础知识和基本技能的培养为主。为降低学习难度,为每篇课文还配写了汉语译文,以提高学生的石油科技英语阅读、翻译及写作能力。

　　《石油资源国经济》分册遵循英语语言能力与经济背景知识相结合的原则,在课文的选材上,注意了以下四个方面:(1)注意英语基础知识和基本技能的培养;(2)对于与石油资源国经济相关的知识进行介绍,使学生掌握石油资源国经济的相关英语知识及文化背景;(3)培养和提高学生的英语阅读与翻译能力;(4)为进一步进行相关专业学习打下基础。

本书共分七个单元:石油与经济、石油工业的现状、石油工业的发展、石油政治经济、石油监管、石油基金、石油运输,分别介绍了石油生产国家与地区的经济发展情况、制约因素以及石油对于经济影响的相关知识。每一单元内,为了能够让学习者更好地掌握课文内容,均列出导读、相关的专业词汇及词组翻译、重点句子讲解,并跟进与重点内容相关的问题,读者在回答问题的同时,可以巩固对课文的理解,进而掌握相关经济背景知识。

本书在强调石油资源国经济的同时,也兼顾了石油系统出国人员对于当地经济状况、环境因素等的了解,如自然资源财富和较差的经济发展、全球视角下的非洲石油和天然气资源地位、英美在中东的主要外交政策、美国的石油管道运输等。

为降低学习的难度,本书对文化背景中所涉及的专业词汇尽可能地作了详细的介绍。

由于作者水平有限,书中内容涉及面较广,可供学习、参考、借鉴的资料不多,所以书中难免出现不足之处,敬请专家和读者批评指正。

丛书主编:吴松林　江淑娟

2014 年 3 月

Contents

Chapter 1　Oil and Economy

1.1　Natural Resource Wealth and Poor Economic Development

⌸ Guidance to Reading

The resource curse literature focuses on the tendency of natural resource abundant countries to suffer from low economic growth and disappointing development outcomes. Dutch Disease theory further highlights the need to integrate economic and political explanations into the analysis of resource exporters. Despite the common Dutch Disease experience, many critics have argued that this ailment affects developed economies far more than it affects under – developed ones and that its effects vary greatly by country.

⌸ Text

The oldest branch of the resource **curse** literature focuses on the tendency of natural resource **abundant** countries to suffer from low economic growth and disappointing development outcomes. Latin American economists Hans Singer and Raul Prebisch were two of the first scholars to address the issue. They argued that primary commodity exporters suffer declining terms of trade over the long run. Prices for commodity exports on the world market will, they **claimed**, fall relative to prices for **manufactured** goods, leaving commodity exporters with balance of payment problems and slow economic growth. Evidence to support their claim has proven mixed, with some studies showing declines and others showing steadier terms of trade. Cuddington and Wei, for instance, found no support for the Prebisch – Singer **hypothesis** in a **statistical** analysis. Sapsford and Balasubramanyan, on the other hand, found evidence to support Prebisch and Singer. Since the 1980s, however, terms of trade have declined worldwide for primary commodities and greater consensus has arisen that, at least for this time period, declining terms of trade have presented a problem for many countries. While declining terms of trade have not yet affected Equatorial

Guinea's oil industry, the economy is becoming **centered around** oil production to such a degree that future declines in the terms of trade would prove **devastating** to the Equato – Guinean economy.

Economists have argued that natural resource wealth may have other **negative** affects on economies. Some have **suspected** that rapid fluctuations in commodity markets might make commodity – dependent economies especially **prone** to **boom and bust cycles** and **discourage** private investment. In volatile markets, such as oil, this may prove especially problematic. We will have to wait for the next fluctuation in oil prices, however, to see if this will affect Equatorial Guinea in any meaningful way, but every indication suggests that a dramatic reduction in oil prices would devastate the country's economy, as ninety percent of all exports come from oil. The very volatile nature of oil markets since 1971 suggests that future fluctuations are likely and that they may prove dangerous for Equatorial Guinea in the future unless the country's leaders can adopt effective policies to **counter** these effects.

Another aspect of resource – led development that has received scholarly attention addresses the **minimal linkages** between the booming sector and the rest of the economy. So far this problem has **bedeviled** Equatorial Guinea greatly. Since most of the inputs needed for the oil industry come from abroad, **indigenous** industry has not benefited from the boom, and even the service industry relies mostly on imports. The oil industry in Equatorial Guinea remains, essentially, an **enclave** with little impact on the rest of the economy. If enclave economies properly invest their resource rents in other parts of the economy as well as in infrastructure and human development, however, they can create growth in other sectors or, improve the quality of health and education services. Theoretically, Equatorial Guinea's **enormous** per – capita oil revenues should make either of these options far easier than in countries with much lower per – capita resource exports. Equatorial Guinea, however, like most oil producers, has failed to act in this direction, leaving the lack of linkages between the oil and non – oil sectors as a fundamental economic problem for the country.

The most well – known and best – studied **variant** of the resource curse literature, Dutch Disease theory, further highlights the need to **integrate** economic and political explanations into the analysis of resource exporters. The Dutch

Disease gets its name from the effects of oil discoveries on the economy of the Netherlands in the 1960s and 1970s. The newfound oil created an export boom, but the domestic economy soon suffered from **inflation** and a decline in manufacturing exports that led to lower economic growth and rising unemployment. The oil boom of the 1970s and 1980s produced similar outcomes in countries as varied as Saudi Arabia, Nigeria, and Mexico. This seemingly **paradoxical** phenomenon **occurs** when the export boom leads to inflation and a **consequent appreciation** of the real exchange rate. This makes domestic producers in fields other than the commodity sector less competitive and, **hence**, less profitable. This decline in the strength of other sectors in the economy is the **crux** of the Dutch Disease.

Corde and Neary have found **ample** support for the hypotheses of Dutch Disease in their theoretical analyses. Other studies confirm the influence of Dutch Disease on economic outcomes **empirically**. In a comprehensive statistical study, Sachs and Warner examine ninety – seven countries over a nineteen – year period and show that states with a high ratio of natural resource exports to GDP in 1971 had unusually slow growth rates between 1971 and 1989. They explain this phenomenon largely through a Dutch Disease effect. Case studies also provide ample support for Dutch Disease. Gelb, for instance, documents six cases of Dutch Disease: Algeria, Ecuador, Indonesia, Nigeria, Trinidad and Tobago, and Venezuela. One of his case studies shows how Nigeria suffered from an extreme instance of the "Disease" in the 1980s. Spikes in oil prices in 1973 – 1974 and 1979 – 1980 led to a large oil **windfall** for the government, but this windfall and its **concomitant** spending increases spurred inflation, an exchange rate **hike** and, consequently, a ninety percent decline in the non – mining sector. Gabon, Equatorial Guinea's neighbor in the Gulf of Guinea, has also suffered from Dutch Disease. While the country has developed a prosperous oil industry, other sectors of the economy, most notably agriculture, have **crumbled** while inequality and poverty persist. Economic growth has **stagnated**. The rapidly approaching end to the country's oil reserves has prompted many to fear almost total economic collapse in the near future unless new reserves are found.

Despite the common Dutch Disease experience, many critics have argued that this **ailment** affects developed economies far more than it affects under – developed ones and that its effects vary greatly by country. Benjamin et al. , for instance, show that in Cameroon Dutch Disease affected agriculture but not manufacturing. Ross further argues that **thoughtful** policies can **counteract** most Dutch Disease effects. In the words of Terry Karl, "The Dutch Disease is not automatic. The **extent** to which it takes effect is largely the result of decision – making in the public **realm**." Furthermore, as Chaudhry points out, the **pursuit** of substantively different **sectoral** and industrial strategies in different oil producers "**belies** the uniform outcomes **posited** by the Dutch Disease". Some countries, including Iraq, Malaysia, Iran and Algeria, have "countered the pressures against investment in **tradeables** by **initiating** industrialization programs".

Words and Expressions

curse	诅咒,咒骂
abundant	丰富的,充裕的
claim	主张,声称,断言
manufacture	制造,生产
hypothesis	假说,假设,前提,猜测 hypotheses (pl.)
statistical	统计的,统计学的
devastate	毁坏,使荒芜,使震惊
negative	否定的,消极的,负面的
suspect	怀疑,猜想
prone	易于……的,有……倾向的
discourage	阻碍
counter	反对,反击
minimal	最小的,最低限度的
linkage	联系,连合,连锁,结合
bedevil	搞糟,搅扰;使苦恼
indigenous	土生土长的,本地的,天生的
enclave	飞地(较大区域内一小块不同民族或人群的聚居地),被包围的领土
enormous	巨大的,庞大的
variant	变体
integrate	整合,结合
inflation	通货膨胀

paradoxical	似是而非的,矛盾的
occur	发生,存在,出现
consequent	作为结果的,随之发生的,合乎逻辑的
appreciation	增值
hence	因此,从此以后
crux	关键,难题
ample	丰富的,充足的
empirically	经验主义地
windfall	风吹落的果实,意外的收获,侥幸所得
concomitant	相伴的,附随的,共存的
hike	提高
crumble	崩溃,弄碎,破灭
stagnate	停止,停滞不前,不景气
ailment	小病,疾病
thoughtful	深思的
counteract	抵制,清除,中和,对抗
extent	广度,宽度,长度,大小,范围,程度
realm	领域
pursuit	追求,追赶
sectoral	(尤指一国经济)领域的
belie	掩饰,与……不符,使……失望
posit	安置,假定
tradeable	可交换的
initiate	开始,创始

Phrases and Expressions

center around	围绕,以……为中心

Proper Names

boom and bust cycles	经济繁荣与萧条的交替循环

Language Focus

1. Prices for commodity exports on the world market will, they claimed, fall relative to prices for manufactured goods, leaving commodity exporters with

balance of payment problems and slow economic growth.

（参考译文：他们声称，世界市场上出口商品的价格相对于制成品的价格下降了，使商品出口国出现了支付和经济增长放缓之间的平衡问题。）

本句中 they claimed 为插入语；for commodity exports on the world market 为 price 的后置定语；主语 price，谓语 will fall；relative to... 进行比较，为状语；随后的 leaving... 分词短语为结果状语，修饰全句。

2. Since the 1980s, however, terms of trade have declined worldwide for primary commodities and greater consensus has arisen that, at least for this time period, declining terms of trade have presented a problem for many countries.

（参考译文：然而，20世纪80年代以来，全球主要商品的贸易条件恶化了，更多共识产生了：至少在这段时间内，贸易条件恶化使许多国家出现了问题。）

本句中 terms of trade have declined... 与 declining terms of trade have presented... 为并列分句。

3. Some have suspected that rapid fluctuations in commodity markets might make commodity – dependent economies especially prone to boom and bust cycles and discourage private investment.

（参考译文：有些人怀疑，商品市场的快速波动可能使依赖商品的经济体容易出现繁荣萧条周期，阻碍私人投资。）

本句基本结构为：might make... and discourage...；其中 prone to sth. / to do sth. 易于……，有……倾向。

4. The very volatile nature of oil markets since 1971 suggests that future fluctuations are likely and that they may prove dangerous for Equatorial Guinea in the future unless the country's leaders can adopt effective policies to counter these effects.

（参考译文：自1971年以来石油市场的极不稳定性表明，石油价格未来的波动是可能的，而且它们可能对未来的赤道几内亚很危险，除非该国的领导人可以采取有效的政策来抵御这些影响。）

本句中 and 连接的两个 that 从句为宾语从句；后者中有 unless 引导的条件状语从句。

5. ... the pursuit of substantively different sectoral and industrial strategies in different oil producers "belies the uniform outcomes posited by the Dutch Disease".

（参考译文：各石油生产国的不同性质的部门战略和工业战略都是为了

“掩盖‘荷兰病’假定的相同结果”。)

本句中 the pursuit 为主语;谓语 belies,宾语 the uniform outcomes;分词短语 posited by the Dutch Disease 为后置定语,修饰 the uniform outcomes。

Reinforced Learning

Ⅰ. **Answer the following questions for a comprehension of the text.**

1. What does the oldest branch of the resource curse literature emphasize?

2. What would prove devastating to the Equato – Guinean economy?

3. What does Dutch Disease theory stress?

4. What do Sachs and Warner' examinations conclude?

5. Between the impact on developed economy and undeveloped economy of Dutch disease, which one is greater?

Ⅱ. **Multiple choice:choose the correct one from the alternative answers to give the exact meaning of the words.**

1. The oldest branch of the resource curse literature focuses on the tendency of natural resource abundant countries to suffer from low economic growth and disappointing development outcomes.

A. scarce　　　B. rich　　　C. various　　　D. exhaustive

2. Prices for commodity exports on the world market will, they claimed, fall relative to prices for manufactured goods.

A. processed　B. advertised　C. man – made　D. produced

3. Some have suspected that rapid fluctuations in commodity markets might make commodity – dependent economies especially prone to boom and bust cycles and discourage private investment.

A. delay　　　B. speculate on C. stimulate　　D. prevent

4. The country's leaders can adopt effective policies to counter these effects.

A. achieve　　　　　　B. enhance

C. ruin　　　　　　　D. lessen or counteract

5. So far this problem has bedeviled Equatorial Guinea greatly.

A. puzzled　　　B. relieved　　C. arisen　　　D. worsened

6. Equatorial Guinea's enormous per – capita oil revenues should make either of these options far easier than in countries with much lower per – capita

resource exports.

    A. national   B. regional   C. large   D. rich

    7. Corde and Neary have found ample support for the hypotheses of Dutch Disease in their theoretical analyses.

    A. sufficient   B. insufficient   C. enthusiastic   D. consistent

    8. Economic growth has stagnated.

    A. decreased   B. been staggering

    C. stood   D. been feeble

    9. Ross further argues that thoughtful policies can counteract most Dutch Disease effects.

    A. positive   B. considerate   C. negative   D. persistent

    10. Some countries have countered the pressures against investment in tradeables by initiating industrialization programs.

    A. imitating   B. coordinating C. undertaking   D. starting up

Ⅲ. Multiple choice：read the four suggested translations and choose the best answer.

    1. Economists have argued that natural resource wealth may have other negative affects on economies.

    A. 主导性的   B. 片面的   C. 消极的   D. 积极的

    2. The domestic economy soon suffered from inflation and a decline in manufacturing exports that led to lower economic growth and rising unemployment.

    A. 重创   B. 萧条   C. 破坏   D. 通货膨胀

    3. This seemingly paradoxical phenomenon occurs when the export boom leads to inflation and a consequent appreciation of the real exchange rate.

    A. 连续的   B. 随之发生的

    C. 按次序的   D. 间接的

    4. This ailment affects developed economies far more than it affects under–developed ones.

    A. 病痛   B. 隐藏   C. 缩短   D. 措施

    5. The extent to which is takes effect is largely the result of decision–making in the public realm.

    A. 事业   B. 场所   C. 工程   D. 领域

Ⅳ. Put the following sentences into Chinese.

1. They argued that primary commodity exporters suffer declining terms of trade over the long run.

2. The newfound oil created an export boom, but the domestic economy soon suffered from inflation and a decline in manufacturing exports that led to lower economic growth and rising unemployment.

3. Some have suspected that rapid fluctuations in commodity markets might make commodity – dependent economies especially prone to boom and bust cycles and discourage private investment.

4. Since most of the inputs needed for the oil industry come from abroad, indigenous industry has not benefited from the boom, and even the service industry relies mostly on imports.

5. Despite the common Dutch Disease experience, many critics have argued that this ailment affects developed economies far more than it affects under – developed ones and that its effects vary greatly by country.

V. Put the following paragraphs into Chinese.

1. In economics, the Dutch disease is a concept that explains the apparent relationship between the increase in exploitation of natural resources and a decline in the manufacturing sector. The mechanism is that an increase in revenues from natural resources (or inflows of foreign aid) will make a given nation's currency stronger compared to that of other nations in an exchange rate, resulting in the nation's other exports becoming more expensive for other countries to buy, making the manufacturing sector less competitive. While it most often refers to natural resource discovery, it can also refer to "any development that results in a large inflow of foreign currency, including a sharp surge (激增) in natural resource prices, foreign assistance, and foreign direct investment".

2. It is rather difficult to definitively say that a country has Dutch Disease because it is difficult to prove the relationship between an increase in natural resource revenues, the real – exchange rate, and a decline in the lagging (滞后的) sector. There are a number of different things that could be causing this appreciation (增值) of the real exchange rate.

1.2 High Oil Prices and Economic Development in Africa

🔲 Guidance to Reading

For the median oil – importing countries in Africa, cumulative output loss resulting from a doubling in the price of oil can be as large as 23 percent in the past five years. However, Africa as a whole has in recent years been enjoying gains from macroeconomic management. This text analyzes in detail the challenges and opportunities of different countries and regions in Africa.

🔲 Text

High oil prices can have very harmful effects on the economy of African oil – importing countries, especially those that are heavily debt – burdened. They lead to a decrease in **output** and consumption, and to a worsening of the net foreign asset position. For the median oil – importing country, the five – year **cumulative** output loss resulting from a doubling in the price of oil can be as large as 23 percent under a **fixed exchange rate regime**, as per the model applied. However, this **recessionary** effect can be **cushioned** through government **intervention** in of shocks, such as productivity shocks, **monetary – policy** shocks, and world – interest – rate shocks.

Africa as a whole has in recent years been enjoying gains from **macroeconomic management**, improved political stability and governance, easing of regional conflicts, strengthening of regional economic blocks, and increased agricultural, mineral, and oil production. Before the financial crisis, many African economies were moving towards fast and steady economic growth. Their performance over 1995 – 2007 **reversed** the collapses over 1975 – 1985 and the **stagnations** over 1985 – 1995. And, for the first time in three decades, African economies were growing at the same rate as the rest of the world economies. The following is about the challenges and problems which main Africa countries have to face.

Net Oil – Importing Countries in Africa

High oil and gas prices have a dramatic impact on net oil – importing countries (NOICs) in Africa. High commodity prices have already been a motive for

riots and demonstrations in many African countries (for example, in Mozambique on February 5, 2008). The main reason for the public outcry is the more than 50 percent rise in public transport costs as a consequence of the increase in the pump prices for diesel and petrol. The rise in the pump price of fuel results in an increase in the general cost of living. The **scenario** is even worse for poor **households** that depend on **kerosene** for lighting and cooking.

Coping with high oil prices, worsened by lack of resources to establish **stabilization** mechanisms and price smoothing, is one of the major challenges facing NOICs. Most countries have opted to either partially or completely pass through the international oil prices; Net Oil – Exporting Countries in Africa with others have introduced **subsidies**. All these mechanisms have proved inefficient in coping with high oil prices in Africa.

Managing Oil Wealth

Oil and gas **exploitation** have caused major economic, social, political, and environmental problems in some net oil – exporting countries. Oil wealth has not supported sustained economic growth and development in most countries. The major challenge is to translate oil wealth into **sustained** economic growth and development.

Particular challenges faced by oil – rich countries include weak governance, low accountability, low capacity for proper budgeting and accounting, and lack of transparency in the oil and gas industry. These lead to high investment uncertainty, and, in some cases, may fuel social conflicts. **The Extractive Industries Transparency Initiative** (EITI) offers an opportunity to address the issue of transparency.

Equitable allocation of the **proceeds** from oil is the key to reducing the risk of social tensions in oil – rich countries. In Nigeria, for example, the federal government passes 13 percent of oil revenues to the nine oil – producing states, primarily to reduce conflict and promote local development. Although this may not fully satisfy the local stakeholders in the Niger Delta, it is a step in the right direction.

Managing Oil Wealth in Nigeria: The Challenge in the Niger Delta

The struggle for the control of oil wealth **dates back to** the 1960s. At stake has been the **quintessential** property rights issue: who owns the oil resources in the Niger Delta? Through legislative **enactments**, most notably the Land Use

Decree of 1978, the federal government has **vested** the ownership of all land in the country to itself, including the minerals, **ores**, oil and gas resources found in them. This has been contested by local communities. There are three inter – related dimensions to the Niger Delta crisis: economic (resource control); environmental (the negative impact of oil exploitation on the environment); and social (health and human rights issues).

In recent years, several factors have **contributed to** the **intensification** of the conflict over the control of resources: the communities' increased sense of **deprivation**, the growing ecological damage, the lack of physical and social infrastructural facilities, the deepening poverty and neglect in the region. A solution to these problems must include community involvement in developing programs for the region, community **empowerment**, and **restoration** of trust between the communities, the oil companies, and the government. In practice, this calls for several initiatives: new or renewed efforts in hiring **indigenes** into operational, managerial, and executive positions in the oil and gas sector, within the government, and in the oil companies; award of maintenance and servicing contracts to indigenes; allocation of oil **blocs** to the communities; involving the communities in the design and **implementation** of programs for the region; and empowering the communities by providing them with financial resources for developing their own businesses and for skills development, so that they are active participants in the **execution** of the various programs being planned for the region.

In addition, **equity** could be promoted through the creation of **decentralized trust funds** for specific programs that address the key issues in the Niger Delta. These can include a physical infrastructure fund, a social infrastructure and training trust, an environmental repair trust, and a small – medium enterprise fund. The trust funds would be managed by corporate governance structures that include federal and community representatives. The arrangement will also enhance government – community partnerships, stimulate competition among the various funds, and generate jobs, especially for youths.

Libyan Reaction to the Challenges

As the major oil producer, the Libyan oil fund has also financed substantial **extrabudgetary** spending. Libyan government is in the process of preparing a financial sector reform program. Recent legislation setting corporate governance standards for financial institutions makes progress towards better management and greater operational independence of public banks. In addition to it, a campaign encouraging conversion of qualified civil servants to **entrepreneurs**, in the face of public sector over employment and declining productivity, does not seem to be producing the desired results thus far.

Words and Expressions

output	产量,生产
cumulative	累积的
recessionary	(经济)衰退的
cushion	缓和……的冲击
intervention	介入,干涉
reverse	倒转,扭转
stagnation	停滞,滞止
riot	暴乱;放纵
scenario	情节,情况
household	家庭
kerosene	煤油,火油
stabilization	稳定,稳定化
subsidies	补贴,津贴
exploitation	开采,利用
sustained	持续的,持久的
equitable	公平的,公正的
proceeds	收入,收益
quintessential	精髓的,典型的
enactment	制定,颁布
vest	归属
ores	矿石
intensification	激烈化
deprivation	剥夺
empowerment	许可,授权
restoration	恢复,复位,归还
indigene	原住民
blocs	集团

implementation	履行,实现
execution	执行,实行
equity	公正,公平
decentralized	分散的,分散化
extrabudgetary	预算外的
entrepreneur	企业家,承包人

Phrases and Expressions

fixed exchange rate regime	固定汇率制度(指汇率水平在一定时期内固定不变,中央银行为任何国际收支赤字和盈余提供融资)
monetary – policy	货币政策
macroeconomic management	宏观经济管理
The Extractive Industries Transparency Initiative	采掘业透明度行动计划
date back to	追溯到
contribute to	有助于;捐献
decentralized trust funds	分散信托基金

Language Focus

1. Coping with high oil prices, worsened by lack of resources to establish stabilization mechanisms and price smoothing, is one of the major challenges facing NOICs.

(参考译文:由于极其缺乏建立稳定机制和价格平滑机制的资源,控制高油价是石油净进口国面临的主要挑战之一。)

本句是简单句,句子的主语是 Coping with high oil prices,动名词短语作主语,系动词是 is,challenges 是表语,而 worsened... 是过去分词作原因状语。

2. In practice, this calls for several initiatives: new or renewed efforts in hiring indigenes into operational, managerial, and executive positions in the oil and gas sector, within the government, and in the oil companies; award of maintenance and servicing contracts to indigenes; allocation of oil blocs to the communities; involving the communities in the design and implementation of programs for the region; and empowering the communities by providing them

with financial resources for developing their own businesses and for skills development, so that they are active participants in the execution of the various programs being planned for the region.

（参考译文：在实践中，还要采取几项举措：在政府和石油公司内部，努力或继续努力启用原住民担任石油和天然气行业营运、管理的行政职位；签订与原住民维护和维修的合约；把油井设施分配给地方；让地方参与该地区项目的设计和实施；通过提供财政资源发展地方企业和培养员工技能；使他们积极地参与该地区正在计划的各种项目。）

本句是简单句，句子主干是 this calls for several initiatives，以下是措施的具体内容，so that 引导结果状语从句，initiatives 都是名词短语。

3. In addition to it, a campaign encouraging conversion of qualified civil servants to entrepreneurs, in the face of public sector over employment and declining productivity, does not seem to be producing the desired results thus far.

（参考译文：除此之外，面对公共部门就业和生产率下降，鼓励有资格的公务员转换企业家的活动，但迄今为止并没有产生预期的效果。）

本句主语是 a campaign，谓语是 does not seem 部分，encouraging... 后是现在分词作定语，修饰主语 a campaign，in the face of ... 是介词短语作状语。

🔲 Reinforced Learning

I. Answer the following questions for a comprehension of the text.

1. What harmful effects are caused by high oil prices for the median oil – importing country?

2. Before the financial crisis, what is about African economies growth?

3. What are particular challenges faced by oil – rich countries?

4. In Nigeria, what measures were taken to reduce the risk of social tensions?

5. According to the passage, which countries are major net oil – exporting countries in Africa?

II. Multiple choice: choose the correct one from the alternative answers to give the exact meaning of the words.

1. They lead to a decrease in <u>output</u> and consumption, and to a worsening of the net foreign asset position.

    A. outset   B. import   C. yield   D. outcry

2. Those rules do not <u>apply to</u> Chinese media organizations, which are controlled and censored by the state.

　　A. put into action　　　　　　　　B. put into force

　　C. put into use　　　　　　　　　　D. put into shape

3. High commodity prices have already been a motive for <u>riots</u> and demonstrations in many African countries (for example, in Mozambique on February 5, 2008).

　　A. rebellions　　　B. resists　　　　C. roils　　　　D. rolls

4. Many investors <u>opt to</u> buy a simple home aimed at the local market and extend or rebuild it to international standards.

　　A. refer to　　　B. consult to　　　C. determine to　　D. choose to

5. The scenario is even worse for poor <u>households</u> that depend on kerosene for lighting and cooking.

　　A. haven　　　　B. hometowns　　　C. housework　　D. families

6. In addition, equity could be promoted through the creation of decentralized trust funds for <u>specific</u> programs that address the key issues in the Niger Delta.

　　A. special　　　　B. detailed　　　　C. precise　　　　D. valid

7. Budgets are not prepared precisely enough, and budget <u>implementation</u> needs to become more uniform.

　　A. distribution　　B. fulfillment　　　C. commitment　　D. approach

8. In addition to it, a campaign encouraging conversion of qualified civil servants to <u>entrepreneurs</u>, in the face of public sector over employment and declining productivity, does not seem to be producing the desired results thus far.

　　A. captains　　　B. leaders　　　　C. enterprisers　　D. conductors

9. The main issues are growth and the <u>restoration</u> of global demand.

　　A. supervision　　B. regulation　　　C. recovery　　　　D. consumption

10. The trust funds would be managed by corporate governance structures that include federal (state government) and community <u>representatives</u>.

　　A. delegates　　　B. executors　　　C. performers　　D. players

III. Multiple choice: read the four suggested translations and choose the best answer.

1. At <u>stake</u> has been the quintessential property rights issue: who owns the oil resources in the Niger Delta?

　　A. 物权　　　　　B. 所有权　　　　C. 准物权　　　D. 财产权

2. However, this recessionary effect can be <u>cushioned</u> through government intervention in of shocks, such as productivity shocks, monetary – policy shocks, and world – interest – rate shocks.

  A. 处理   B. 化解   C. 解决   D. 缓冲

3. As the major oil producer, the Libyan oil fund has also financed substantial <u>extrabudgetary</u> spending. Libyan government is in the process of preparing a financial sector reform program.

  A. 收支外的 B. 预算外的 C. 预算内的 D. 收支内的

4. In addition, equity could be promoted through the creation of <u>decentralized</u> trust funds for specific programs that address the key issues in the Niger Delta.

  A. 中心的   B. 密集的   C. 分散的   D. 下放的

5. The major challenge is to <u>translate</u> oil wealth into sustained economic growth and development.

  A. 调动   B. 转化   C. 翻译   D. 解释

Ⅳ. Put the following sentences into Chinese

1. High oil prices can have very harmful effects on the economy of African oil – importing countries, especially those that are heavily debt – burdened.

2. Africa as a whole has in recent years been enjoying gains from macroeconomic management, improved political stability and governance, easing of regional conflicts, strengthening of regional economic blocks, and increased agricultural, mineral, and oil production.

3. Oil and gas exploitation have caused major economic, social, political, and environmental problems in some net oil – exporting countries.

4. In Nigeria, for example, the federal government passes 13 percent of oil revenues to the nine oil – producing states, primarily to reduce conflict and promote local development.

5. In addition, equity could be promoted through the creation of decentralized trust funds for specific programs that address the key issues in the Niger Delta.

Ⅴ. Put the following paragraphs into Chinese

1. Average growth in the Sub – Saharan economies was 5. 4 percent in 2005 and 2006. However, sustaining（持续的）high growth rates has been a

chronic（长期的）challenge for African countries as they confront shocks including high oil prices. Coping with high oil prices requires a set of measures to maximize the positive impacts and mitigate（缓和）the negative impacts. The negative impacts are more intense for net oil importers, but can be mitigated through government initiatives or through foreign aid.

2. In a completely deregulated（解除管制）market, price increases are passed on fully to consumers. Linking domestic prices to international prices in a pricing formula attempts to mimic（模仿）a deregulated market. Given the volatility of world product prices, in countries where governments wish to exercise some measure of control over pricing, it may be reasonable to take a moving average of actual prices spread over a period of more than one month.

1.3　Potential for Asian – Pacific Markets

🔲 Guidance to Reading

China, South Korea, and Japan are the main crude oil consumers in the Asia Pacific region. The text introduces oil source and refining capacity of these three countries briefly and respectively. It also points out the importance of establishing a fully – developed emergency response system to secure economic development. Finally, it mentions about the three countries' cooperative prospects with Alberta of Canada in oil resource utilization.

🔲 Text

The largest markets for crude oil in the Asian – Pacific region are Japan, Korea, and China. All of these countries are currently heavily dependent on imports from the Middle East to meet their energy requirements, chiefly from Saudi Arabia. Despite the increasing energy demand and dependence on **external** sources of energy, this region has become increasingly **vulnerable** to a reduction in supply, due to the lack of a fully – developed **emergency response system**, such as an oil **stockpile**. Other risk factors affecting Asian petroleum imports include **territorial** disputes, political **turmoil**, and increasing unemployment in the Middle East, as well as increasing demand for tankers to transport crude oil and global **volatility** of oil prices. Canada's political stability and competitive oil prices are of increasing interest to Asian countries interested in a secure long – term energy supply.

Japan

In 2002, Japan imported a total of 4. 0 million b/d of crude oil, of which 86. 8% of that was from the Middle East. The remaining imports were from Africa (3. 8%), other Asian sources, **primarily** China (7. 5%), and other sources such as Russia (1. 9%). Although major efforts have been made in Japan to focus more on alternate energy sources such as natural gas, coal, and nuclear, crude imports have decreased only slightly since a peak in 1995, and the Middle East remains a key supplier. For example, in February 2004, Middle East sources supplied 92. 6% of Japanese crude oil imports.

Japan has 33 refineries, with a charge capacity of 4. 7 million b/d. Due to the increasing use of natural gas and coal to supply power, these refineries are not fully utilized (81. 4% utilization ratio in 2002), and a projected drop in fuel oil demand by approximately 1. 4% per year to 2007 is expected to reduce the utilization ratio even further. Further reductions could take place if **initiatives** to introduce higher levels of ethanol in gasoline, are successful.

The majority of Japanese crude oil imports can be **classified** as **medium or light sour**. However, close to 95% of Japan's **distillation** capacity has been **equipped with desulphurization units** to meet increasingly stringent fuel sulphur specifications. The sulphur content of gasoline must drop from 100 ppm to 50 ppm at the end of 2004, and must be sulphur free (below 10 ppm) by 2008. Diesel sulphur content will be reduced to 50 ppm by the end of 2004 from the current value of 500 ppm, and must be sulphur free after 2007. Japanese refineries will **voluntarily** supply sulphur free gasoline and diesel in limited areas by 2005.

Japan has already indicated an interest in pursuing a long – term relationship with Alberta through a 75% ownership of the Hangingstone SAGD project by **Japan Canada Oil Sands Ltd**. With an **excess** in refinery capacity designed to handle medium sour crude, and extensive desulphurization capability, Japan could easily meet its import requirements with Canadian "**dilbit**" **or** "**synbit**" blends. However, the decline in annual growth of oil demand, which will primarily be due to Japanese government efforts to reduce its dependence on petroleum as an energy source. Although gasoline demand is expected to increase, a drop in diesel as well as fuel oil demand will be the primary reason for the decline. The **naphthenic** nature of Alberta bitumen will therefore make it a somewhat less desirable **feedstock** for Japanese refineries.

Korea

Korea imported 2. 1 million b/d of crude oil in 2002, with 74. 5% of the oil deriving from Middle East sources. The two other largest suppliers were Indonesia (5. 5%) and the Congo (2. 7%), with the **remainder** coming from a variety of suppliers including Canada (0. 1%). Korea has a total of 6 refineries, with a charge capacity of 2. 5 million b/d; these refineries run at a near 100% utilization rate, and any excess products are exported.

Oil demand in Korea is expected to hold steady, with forecasted increases for all refinery products except for kerosene based **on the assumption of** strong industry and transportation sectors. Fuel sulphur **specifications** are not as **stringent** as those in Japan; gasoline **sulphur** content will drop to 50 ppm from the current level of 130 ppm by 2006, and that of diesel to 30 ppm from 430 ppm. The existing import relationship with Canada, and the projected increase in demand for diesel and boiler feed, should make Alberta bitumen an attractive **option** for Korean refineries.

China

Unlike Japan and Korea, China has a strong **domestic** petroleum industry, dominated by two major companies: **China National Petroleum Corporation** (**CNPC**), which controls about two thirds of domestic crude oil production capacity, and **China Petroleum & Chemical Corporation** (**SINOPEC**), which controls more than half of the refining capacity. The majority of CNPC's assets are under the umbrella of **PetroChina**, which is a public corporation. Offshore exploration and production is the **mandate** of the **China National Offshore Oil Corporation** (**CNOOC**); however, this company only accounts for about 10% of domestic production.

Prior to 1993, China was a net exporter of crude oil. Since then, China's explosive economic growth has fuelled a dependence on foreign oil, which has grown by approximately 5% per year. In 2004, imports are projected to make up 41% of China's total oil requirements. This trend is expected to continue through 2020, with **incremental** oil demand growing by 5. 7 million b/d between 2000 and 2020.

China is slightly less vulnerable to **fluctuations** in Middle East oil exports than are most of the other Asian – Pacific countries. In 2002, China imported a total of 1. 4 million b/d of crude oil, of which only 49. 5% was shipped from the Middle East. However, by the end of 2003, imports had risen to an average of 1. 9 million b/d, with 56% from Middle Eastern producers. Other major exporters of crude oil to China are Angola, Sudan, Vietnam, Indonesia, Malaysia, and Russia; however, oil has been imported from as far away as the North Sea, to ensure a **diversity** of supply. China is also implementing an emergency response system, by dedicating six sites, most of them near major refining and transportation centres, with a storage capacity of 350 million barrels to provide 30 days of import cover by 2005, and 50 days of import cover in 2010.

Due to its domestic production, China's imports of crude oil are less than those of Japan and Korea. However, if its economy continues to grow as projected, China will eventually **outstrip** them as a major oil importer in the Asian – Pacific region. In terms of sustained market growth, China is an attractive export market for Alberta producers. However, China's inadequate heavy crude refining capability and lack of desulphurization units make it a poor receptor for "dilbit" or "synbit" blends. On the other hand, as production of **synthetic** crude oil outstrips the ability of Alberta refineries to absorb it, synthetic crude oil (**SCO**) would be a desirable feedstock for Chinese refineries, due to its higher diesel yield and low sulphur.

Words and Expressions

external	外部的
vulnerable	易受……的攻击
stockpile	积蓄;库存
territorial	领土的
turmoil	动荡,骚动
volatility	易变
primarily	首先;首要地
initiative	举措,倡议
classify	把……分类
distillation	蒸馏,净化
voluntarily	自动地
excess	过量的,过度的

naphthenic	环烷的;脂环烃的
feedstock	原料;给料
remainder	剩余;余数
specification	规格;说明书
stringent	严厉的;迫切的
sulphur	硫黄;硫黄色
option	选项,选择权
domestic	家庭的;国内的
mandate	授权;委托
incremental	增加的,增值的
fluctuation	起伏,波动
diversity	多样性
outstrip	胜过,超过
synthetic	合成的

Phrases and Expressions

emergency response system	应急响应体系
medium or light sour	中度或轻度含硫
equip with	配备,装备
desulphurization units	脱硫装置
"dilbit" or "synbit"	油砂沥青的原料
on the assumption of	在……前提下

Proper Names

Japan Canada Oil Sands Ltd	日本加拿大含油砂有限责任公司
CNPC	中国石油天然气集团公司
SINOPEC	中国石油化工集团公司
PetroChina	中国石油天然气股份有限公司
CNOOC	中国海洋石油总公司
SCO	合成原油

Language Focus

1. Further reductions could take place if initiatives to introduce higher levels of ethanol in gasoline, and biodiesel, are successful.

（参考译文:如果引进高浓度乙醇汽油的举措成功的话,燃油需求会进一步减少。)

本句是一个复合句,Further reductions could take place 是主句,if 引导条件状语从句,其中 to introduce higher levels of ethanol in gasoline, and biodiesel 不定式作定语修饰从句的主语 initiatives。

2. Although gasoline demand is expected to increase, a drop in diesel as well as fuel oil demand will be the primary reason for the decline.

（参考译文:虽然汽油需求有望增长,但燃油和柴油需求下降是石油需求减少的首要原因。)

本句是一个复合句,Although 引导让步状语从句,主句的主语 a drop,介词短语 in diesel as well as fuel oil demand 修饰 a drop。

3. On the other hand, as production of synthetic crude oil outstrips the ability of Alberta refineries to absorb it, synthetic crude oil（SCO）would be a desirable feedstock for Chinese refineries, due to its higher diesel yield and low sulphur.

（参考译文:另一方面,艾伯塔炼油厂不能提取合成原油产品,鉴于合成原油产品高柴油产量和低含硫量,因此它将成为中国炼油厂的理想原料。)

本句是一个复合句,as 引导原因状语从句,SCO would be a desirable feedstock for Chinese refineries 是主句,due to 表示原因。

🔲 Reinforced Learning

Ⅰ. Answer the following questions for a comprehension of the text.

1. What are other risk factors affecting Asian petroleum imports according to text?

2. What is about Japan oil resource import according to article?

3. How many percent of Japan refineries are utilized in 2002, due to the increasing use of natural gas and coal to supply power?

4. For Korea how is cooperative prospect with Alberta of Canada?

5. How many and what petroleum corporation are dominated petroleum industry in China?

Ⅱ. Multiple choice: choose the correct one from the alternative answers to give the exact meaning of the words.

1. These trade disputes between China and Britain resulted in China being forced to open more of its ports to trade with western countries.

A. objections   B. fights   C. combats   D. conflicts

2. Other risk factors affecting Asian petroleum imports include territorial disputes, political turmoil, and increasing unemployment in the Middle East.

A. disaster   B. chaos   C. mass   D. trap

3. Questions can help children learn to compare and classify things.

A. dispose   B. comprehend   C. categorize   D. divide

4. China accounts for 23 per cent of all foreign holdings of US Treasuries and is the largest single investor.

A. counts to   B. takes up

C. counts on   D. takes down

5. The majority of CNPC's assets are under the umbrella of PetroChina, which is a public corporation.

A. executions   B. properties   C. advantages   D. means

6. Citroen has faced its own difficulties in recent years, producing products that outstrip the brand's reputation.

A. surpass   B. flourish   C. displace   D. overlook

7. Lenders demand higher credit scores, bigger deposits and more stringent proof of income.

A. appropriate   B. precise   C. solemn   D. rigorous

8. The naphthenic nature of Alberta bitumen will therefore make it a somewhat less desirable feedstock for Japanese refineries.

A. outcome   B. material   C. origin   D. feedback

9. Offshore exploration and production is the mandate of the China National Offshore Oil Corporation (CNOOC).

A. approval   B. authorization   C. recognation   D. control

10. Oil has been imported from as far away as the North Sea, to ensure a diversity of supply.

A. assume   B. facilitate   C. inflate   D. assure

III. Multiple choice: read the four suggested translations and choose the best answer.

1. Despite the increasing energy demand and dependence on external sources of energy, this region has become increasingly vulnerable to a reduction in supply, due to the lack of a fully - developed emergency response system, such as an oil stockpile.

A. 有弱点的 　　　　　　　　B. 易受冲击的
C. 有缺点的 　　　　　　　　D. 易破碎的

2. The majority of Japanese crude oil imports can be classified as medium or light sour.

A. 中度或轻度酸 　　　　　　　B. 中度或轻度发酵
C. 中度或轻度含硫 　　　　　　D. 中度或轻度含酸

3. The majority of CNPC's assets are under the umbrella of PetroChina, which is a public corporation.

A. 公众公司 　　　　　　　　　B. 上市公司
C. 公营公司 　　　　　　　　　D. 公交公司

4. Gasoline sulphur content will drop to 50 ppm from the current level of 130 ppm by 2006, and that of diesel to 30 ppm from 430 ppm.

A. 百分之…… 　　　　　　　　B. 百万分之……
C. 十万分之…… 　　　　　　　D. 千万分之……

5. Fuel sulphur specifications are not as stringent as those in Japan; gasoline sulphur content will drop to 50 ppm from the current level of 130 ppm.

A. 硫说明 　　　B. 硫规格 　　　C. 硫特性 　　　D. 硫型号

IV. Put the following sentences into Chinese.

1. The largest markets for crude oil in the Asian – Pacific region are Japan, Korea, and China. All of these countries are currently heavily dependent on imports from the Middle East to meet their energy requirements, chiefly from Saudi Arabia.

2. Canada's political stability and competitive oil prices are of increasing interest to Asian countries interested in a secure long – term energy supply.

3. Japanese refineries will voluntarily supply sulphur free gasoline and diesel in limited areas by 2005.

4. Oil demand in Korea is expected to hold steady, with forecasted increases for all refinery products except for kerosene based on the assumption of strong industry and transportation sectors.

5. Since then, China's explosive economic growth has fuelled a dependence on foreign oil, which has grown by approximately 5% per year.

V. Put the following paragraphs into Chinese.

1. Chinese gas production is growing rapidly both onshore and offshore.

Due to its large reserves of coal, China has only recently begun full exploitation of its gas reserves with new pipelines and exploration of gas – prone basins in the western interior and offshore.

2. China doubled its oil consumption between 1995 and 2005, while during the same period world demand grew by 20%. Since 2003, China has been consuming more oil than Japan and in 1993 it became a net importer.

1. 4 The Economic Impacts of GOM Oil and Natural Gas Industry on the U. S. Economy

⌐⊔ Guidance to Reading

GOM provides energy security for the U. S. economy. Further on it, the offshore GOM oil and natural gas industry promotes the development of the U. S. economy, boosts GDP, creates jobs and generates tax revenues at all levels of government. Many industries benefit from it and have a great boom due to offshore GOM oil and natural gas industry activity.

⌐⊔ Text

Executive Summary

The offshore oil and natural gas industry is **instrumental** to the United States both from an energy supply perspective and due to its contribution to U. S. GDP and job creation. In 2010, over 30 percent of the oil and 11 percent of the natural gas produced in the United States was produced in the Gulf of Mexico (GOM). This production is crucial to U. S. energy **security**. In addition, capital investment and **purchases** of **intermediate inputs** of the oil and natural gas industry **stimulate** its **entire value chain** and ripple through many sectors of the economy, creating jobs, contributing to GDP and **generating tax revenue at all levels of** government. Oil and natural gas industry activity supports employment across **a wide swath of** industries in manufacturing and services, including oil and natural gas **machinery**, air and **marine** transport, legal and insurance services.

National Impacts

Overall spending for the Gulf of Mexico offshore industry in 2008 was over $ 28. 5 billion which translated into a total GDP impact of over $ 30. 8 billion. This impact was felt throughout the country and supported over 305 thousand jobs nationwide. Approximately 90 thousand of those jobs were directly related to the industry (meaning jobs working directly for oil and natural gas companies or for **contractors** that are directly paid by the oil and natural gas industry) while 220 thousand were indirect (meaning jobs providing goods and services to oil companies such as components for manufacturing, legal and financial services, etc.) and **induced** jobs (meaning jobs throughout the economy that result from the spending of income from direct and indirect **employment** such as waiters, **retail** workers, **automobile** manufacturers, service providers, etc).

In 2009, in part due to the effects of the economic **recession**, industry capital investment and operational spending fell to $ 27. 1 billion with an associated GDP impact of just over $ 29. 3 billion. This economic activity supported approximately 285 thousand jobs in total of which 80 thousand were direct, and 205 thousand were indirect and induced jobs. The year 2010 saw capital investment and operational spending fall to its lower level of interest to $ 24. 2 billion. This was **primarily** due to the **moratorium** on drilling in the deepwater GOM and the **subsequent** lack of deepwater **drilling permits issued** and the associated **slow down** in drilling in the shallow water due to the decrease in permits issued. **As a result of** the decrease in capital investment and operational spending in 2010, the total GDP impact decreased to $ 26. 1 billion despite the **stirrings** of **economic recovery**. This led to total employment levels associated with GOM offshore oil and natural gas development falling to **roughly** 240 thousand jobs of which 60 thousand were direct jobs and 180 thousand were indirect and induced jobs. Overall this was a 21 percent decline nationwide from supported employment levels in 2008, contributions to GDP fell 15 percent nationwide.

State and Regional Impacts

The Gulf Coast states, with the primary four being Texas, Louisiana, Mississippi, and Alabama (including the federal waters of these states), are areas which produce oil and natural gas and receive the majority of the spending from the offshore oil and natural gas industry in the Gulf of Mexico. These states are the **location** of most of the primary spending for capital **equipment** and purchases of intermediate inputs needed for the operational activities of the Gulf of Mexico oil and natural gas industry.

Throughout the Gulf Coast, activities such as engineering and management, manufacturing of equipment, support of offshore activities, and **fabrication** of platforms and **topsides** are widespread. Due to this **concentration** of primary investment and spending, the offshore Gulf of Mexico oil and natural gas industry is instrumental in the economic health of these states. In 2010, capital investment and operational spending in these four states totaled $17.5 billion, with Alabama accounting for $2.7 billion of spending, Louisiana accounting for $7.3 billion, Mississippi accounting for $0.3 billion of spending and Texas $7.3 billion. The total contribution to GDP of these states associated with GOM offshore oil and natural gas activity **stood at** just over $19.1 billion in 2010 with $2.6 billion **centered** in Alabama, $7.4 billion in Louisiana, $0.2 billion in Mississippi and $8.9 billion in Texas.

In 2010 the Gulf Coast States, defined as Alabama, Louisiana, Mississippi, and Texas, saw employment levels of 175 thousand due to Gulf of Mexico offshore oil and natural gas industry activity. Jobs **tied** directly **to** the industry were estimated at 42 thousand while indirect and induced jobs were estimated at 133 thousand. These states see the highest employment levels due to the concentration of spending in the region as many goods and services providers to the industry are located near to the Gulf coast. Employees on **drilling rigs** and other offshore **personnel** who often work offshore for two week **stretches** normally live **close to** their onshore bases for ease of transportation.

At the time of the moratorium the Louisiana Mid – Continent Oil and Natural Gas Association stated that for every **idle** rig platform there were 800 – 1400 jobs **at risk**. According to the association wages lost for these jobs could exceed $5 to $10 million for one month per platform, with a maximum of 33 rigs having been idled **at the peak**.

Outside of the Gulf States, Quest estimated that offshore Gulf of Mexico oil and natural gas industry activity supported 65 thousand jobs in 36 other states in 2010. Total contribution to GDP from these states due to offshore GOM oil and natural gas industry activity was estimated at $7.0 billion in 2010 based on total spending in these states of $6.7 billion. The non – Gulf of Mexico States, which primarily provide manufactured goods, **component parts** and services to the industry, are expected to see spending levels rise 61 percent to $10.8 billion in 2013 from 2010 levels. This spending rise is expected to yield a 61 percent increase in contributions to GDP to ＄11.3 billion and a 67 percent increase in employment to 105 thousand jobs.

Impacts on Other Industries

While the economic impact of the offshore Gulf of Mexico oil and natural gas industry is felt across many sectors, certain industries are impacted more than others. The largest other industry **beneficiary**, due to the investment and operations of the offshore Gulf of Mexico oil and natural gas industry, was the **real estate** and **rental and leasing industry**. Activity in this sector was nearly ＄3.5 billion and over 18,500 jobs were supported due to offshore GOM oil and natural gas industry activity.

Other industries in 2010 which were beneficially supported include the manufacturing sector, with a GDP impact of approximately ＄2.0 billion and over 23 thousand jobs supported and the **professional**, scientific and technical services sector with GDP impact in 2010 of ＄1.2 billion and supported employment of approximately 14 thousand jobs. The GOM oil and natural gas industry also supports jobs in the real estate and construction sectors.

Total indirect and induced jobs due to offshore GOM oil and natural gas industry activity stood at 180 thousand jobs in 2010. The large impacts of oil and natural gas industry activity on other sectors make up a large **share** of the total **economy – wide** economic impacts.

Words and Expressions

instrumental	有帮助的,起作用的
security	安全
purchase	购买,进货
stimulate	刺激;鼓舞,激励
entire	全部的,整个的;全体的
generate	产生,使(某物)存在或发生
machinery	机械;机器;机构;机械装置
marine	航海的,海运的,海上的,海洋的
contractor	承包人,承建商
induced	引发的,产生的,造成的;诱导的
employment	雇用,就业
retail	零售的

automobile	汽车
recession	衰退;不景气
primarily	首先;主要地,根本上
moratorium	暂停,中止
subsequent	后来的,随后的
issue	发行,发布;发给
stirrings	渐起;萌芽
roughly	概略地,大致
location	位置,地点,所在地
equipment	设备,装备;器材
fabrication	制造,建造;装配
topside	上部
concentration	集中
center	集中,置于中心
personnel	人事部门;全体人员
stretch	伸展,延伸
idle	闲置的
beneficiary	受益人,受惠者
professional	专业的;职业的
share	份额;股份
economy – wide	全体经济的;整个经济体的

Phrases and Expressions

at all levels of	各级
a swath of	一连串的,一片的
as a result of	因此,由于;作为……的结果
stand at	处于某水平
tie to	与……联系在一起
close（adj.）to	接近于;在附近
at risk	处于危险中
at the peak（of）	在高峰期

Proper Names

executive summary	概述,摘要

intermediate inputs	中间投入
value chain	价值链
tax revenue	税收
drilling permits	钻探许可证
slow down	减缓,减慢
economic recovery	经济复苏
drilling rig	钻机,钻探装置,钻井平台
component parts	零部件;元件部分
real estate	不动产,房地产
rental and leasing industry	租赁行业

Language Focus

1. The offshore oil and natural gas industry is instrumental to the United States both from an energy supply perspective and due to its contribution to U. S. GDP and job creation.

（参考译文:对美国而言,近海油气工业无论对能源供应,还是对国内生产总值的贡献和创造的就业机会,都是具有重要意义的。）

本句中的结构 both... and... 为状语。

2. ... capital investment and purchases of intermediate inputs of the oil and natural gas industry stimulate its entire value chain and ripple through many sectors of the economy, creating jobs, contributing to GDP and generating tax revenue at all levels of government.

（参考译文:资本投资与油气工业的中间投入刺激了整个价值链,波及许多经济部门,创造了就业机会,促进了国内生产总值的增长,并且产生了各级政府的税收收入。）

本句中 and 引导的并列名词性短语为句子主语;且 stimulate... and ripple... 为并列谓语;后面的并列分词性短语为状语,表示补充说明。

3. This was primarily due to the moratorium on drilling in the deepwater GOM and the subsequent lack of deepwater drilling permits issued and the associated slow down in drilling in the shallow water due to the decrease in permits issued.

（参考译文:这主要是因为墨西哥湾的深水钻井暂停、后续缺乏深水钻井许可和由于减少浅水钻井的许可而相应地减缓了浅水钻井。）

本句 be due to 中 due 是形容词;而后者 due to 与 owing to 用法相同,但

due to 可用在名词后,如：Accidents due to driving at a high speed were very common that weekend. (那个周末因高速驾驶造成的交通事故很多。)

slow down 是名词,"生产放慢",如：a slow down in the dairy industry. (奶制品工业的生产放慢。)

4. These states are the location of most of the primary spending for capital equipment and purchases of intermediate inputs needed for the operational activities of the Gulf of Mexico oil and natural gas industry.

(参考译文:墨西哥湾油气工业的业务活动需要资本设备和中间投入的购买,而这几个州正处于业务活动绝大部分主要支出的位置。)

本句中分词短语 needed. . . 为后置定语,修饰前面并列的名词性短语 the primary spending. . . and purchases. . . 。

5. Other industries in 2010 which were beneficially supported include the manufacturing sector, with a GDP impact of approximately ＄2. 0 billion and over 23 thousand jobs supported and the professional, scientific and technical services sector with GDP impact in 2010 of ＄1. 2 billion and supported employment of approximately 14 thousand jobs.

(参考译文:2010 年,获得大力支持的产业包括制造业,所创造的国内生产总值约 20 亿美元,并提供超过 2.3 万个就业机会,并且在专业、科技服务业的国内生产总值达 12 亿美元,支持约 1.4 万人就业。)

本句基本结构:Other industries include the manufacturing sector and the professional, scientific and technical services sector;其中 which 引导的限制性定语从句修饰限制 Other industries;with 的复合结构为独立主格,作状语,表示补充说明。

🔲 Reinforced Learning

Ⅰ. Answer the following questions for a comprehension of the text.

1. Why is the Gulf of Mexico (GOM) crucial to U. S. energy security?

2. Why did the year 2010 see capital investment and operational spending fall to its lower level of interest to ＄24. 2 billion in U. S. ?

3. What do the Gulf Coast states mainly include?

4. What factors contribute to the highest employment levels among the Gulf Coast states?

5. What is the largest other industry beneficiary, due to the investment and operations of the offshore Gulf of Mexico oil and natural gas industry?

Ⅱ. **Multiple choice**: **choose the correct one from the alternative answers to give the exact meaning of the words.**

1. This production is crucial to U. S. energy underline{security}.

A. exploration   B. accumulation

C. consumption   D. safety

2. It underline{generated} tax revenue at all levels of government.

A. got   B. increased   C. drained   D. brought

3. In 2009, in part due to the effects of the economic underline{recession}, industry capital investment and operational spending fell to $ 27. 1 billion with an associated GDP impact of just over $ 29. 3 billion.

A. reaction   B. depression   C. stagnation   D. circulation

4. This led to total employment levels associated with GOM offshore oil and natural gas development falling to underline{roughly} 240 thousand jobs of which 60 thousand were direct jobs and 180 thousand were indirect and induced jobs.

A. approximately   B. incompletely

C. physically   D. brutally

5. Throughout the Gulf Coast, activities such as engineering and management, manufacturing of equipment, support of offshore activities, and underline{fabrication} of platforms and topsides are widespread.

A. leasing   B. operation   C. explosion   D. manufacture

6. Due to this underline{concentration} of primary investment and spending, the offshore Gulf of Mexico oil and natural gas industry is instrumental in the economic health of these states.

A. condensation   B. centralization

C. absorption   D. attention

7. Other offshore personnel often work offshore for two week underline{stretches}.

A. elasticity   B. spread   C. period   D. strain

8. Employees on drilling rigs and other offshore personnel normally live underline{close to} their onshore bases for ease of transportation.

A. near to   B. almost do   C. intimate with   D. almost in

9. The Louisiana Mid – Continent Oil and Natural Gas Association stated that for every underline{idle} rig platform there were 800 – 1400 jobs at risk.

A. lazy   B. single   C. empty   D. inactive

10. They make up a large underline{share} of the total economy – wide economic

impacts.

    A. part   B. stock   C. amount   D. payment

Ⅲ. Multiple choice: read the four suggested translations and choose the best answer.

1. Capital investment and purchases of <u>intermediate inputs</u> of the oil and natural gas industry stimulate its entire value chain and ripple through many sectors of the economy.

    A. 要素投入   B. 中间投入   C. 媒介投入   D. 调停介入

2. This was primarily due to the <u>moratorium</u> on drilling in the deepwater GOM and the subsequent lack of deepwater drilling permits issued.

    A. 作业   B. 禁止   C. 暂停   D. 泄漏

3. According to the association wages lost for these jobs could exceed ＄5 to ＄10 million for one month per platform, with a maximum of 33 rigs having been idled <u>at the peak</u>.

    A. 高峰期   B. 闲置时   C. 漏油时   D. 停产时

4. The non – Gulf of Mexico States primarily provide manufactured goods, <u>component parts</u> and services to the industry.

    A. 部分   B. 零部件   C. 组成成分   D. 中和成分

5. The largest other industry <u>beneficiary</u>, due to the investment and operations of the offshore Gulf of Mexico oil and natural gas industry, was the real estate and rental and leasing industry.

    A. 受害者   B. 收款人   C. 受惠者   D. 受托人

Ⅳ. Put the following sentences into Chinese.

1. The year 2010 saw capital investment and operational spending fall to its lower level of interest to ＄24. 2 billion.

2. As a result of the decrease in capital investment and operational spending in 2010, the total GDP impact decreased to ＄26. 1 billion despite the stirrings of economic recovery.

3. Throughout the Gulf Coast, activities such as engineering and management, manufacturing of equipment, support of offshore activities, and fabrication of platforms and topsides are widespread.

4. This spending rise is expected to yield a 61 percent increase in contributions to GDP to ＄11. 3 billion and a 67 percent increase in employment to 105

thousand jobs.

5. The large impacts of oil and natural gas industry activity on other sectors make up a large share of the total economy – wide economic impacts.

V. Put the following paragraphs into Chinese.

1. The Deepwater Horizon oil spill also referred to as the BP oil spill, the Gulf of Mexico oil spill, the BP oil disaster, or the Macondo（马贡多油井） blowout is an oil spill in the Gulf of Mexico which flowed unabated（不减弱的，不衰退的） for three months in 2010. It is the largest accidental marine oil spill in the history of the petroleum industry.

2. In January 2011 the White House oil spill commission released its final report on the causes of the oil spill. They blamed BP and its partners for making a series of cost – cutting decisions and the lack of a system to ensure well safety. They also concluded that the spill was not an isolated incident caused by "rogue（无耻之徒）industry or government officials", but that "The root causes are systemic and, absent significant reform in both industry practices and government policies, might well recur". After its own internal probe, BP admitted that it made mistakes which led to the Gulf of Mexico oil spill. In June 2010 BP set up a ＄20 billion fund to compensate victims of the oil spill. To July 2011, the fund has paid ＄4. 7 billion to 198,475 claimants. In all, the fund has nearly 1 million claims and continues to receive thousands of claims each week. In September 2011, the U. S. government published its final investigative report on the accident. In essence, that report states that the main cause was the defective cement job, and Halliburton（承包商哈利伯顿）, BP and Transocean（钻探设备商越洋公司）were, in different ways, responsible for the accident.

1. 5　Venezuela's Oil – Based Economy

⊞ Guidance to Reading

Venezuela is one of the world's major oil – producing and exporting countries, which has massive potential market for oil exporting. Venezuela has expanded international energy trade through diversified channels, and been committed to further economic integration with the other countries of South America. In recent years, U. S. has increasingly become dependent on Venezuelan oil and Venezuela has been America's largest supplier of crude oil. Venezuela's economy is largely based on its petroleum sector, which accounts for a certain percentage of GDP, government finances and the state foreign exchange. Petroleum sector is the pillar of national economy of Venezuela. As one of the largest state – owned enterprises, Petroleos de Venezuela (PDVSA) has become the world's influential enterprise in oil and gas industry, which has greatly promoted the economic development of Venezuela.

🔲 Text

Introduction

Venezuela's proven oil reserves are among the top ten in the world. Oil generates about 80 percent of the country's total export revenue, contributes about half of the central government's income, and **is responsible for** about one – third of GDP. Increases in world oil prices in recent years have allowed Venezuelan President Hugo Chavez to expand social program spending, **bolster commercial** ties with other countries, and **boost** his own international profile. The medium – term **outlook** for state oil company **PDVSA** is **questionable**, however, and analysts draw links between PDVSA's **profitability** and the political stability of the country. Analysts say the recent global financial **crisis** and sudden drop in oil prices are adding to the oil company's financial turmoil.

Venezuela's Economy under Chavez

Hugo Chavez took office in 1999. Since then, Venezuela's economy has remained **squarely** centered on oil production. In 2006, Chavez **announced** a **nationalization** of oil fields managed by foreign companies, which resulted in an increase of the government's shares in these projects from 40 percent to 60 percent. Government officials argue, however, that economic growth efforts are not **solely** focused on oil. Venezuela's ambassador to the United States, Bernardo Alvarez Herrera, wrote in a 2006 Foreign Affairs essay that the non – oil sector, which includes mining, manufacturing, and agriculture, grew 10. 6 percent in 2005, "indicating an important **diversification** of the country's economy. " Yet even if the country is working to diversify, "oil still **predominates**," says Miguel Tinker – Salas, a professor of Latin American history at Pomona College.

PDVSA

PDVSA (Petróleos de Venezuela, S. A.), Venezuela's state – owned petroleum company, oversees the exploration, production, refinement, and export of oil as well as the exploration and production of natural gas. It is the world's third – largest oil company, behind **Saudi Aramco** and **ExxonMobil**. According to **Tinker – Salas**, after the nationalization of Venezuela's oil in 1976, PDVSA was very much like a "state within a state." It "insulated itself from the government" and **functioned** largely as its own **entity** with control of the nation's wealth. In 1980, PDVSA acquired CITGO, a U. S. – based refinery, and it is now one of the world's largest refiners.

PDVSA's Production Levels and Fiscal Health

A report by the International Energy Agency examining Venezuela's **extra – heavy crude oil** production **put** PDVSA's 2005 production rate **at** 3. 2 million barrels per day but showed a decreased rate of 2. 55 million in September 2006. Currently, OPEC, the U. S. government, and the International Energy Agency agree that Venezuelan oil production **amounts t**o roughly 2. 4 million barrels per day. The Venezuelan government, however, says PDVSA's production is about 3. 3 million barrels per day.

Either way, there are new signs that all isn't **rosy** at PDVSA. In 2008, Venezuela's energy ministry **released unaudited** results documenting a 35 percent fall in profits by PDVSA the previous year. A few months later, audited figures were released that indicated profits increased 15 percent in 2007. The International Energy Agency, however, shows a $7. 9 billion loss in 2007. Oil prices, which were extraordinarily high through much of 2008, helped mask some of the company's financial **woes**. Since they began to drop dramatically PDVSA has **struggled to keep up with** its financial obligations, especially once it lost a $5 billion line of **credit** (CNBC) with the Royal Bank of Scotland in October 2008. The company had about $7. 9 billion in **unsettled accounts** between January and September 2008, up from $5. 7 billion during all of 2007, but analysts say **so far** the company is unlikely to **default** on its **creditors**. However, the company may need to make serious **cutbacks** or possibly even sell assets.

Venezuela has an estimated 78 billion barrels of proven conventional crude oil reserves and an additional estimated 235 billion barrels of **unconventional** extra – heavy crude oil in the **Orinoco Belt region** located southeast of **Caracas**. If development in the region can turn this **extra – heavy tar – like** oil into a more **marketable commodity**, Venezuela's total reserves could **rival**, reports the New York Times. **Oxford Analytica** notes, however, that PDVSA will struggle to develop its heavy – oil reserves **a timely fashion** given its lack of infrastructure investment and the **ongoing** oil nationalizations. Oil industry experts suggest that PDVSA needs to invest at least $ 3 billion annually into its existing fields just to maintain current production levels.

Regional Ventures

Venezuela is South America's third – largest market and is actively pursuing further economic integration with other countries in the region. In July 2006 it became a member of the South American trade group **Mercosur** (Mercado Común del Sur), joining Brazil, Argentina, Uruguay, and Paraguay. Chavez has also **spurred** the creation of a regional development bank, known as **Banco del Sur**. **Highlights** of Venezuela's recent regional agreements include:

Argentina. Venezuela and Argentina have made agreements to create an investment bank for infrastructure development, as well as joint hydrocarbon exploration and development in both countries. Venezuela has also purchased $ 3.5 billion in bonds to help **pay off** Argentina's debt.

Brazil. In May 2008, Petrobras and PDVSA signed an agreement to build an oil refinery in northeastern Brazil, which is **anticipated** to require $ 4.05 billion in investment. **Petrobras** will hold 60 percent of the refinery's shares. Crude oil will be supplied by both countries to refine a projected 200,000 barrels per day.

Colombia. In 2007, Venezuela and Colombia opened a natural gas pipeline that links northern Colombia's **La Guajira gas fields** to the **Paraguana refining complex** in western Venezuela. Tensions between the two countries have **heightened**, however, since a March 2008 **standoff** in which Chavez sent troops to the Colombian border and **temporarily severed diplomatic ties**.

Bolivia. Venezuela and Bolivia signed agreements in January and May 2006 for Venezuela to supply **preferentially** priced **diesel** and invest $ 1.5 billion in the Bolivian oil and gas sector **in exchange for** Bolivian goods and services, according to Oxford Analytica.

Ecuador. In February 2008, Venezuela and Ecuador agreed to **collaborate** on an oil refinery in Ecuador estimated to cost $ 5.5 billion. Under agreements signed in May 2006, Venezuela is expected to refine up to 100,000 barrels of

Ecuadorean crude oil per day at **discount** prices.

Cuba. **Commerce** between Venezuela and Cuba **soared** to $ 7 billion in 2007, according to the Cuban government (in 2006, trade was $ 1. 7 billion). Venezuela is selling up to 100,000 barrels of oil per day to Cuba, discounted by as much as 40 percent. In exchange, thousands of Venezuelans have traveled to Cuba for medical treatment, and Cuban doctors help **administer health care** programs for low – income Venezuelans.

U. S. – Venezuela Oil Ties

Though Venezuela has repeatedly threatened to cut off its oil exports to the United States, analysts say the two countries are mutually dependent. Venezuela supplies about 1. 5 million barrels of crude oil and refined petroleum products to the U. S. market every day, according to the EIA. Venezuelan oil **comprises** about 11 percent of U. S. crude oil imports, which amounts to 60 percent of Venezuela's total exports. PDVSA also **wholly** owns five refineries in the United States and partly owns four refineries, either through partnerships with U. S. companies or through PDVSA's U. S. **subsidiary**, CITGO. **U. S. Government Accountability Office** (**GAO**) says Venezuela's exports of crude oil and refined petroleum products to the United States have been relatively stable **with the exception of** the strike period.

The World Bank's Frepes – Cibils says "Venezuela will continue to be a key player in the U. S. market. " He argues that in the short term it will be very difficult for Venezuela to make a significant **shift** in supply from the United States. Nevertheless, Chavez has increasingly made efforts to diversify his oil clients in order to lessen the country's dependence on the United States. The GAO report says the sudden loss of Venezuelan oil in the world market would raise world oil prices and slow the economic growth of the United States.

Words and Expressions

bolster	支持；支撑；加强
commercial	商业的；营利的
boost	促进；增加
outlook	展望
questionable	可疑的；有问题的
profitability	盈利能力；收益性；利益率

crisis	危机;危险期
squarely	干脆地;明确无误地;毫不含糊地
announce	宣布,宣告;通知
nationalization	国有化
solely	单独地,唯一地
diversification	多样化;变化
predominate	占主导(或支配)地位;占优势
function	运行;活动;行使职责
entity	实体;存在;本质
rosy	美好的;乐观的
release	发布,允许发表
unaudited	未审计的;未稽核的
woe	悲哀,悲痛;灾难
credit	贷款
default	拖欠;不履行
creditor	债权人,贷方
cutback	减少,削减
unconventional	非常规的;非传统的;不依惯例的
marketable	市场的;可销售的;有销路的
commodity	商品,货物;日用品
rival	竞争
ongoing	不间断的,进行的;前进的
spur	激励,鞭策
highlight	最精彩的部分;最重要的事情
anticipate	预期,期望;占先,抢先;提前使用
heighten	升高;变强
standoff	和局;僵持
temporarily	临时地
severed	切断的;隔断的
preferentially	优先地;优惠地
diesel	柴油
collaborate	合作
discount	折扣;贴现率
commerce	贸易,商业

soar	上升,高涨,飞涨
administer	管理;执行;给予
comprise	包含;由……组成
wholly	完全地;全部;统统
subsidiary	子公司,辅助者
shift	移动;变化

Phrases and Expressions

be responsible for	对……负责;是……的原因
put sth. at sth.	计算,估计(某物之大小、价值等)
amount to	相当于,总计为
struggle to do sth.	努力做某事
keep up with	赶得上;和……保持联系
unsettled account	悬账,未决账项,未结账
so far	到目前为止,迄今为止
a timely fashion	及时地
pay off	付清
diplomatic ties	外交关系;邦交
in exchange for	作为……的交换
with the exception of	除了……以外

Proper Names

PDVSA	委内瑞拉国家石油公司
Saudi Aramco	沙特阿美(沙特阿拉伯国家石油公司)
ExxonMobil	埃克森美孚公司(世界最大的非政府石油天然气生产商)
Tinker – Salas	廷克·萨拉斯(加利福尼亚州波莫纳学院拉美问题专家)
extra – heavy crude oil	超重原油
Orinoco Belt region	奥里诺科河带地区
Caracas	加拉加斯 委内瑞拉首都
extra – heavy tar – like oil	焦油状超重原油
Oxford Analytica	牛津分析;牛津分析公司;牛津分析顾问公司

Mercosur	南方共同市场（南美地区最大的经济一体化组织）
Banco del Sur	南方银行（由南美国家共同出资，致力于地区经济发展）
Petrobras	巴西国家石油公司（全球最大的综合能源公司之一）
La Guajira gas fields	拉瓜希拉油气田
Paraguana refining complex	帕拉瓜纳炼油基地
health care	卫生保健
GAO	美国政府问责办公室
The World Bank	世界银行

Language Focus

1. Increases in world oil prices in recent years have allowed Venezuelan President Hugo Chavez to expand social program spending, bolster commercial ties with other countries, and boost his own international profile.

（参考译文：近年来，世界石油价格的上涨已使委内瑞拉总统查韦斯扩大社会计划开支，加强与其他国家的商业关系，提升自己的国际形象。）

本句的基本结构为 allow... to expand..., bolster..., and boost...。

2. Venezuela's ambassador to the United States, Bernardo Alvarez Herrera, wrote in a 2006 Foreign Affairs essay that the non – oil sector, which includes mining, manufacturing, and agriculture, grew 10. 6 percent in 2005,...

（参考译文：委内瑞拉驻美国大使贝尔纳多·阿尔瓦雷斯·埃雷拉，在2006年外交事务的文章中写道，2005年，包括包括采矿业、制造业和农业在内的非石油部门增长 10. 6% ，……）

本句中 Venezuela's ambassador 与 Bernardo Alvarez Herrera 是同位语，随后的 that 从句中 which 引导的非限制性定语从句，修饰限定 the non – oil sector。

3. It "insulated itself from the government" and functioned largely as its own entity with control of the nation's wealth.

（参考译文：它"不受政府影响"，兼为控制国家财富独立的实体。）

本句中并列谓语 insulated... and functioned..., with 引导的介词结构为状语，表示补充说明。

4. Since they began to drop dramatically PDVSA has struggled to keep up

with its financial obligations, especially once it lost a $5 billion line of credit (CNBC) with the Royal Bank of Scotland in October 2008.

（参考译文：自从他们开始急剧下降以来，尤其是 2008 年 10 月，当 PDV-SA 失去向苏格兰皇家银行(CNBC)信贷的 50 亿美元后，它一直在努力维持其财政上的义务。）

本句中 since 引导时间状语从句，副词 once 在此处为"一度、曾经"。

5. Tensions between the two countries have heightened, however, since a March 2008 standoff in which Chavez sent troops to the Colombian border and temporarily severed diplomatic ties.

（参考译文：然而，在 2008 年 3 月的对峙中，查韦斯派遣军队到哥伦比亚边境，并暂时断绝外交关系，两国之间的紧张局势加剧。）

本句中 since 是介词，a March 2008 standoff 为其介词宾语，which 引导的定语从句修饰 standoff。

Reinforced Learning

I. Answer the following questions for a comprehension of the text.

1. What factors contribute to PDVSA's financial turmoil according to analysts?

2. In 2006, what did Chavez announce to increase governmental shares in oil sector?

3. What are the largest oil companies in the world the passage mentioned?

4. What countries do Venezuela's recent regional agreements involve?

5. Why did tensions between Venezuela and Colombia suddenly heighten in March 2008?

II. Multiple choice: choose the correct one from the alternative answers to give the exact meaning of the words.

1. Increases in world oil prices have allowed Chavez to bolster commercial ties with other countries.

　　A. split　　　　B. create　　　　C. reinforce　　　　D. determine

2. Economic growth efforts are not solely focused on oil.

　　A. exclusively　B. inevitably　　C. specially　　　　D. only

3. Oil still predominates.

　　A. prevails　　　B. remains　　　C. soars　　　　　D. preponderates

4. The International Energy Agency agree that Venezuelan oil production amounts to roughly 2. 4 million barrels per day.

    A. adds up to   B. declines   C. resumes   D. speeds up

5. Venezuela's energy ministry released unaudited results documenting a 35 percent fall in profits by PDVSA the previous year.

    A. discharged   B. estimated   C. concluded   D. issued

6. Increases in oil prices helped mask some of the company's financial woes.

    A. adventures   B. troubles   C. deficits   D. losses

7. So far the company is unlikely to default on its creditors.

    A. deceive   B. not pay   C. compensate   D. stave off

8. The company may need to make serious cutbacks or possibly even sell assets.

    A. efforts   B. commitments C. reduction   D. money

9. Venezuela has also purchased $ 3. 5 billion in bonds to help pay off Argentina's debt.

    A. clear off   B. collect   C. recover   D. run up

10. Cuban doctors help administer health care programs for low – income Venezuelans.

    A. organize   B. provide   C. hit or kick   D. govern

Ⅲ. Multiple choice: read the four suggested translations and choose the best answer.

1. Analysts draw links between PDVSA's profitability and the political stability of the country.

    A. 成效   B. 补贴   C. 前景   D. 收益

2. In 2006, Chavez announced a nationalization of oil fields managed by foreign companies.

    A. 国际化   B. 国有化   C. 民族化   D. 大众化

3. The International Energy Agency examined that Venezuela's extra – heavy crude oil production put PDVSA's 2005 production rate at 3. 2 million barrels per day.

    A. 轻质原油 B. 中质原油   C. 重质原油   D. 超重原油

4. Venezuela has an additional estimated 235 billion barrels of unconventional extra – heavy crude oil in the Orinoco Belt region.

A. 非传统的   B. 非常规的

C. 非世俗的   D. 不合惯例的

5. The development in the region can turn this extra – heavy tar – like oil into a more marketable commodity.

A. 商品   B. 平台   C. 条件   D. 业务

Ⅳ. Put the following sentences into Chinese.

1. A report by the International Energy Agency examining Venezuela's extra – heavy crude oil production put PDVSA's 2005 production rate at 3. 2 million barrels per day but showed a decreased rate of 2. 55 million in September 2006.

2. If development in the region can turn this extra – heavy tar – like oil into a more marketable commodity, Venezuela's total reserves could rival.

3. Oxford Analytica notes, however, that PDVSA will struggle to develop its heavy – oil reserves a timely fashion given its lack of infrastructure investment and the ongoing oil nationalizations.

4. Venezuela is South America's third – largest market and is actively pursuing further economic integration with other countries in the region.

5. Venezuela and Argentina have made agreements to create an investment bank for infrastructure development, as well as joint hydrocarbon exploration and development in both countries.

Ⅴ. Put the following paragraphs into Chinese.

1. Under Chavez, however, the company's mandate (授权) has drastically expanded. In 2002, Chavez redefined PDVSA's role to include the government's social priorities. PDVSA must now spend at least 10 percent of its annual investment budget on social programs. This money is funneled through the National Development Fund, or Fonden, an investment fund set up in 2005 that is not included in the government's budget. Peter Hakim, president of the Inter – American Dialogue, a Washington – based center for policy analysis, says that Chavez's gradual takeover of PDVSA has given him an enormous bankroll (资金) to pursue his political and economic ambitions.

2. Opinion is divided over the effect of Chavez's policies on Venezuela's economy. Some economists say the tremendous rise in social spending under Chavez has greatly reduced poverty and pushed unemployment below 10 percent, its lowest level in more than a decade. But other economists express

concerns about the country's high inflation levels. The IMF（国际货币基金组织）has forecast inflation of 25. 7 percent in 2008 and 31 percent in 2009—among the highest rates for any country in the world—and according to news reports, the country is already experiencing food shortages of goods such as sugar and milk. Francisco Rodriguez, former（以前的）chief economist of the Venezuelan National Assembly, writes in a 2008 *Foreign Affairs*（《外交事务》）article that income inequality has increased during Chavez's tenure（任期）.

Chapter 2　Status of Oil Industry

2.1　The Oil Industry in the Middle East

🔲 Guidance to Reading

Different from the United States, in the nations of the Middle East, mineral rights belong to the state. Oil companies must negotiate with governments to get concessions, or rights to produce oil, while Middle Eastern countries had to compete for the investment of oil company. In general oil company partnerships and concession patterns also limited the leverage of governments in the Middle East, which is illustrated by the example of Kuwait and Iran. The one company – one country pattern of concessions and Joint participation concessions are main patterns conducted in the Middle East.

🔲 Text

In the nations of the Middle East, as in many other countries, mineral rights belong to the state. Oil companies must **negotiate** with governments to get **concessions**, or rights to produce oil, in exchange for **lump – sum payments**, rents, and/or **royalties**, payments per unit (barrels or tons) of oil produced.

In most of the United States, mineral rights **go with** land ownership and oil companies can pick and choose among individual "sellers" of rights to explore for or produce oil on their land. But even though there may be more than one oil company "buyer", in reality each seller faces a concentrated market and none has leverage unless an individual's holdings are extremely large and/or strategically located. These structural **criteria** show why land owners in the United States are at a disadvantage in their bargaining with oil companies **as compared to** governments in the Middle East. This is true today but it was not always the case.

Before the Second World War, Middle Eastern countries had to compete for oil company investment in much the same way as **ranchers** in Texas or Oklahoma. The large companies were more afraid of a **glut** of oil than oil shortages. Under the "**Red Line Agreement**" of 1928, the three largest, Exxon, Shell, and BP, along with a few smaller partners, agreed that none of them would explore for or develop new oil in the old Ottoman Empire unless all the partners **consented**.

Countries inside the Red Line had difficulty getting these companies to find the new oil that could increase national income because the Red Line companies were **reluctant** to do anything that might increase world oil supplies and thus depress prices.

Oil company partnerships and concession patterns also limited the **leverage** of governments in the Middle East. Instead of one government being able to deal with several oil companies competing to operate in various parts of its territory, each government generally faced a single operating company, often a **joint venture** or partnership, on the other side of the bargaining table. Joint ventures are common in the oil industry because of its capital intensity and because oil investments are highly risky. Individual parent companies, like Gulf and **BP**, set up operating companies, like the **Kuwait Oil Company** (**KOC**), which they jointly owned. Even though two separate parents invested the capital and took the profits from Kuwait's oil, their business in Kuwait was conducted by a single company, KOC. Such partnerships allowed the large **multinational** oil companies to exercise more control over total world oil supplies by providing them with information about one another's production. They also discouraged competition among the partners to develop new concessions, and provided a means to coordinate their global operations.

Kuwait's ability to choose which company would get its concession was limited by the British government, which had signed treaties with Kuwait giving it the final authority to determine who would exploit any oil found there. The British would not permit the Kuwaitis to contract with a non–British company, though the amir held out for a company that had at least one non–British partner. After the concession was granted, Kuwait's **autonomy** was even more limited. The terms of its contract with KOC gave the company exclusive rights for 90 years to find and produce oil over the entire land area of the country. If the government were to try to get better terms from another company during the period of the KOC concession, that company would face legal challenges from BP and Gulf. Even more of a threat was the possibility of intervention by one of the home governments, Britain and the United States. If Kuwait should try to remove KOC from its **privileged** position, it could expect one or both to react unfavorably.

This is what happened in the early 1950s in Iran. The Iranian government, under Prime Minister Mohammad Mossadeq, nationalized Iran's oil in 1951. Iran's concession was unusual for the Middle East in that there was only one parent company, BP. When its holdings were nationalized, BP obtained court orders **enjoining** other companies from buying oil from the Iranian government. Afraid of the example that a successful nationalization might set for other Middle Eastern oil exporting states, the British and American governments worked to **destabilize** and eventually to **overthrow** the Mossadeq regime. The restoration of the Shah in 1953 following a brief period of **ouster** also **reinstated** foreign oil companies as managers of the nationalized Iranian oil company. However, instead of restoring BP to its former position as sole owner, the Iranian government sought a "Kuwait solution." The Shah invited non – British participation in the **National Iranian Oil Company** (**NIOC**). When NIOC was reorganized, American companies and the French national oil company, CFP, were given 60 percent of the **shares**, and BP was left with only 40 percent.

The one company – one country pattern of concessions through much of the Middle East helped to make the region the **marginal** supplier of oil to the international market, that is, the source of however much oil was needed to balance global supply and demand. This balancing act was made possible by the participation of all the very large companies, whose production holdings stretched across the globe, in one or another Middle Eastern concession. The solution of the Iranian crisis in the 1950s made this control even easier because the reorganized NIOC was the first operating consortium in the Middle East that included every one of the major oil companies, the "seven sisters" who dominated the industry from the end of the Second World War.

Joint participation in Middle Eastern concessions enabled oil companies to share information. Even more important for supply management was the leverage the companies could exercise against the host governments. Once they had decided what total supply should be, the companies could regulate production by increasing or decreasing off take in a few countries whose governments could not easily **retaliate** against them. The one company – one country pattern did not hold in Libya, whose oil was discovered and developed much later than that of most of the Gulf countries. As we shall see, this enabled the Libyan government to spearhead the assault on the oil companies that triggered the oil revolution of the 1970s.

The large oil companies **refrained** from competing with one another over concession terms to avoid setting an example that might persuade other governments to try to get better terms as well. They also agreed to avoid competing in other ways, such as in setting prices to transport oil and prices for oil products like gasoline. The regulation of oil company competition was outlined in another 1928 cartel arrangement, the *"As Is Agreement."*

The *As Is agreement*, **ostensibly** global in nature, actually required the individual negotiation of little *As Is arrangement* in each regional market but it was not rigidly followed anywhere. Large companies challenged it on occasion, but the most constant **violators** were small companies who behaved as though nothing they did could affect the overall price structure of the **cartel regime**.

🔲 Words and Expressions

negotiate	谈判,交涉
concession	特许(权)
royalties	特许使用权费
criteria	标准,条件
rancher	大农场经营者
glut	(商品)供过于求
consent	同意,答应
reluctant	不情愿的;勉强的
leverage	杠杆作用;影响力
multinational	多国的,跨国公司的
autonomy	自治,自治权
privileged	享有特权的
enjoin	禁止
destabilize	使动摇
overthrow	推翻,打倒
ouster	驱逐;剥夺

reinstate	使恢复,使复原
share	股份;份额
marginal	边缘的;临界的
retaliate	报复;回敬
refrain	避免;克制
ostensibly	表面上;外表
violator	违反者

Phrases and Expressions

lump – sum payments	一次性支付
go with	伴随
as compared to	同……相比
joint venture	合资企业

Proper Names

Red Line Agreement	红线协定(美英等石油企业为瓜分中东石油资源而达成的第一协议,是美国冲破英法防线,涉足中东石油资源的重要一步)
BP	英国石油公司
KOC	科威特石油公司
NIOC	伊朗国家石油公司
cartel regime	卡特尔体制(指生产同类商品的企业,为了获取高额利润,在划分销售市场、规定商品产量、确定商品价格等方面达成协议而形成的一种垄断联合)

Language Focus

1. Countries inside the Red Line had difficulty getting these companies to find the new oil that could increase national income because the Red Line companies were reluctant to do anything that might increase world oil supplies and thus depress prices.

（参考译文:因为红线(即签协议)公司都不愿意做那些可能增加世界石油供应,从而压低油价的事情,所以,被划分到红线以内的国家在寻找勘探新油田的公司上困难重重,而新油田可以增加国家收入。)

本句是复合句,because 引导原因状语从句,主句中的 that 引导定语从句修饰 the new oil,原因状语从句中的 that 引导定语从句,修饰 anything。

2. Instead of one government being able deal with several oil companies competing to operate in various parts of its territory, each government generally faced a single operating company, often a joint venture or partnership, on the other side of the bargaining table.

(参考译文:政府不是解决几个公司在其领土的不同地区的竞争,而是每个政府普遍面对一个单一的经营公司,其往往是谈判桌对面的一个合资企业或合作伙伴。)

本句是简单句, Instead of 是介词短语表示"替代,不是",句子的主谓部分是 each government generally faced,而 often a joint venture or partnership 是插入语,说明句子的宾语,on the other side of the bargaining table 是介词短语,修饰句子的宾语。

3. Kuwait's ability to choose which company would get its concession was limited by the British government, which had signed treaties with Kuwait giving it the final authority to determine who would exploit any oil found there.

(参考译文:科威特选择哪家公司获得特许权将受到英国政府的限制,英国政府与科威特已签署条约,赋予英国最终权力,决定谁可以开发特威特石油。)

本句是复合句,句子的主语是 Kuwait's ability,to... 是不定式作定语,修饰主语,逗号后的 which 引导非限定性定语从句,修饰 the British government,而定语从句中包含一个 who 引导的宾语从句。

4. The solution of the Iranian crisis in the 1950s made this control even easier because the reorganized NIOC was the first operating consortium in the Middle East that included every one of the major oil companies, the "seven sisters" who dominated the industry from the end of the Second World War until the oil revolution.

(参考译文:20世纪50年代的伊朗危机的解决方案使得这种控制更加容易,因为伊朗国家石油公司(NIOC)的重组由中东地区的第一经营财团进行,该财团包括在第二次世界大战后期主导石油产业的"七姐妹"——大型石油公司中的每一个成员。)

本句是复合句,because 引导原因状语从句,状语从句中包含一个由 that 引导的定语从句,修饰 operating consortium,同位成分 the "seven sisters" 后接定语从句。

5. Large companies challenged it on occasion, but the most constant violators were small companies who behaved as though nothing they did could affect the overall price structure of the cartel regime.

（参考译文：有时大公司会挑战此协议，但最经常违反该协议的是一些小公司，似乎他们做什么都不可能影响卡特尔体制的整体价格结构。）

本句是并列句，but 连接一个简单句和一个复合句，who 引导定语从句修饰 small companies，其中 they did 是省略 that 的定语从句，修饰 nothing。

Reinforced Learning

I. Answer the following questions for a comprehension of the text.

1. Under the "Red Line Agreement" of 1928, what agreement was reached for oil company?

2. Why were joint ventures so common in the oil industry in the Middle East?

3. Why did the British and American governments work to destabilize and eventually to overthrow the Mossadeq regime?

4. What are the advantages of the one company – one country pattern of concessions conducted in the Middle East countries?

5. What are the advantages of joint participation conducted in Middle Eastern countries?

II. Multiple choice: choose the correct one from the alternative answers to give the exact meaning of the words.

1. In most of the United States, mineral rights go with land ownership and oil companies can pick and choose among individual "sellers" of rights to explore for or produce oil on their land.

    A. correspond   B. consistent

    C. accompany   D. match

2. Registering to join Wal – Mart's Hubster community also requires parental consent.

    A. pleasure   B. approval

    C. understanding   D. support

3. At the moment, diesel is in short supply and there is a glut of fuel oil.

    A. supply with an excess   B. supply with a shortage

C. supply with a moderate amount D. supply with an enough amount

4. But China was <u>reluctant</u> to sign up to the 2050 target without first gaining key concessions.

    A. unwilling B. narrow

    C. dissatisfied D. grouchy

5. This would preserve the <u>autonomy</u> of fees, while creating what many consider greater fairness.

    A. self – help B. self – fulfilling

    C. self – possessed D. self – rule

6. Even domestic investors might reflect on the potential for inflation to erode the real value of their <u>holdings</u>.

    A. possession of the property B. possession of the security

    C. possession of the credit D. possession of the loan

7. He warned that the fighting in Lebanon could <u>destabilize</u> the Middle East.

    A. threaten B. persecute C. unsettle D. unease

8. The restoration of the Shah in 1953 following a brief period of <u>ouster</u> also reinstated foreign oil companies as managers of the nationalized Iranian oil company.

    A. downfall B. divergence C. expulsion D. deviation

9. The meeting was <u>ostensibly</u> to discuss a potential acquisition of the German automaker.

    A. explicitly B. apparently C. particularly D. definitely

10. If Kuwait should try to remove KOC from its privileged position, it could expect one or both to react <u>unfavorably</u>.

    A. energetically B. wrongfully C. adversely D. restlessly

III. Multiple choice: read the four suggested translations and choose the best answer.

1. Oil companies must negotiate with governments to get concessions, or rights to produce oil, in exchange for lump – sum payments, rents, and/or <u>royalties</u>, payments per unit (barrels or tons) of oil produced.

    A. 关税权使用费 B. 专利权使用费

    C. 特许使用权费 D. 版税使用费

2. But even though there may be more than one oil company "buyer," in

reality each seller faces a concentrated market and none has leverage unless an individual's holdings are extremely large and/or strategically located.

 A. 杠杆作用 B. 影响力 C. 手段 D. 效应

 3. Joint ventures are common in the oil industry because of its capital intensity and because oil investments are highly risky.

 A. 资本密集 B. 资本集中 C. 资本运用 D. 资本力度

 4. The one company – one country pattern of concessions through much of the Middle East helped to make the region the marginal supplier of oil to the international market, that is, the source of however much oil was needed to balance global supply and demand.

 A. 边际供应商   B. 末端供应商
 C. 临界供应商   D. 边缘供应商

 5. Once they had decided what total supply should be, the companies could regulate production by increasing or decreasing off take in a few countries whose governments could not easily retaliate against them.

 A. 生产 B. 委托 C. 承购 D. 包销

Ⅳ. Put the following sentences into Chinese.

 1. Under the "Red Line Agreement" of 1928, the three largest, Exxon, Shell, and BP, along with a few smaller partners, agreed that none of them would explore for or develop new oil in the old Ottoman Empire unless all the partners consented.

 2. They also discouraged competition among the partners to develop new concessions elsewhere, and provided a means to coordinate their global operations.

 3. Iran's concession was unusual for the Middle East in that there was only one parent company, BP.

 4. The one company – one country pattern did not hold in Libya, whose oil was discovered and developed much later than that of most of the Gulf countries.

 5. The large oil companies refrained from competing with one another over concession terms to avoid setting an example that might persuade other governments to try to get better terms as well.

V. Put the following paragraphs into Chinese.

1. The Middle East is the geographic "center of gravity" of the world oil industry. Oil is of integral (完整的,不可缺少的) importance in both the foreign and the domestic politics of nearly every country in the region, oil importers as well as oil exporters.

2. Upstream from production are exploration, the search for oil – bearing lands, and development, the construction of production infrastructure (基础设施) like oil wells and gas separators. Downstream from production are transportation, including pipelines, tankers, and railroads; refining, which turns crude oil into usable products like gasoline and fuel oil; and marketing—gasoline/petrol stations, among other things.

2.2 Africa's oil refinery

⌐┐ Guidance to Reading

The major refining centers in Africa are located in South Africa, Nigeria, Egypt, and Algeria. Since the early 1980s, many of the remaining refineries in Africa have faced significant challenges and even some African refineries have been forced to close. The text gives a presentation about governments polices in developing refinery industry and major projects in four countries.

⌐┐ Text

The downstream industry includes refining and retail activities. Oil refineries **convert** crude oil **into** fuel products, **lubricating oils**, bitumen, chemical feedstocks and other oil products. The major refining centers in Africa are located in South Africa (4 refineries and 3 synthetic fuel plants), Nigeria (3 refineries), Egypt (9 refineries), and Algeria (4 refineries). The largest single refinery is the Skikda refinery in Algeria (300 million bpd), whereas the smallest **operating** refinery is the Solimar refinery in Madagascar, with a capacity of 14 million bpd.

Many African refineries have been forced to close because of low worldwide refining **margins**, small local markets, high operating costs (due to small size), and poor yields. Following the World Bank/**IMF insistence** on market liberalization in the early 1980s, many of the remaining refineries have faced significant challenges. Although **installed** capacity in Africa is higher than present consumption, the continent still faces high shortages in refined products that are **balanced** by imports. As a consequence of the short – ages and of the need to maximize economic profit by placing the refinery close to the source, several initiatives and plans are **underway** to install new refineries in such countries as Nigeria, Sudan, Uganda, and Mozambique.

The Example of Nigeria's Refinery Industry

There are considerable investment opportunities in Nigeria's downstream oil and gas sector. The government's focus is on **deregulating** the sector by licensing private refineries, **eliminating** government subsidies to the downstream sector, and privatizing existing ones. Through such strategic action, domestic capacity is expected to at least meet demand. The four existing refineries have significantly and consistently produced below capacity, owing to **a host of** factors, including poor management and maintenance.

The deregulation of the downstream oil and gas sector (Petroleum Refining & Marketing) has been in focus for a number of years. Indeed, **scarcity** of petroleum products and gradual deregulation of petroleum product prices have generated heated controversies in Nigeria. The government is determined to **nurture** private – sector participation and engage local companies in the oil and gas sector—hence the licensing of private refineries and deregulation of petroleum product prices—to improve local capacity. In the coming years, **consolidation** is expected in the oil refining and marketing sector, with new **entrants**. There are significant investment opportunities for both local and international funding.

Sahara Petroleum Exploration, a subsidiary of Global Environmental Energy, has been **contracted** to build a 70,000 bpd oil refinery at Eket, Akwa Ibom state, Nigeria.

This is an approximately $4 billion project that represents cash flow at today's market rate of approximately $1.5 billion **per annum**. Such plans to increase Nigeria's refining capacity will also provide considerable cost savings to operators (such as Sahara Petroleum) by refining oil products close to source. At present, the country has four main refineries with a **nameplate** capacity of 438,750 bpd.

Tullow Oil Refinery Plan in Uganda

Tullow Oil is currently working to find out the quantity and quality of oil that has been discovered in the Albertine Graben in Uganda before a decision is made to build a multi – billion dollar refinery or not.

The Uganda government and Tullow Oil have agreed to build a **mini refinery** in an early production scheme that will enable installation of a 100 MW heavy fuel oil thermal power plant. The mini refinery (with a capacity of about 5,000 barrels of oil per day) will cost Tullow US $ 200 million.

Sudan to Double its Oil – refining Capacity

Sudan is planning to double its oil refining capacity, with a short, three – year investment plan, to handle increased production, having reached an agreement to end its 21 – year civil war. A new 100,000 bpd refinery will be built in Port Sudan, on the Red Sea coast, and the capacity of two existing refineries will be increased. Talks have been held with India's Oil & Natural Gas, China's Sinopec, Malaysia's Petronas, and an **unidentified** Turkish company to build the new refinery. Boosting refinery capacity is especially timely since Sudan expects crude oil production to increase significantly in the coming years.

New Mozambique Oil Refinery Approved

The Mozambican **Council of Ministers** has approved the **construction** of an oil refinery, valued at more than $ 1.3 billion, in the northern province of Nampula. **Dubbed** the 'Ayr Logistics Limited—Nacala', the project is **spearheaded** by a privately owned American company, Ayr Logistics, in partnership with one Mozambican and three South African investors. The project is expected to create about 450 jobs and generate extra tax revenue for the Mozambican government. With an installed capacity of about 100,000 bbl/d, most of the product will be exported to Malawi, Zimbabwe, and Zambia. The project also includes the construction of several **infrastructures** that will support the main activity of the project, which will be implemented over an area of 838 ha and will be situated in the district of the Nacala port, which is also home to Mozambique's deepest and busiest port.

Despite the **illustration** of the above plans and visions, the fact remains that very little global refining capacity has been added in the last three years, including in 2007.

Nevertheless, significant refinery capacity additions are still planned, although a major concern is that construction costs are rising with **inflationary** prices. Other non – economic reasons—in Africa, as elsewhere—for the slow growth in refining capacity（worldwide）are environmental and local concerns，more stringent environmental laws，and effective community organizing，which have made it very difficult to build new refineries.

Some **analysts** consider refinery capacity a significant factor of high oil prices. It thus **makes sense** to increase refinery capacity in Africa as a way to reduce the costs of refined oil products. However，this needs to be done in an environment – friendly manner.

Words and Expressions

operating	运营的；操作的
margin	利润
insistence	坚持，坚决主张
installed	安装的，已装入的
balance	使平衡
underway	进行中的
deregulate	解除对……的管制
eliminate	消除，排除
scarcity	缺乏，不足
nurture	鼓励，扶植
consolidation	巩固；合并
entrant	进入者；新会员
contract	订约，合同
nameplate	标示牌
unidentified	未经确认的
construction	建设
dubbed	被称为的
spearhead	带头，牵头
infrastructure	基础设施
illustration	说明，例证
inflationary	通货膨胀引起的；通货膨胀倾向的
analysts	分析师，分析家

Phrases and Expressions

convert into	把……转化成

a host of	众多,大量
per annum	每年
make sense	有意义

▣ Proper Names

the downstream industry	下游产业(在整个产业链的末端,加工原材料和零部件,制造成品和从事生产、服务的行业)
lubricating oils	润滑油
IMF	(联合国)国际货币基金组织
Tullow Oil	塔洛石油公司(全称英国图洛石油公司,欧洲最大的独立石油和天然气勘探公司之一)
mini refinery	微型炼油厂
Council of Ministers	内阁
Ayr Logistics Limited	艾尔物流有限公司

▣ Language Focus

1. As a consequence of the short – ages and of the need to maximize economic profit by placing the refinery close to the source, several initiatives and plans are underway to install new refineries in such countries as Nigeria, Sudan, Uganda, and Mozambique.

(参考译文:受精炼产品短缺,及经济利润最大化的吸引,炼油厂设在石油资源附近, 尼日利亚、苏丹、乌干达和莫桑比克等国家正在计划建立新的炼油厂。)

本句是简单句,As a consequence of 引导原因状语,主谓部分是 several initiatives and plans are underway。

2. Sudan is planning to double its oil refining capacity, with a short, three – year investment plan, to handle increased production, having reached an agreement to end its 21 – year civil war.

(参考译文:由于已经达成了结束21年内战的协议,为了提高产量,在三年短期的投资计划中,苏丹计划炼油能力提高一倍。)

本句是简单句,having reached an agreement to end its 21 – year civil war 是过去分词,作原因状语。

3. The project also includes the construction of several infrastructures that will support the main activity of the project, which will be implemented over an

area of 838 ha and will be situated in the district of the Nacala port, which is also home to Mozambique's deepest and busiest port.

（参考译文：该项目还包括建设几个基础设施，以支持其主要生产，该项目占地面积 838 公顷，位于纳卡拉港口地区，此港口也是莫桑比克最深且最繁忙的港口。）

本句是复合句，that 引导限定性定语从句修饰 the construction of several infrastructures，而 which 引导非限定性定语从句，修饰前面整个句子。

4. Other non – economic reasons—in Africa, as elsewhere—for the slow growth in refining capacity (worldwide) are environmental and local concerns, more stringent environmental laws, and effective community organizing, which have made it very difficult to build new refineries.

（参考译文：像其他地方一样，非洲（世界各地）炼油能力增长缓慢有其他非经济原因：对地方及环境的担忧、更严格的环保法规及有效的地区规划，这些原因使得建立新炼油厂很难。）

本句是复合句，in Africa, as elsewhere 是作地点状语，主句的主语是 Other non – economic reasons for the slow growth in refining capacity (worldwide)，后面的三个名词短语作并列表语，而 which 引导非限定性定语从句，修饰前面整个句子。

Reinforced Learning

I. Answer the following questions for a comprehension of the text.

1. Why have been many African refineries forced to close?

2. What's the government's focus in Nigeria's to improve local capacity?

3. What's the goal of Sudan in oil refining capacity?

4. How to describe the project dubbed the 'Ayr Logistics Limited—Nacala' in Mozambique according to text?

5. In Africa, what do other non – economic reasons of the slow growth of refining capacity refer to?

II. Multiple choice: choose the correct one from the alternative answers to give the exact meaning of the words.

1. Current assets refer to the companies who want to <u>convert into</u> cash within the accounting period.

A. communicate to   B. change to

C. accelerate to   D. translate to

2. Many African refineries have been forced to close because of low world-wide refining margins, small local markets, high operating costs (due to small size), and poor yields.

A. edges   B. profits   C. brinks   D. suburbs

3. Astronauts will conduct three space walks during the mission to install some of the equipment to the station.

A. build   B. establish   C. place   D. constitute

4. We applaud the president's insistence on tough environmental laws.

A. adherence   B. duration   C. resistance   D. response

5. Some industries, including airlines and trucking have already started to deregulate.

A. put the regulations on   B. lift the regulations on

C. impose the regulations on   D. ease the regulations on

6. The government is determined to nurture private – sector participation and engage local companies in the oil and gas sector.

A. assist   B. support   C. educate   D. foster

7. The vast consolidation within the rail industry means that most shippers are served by only one rail company.

A. convention   B. purchase   C. alliance   D. merger

8. Indeed, scarcity of petroleum products and gradual deregulation of petroleum product prices have generated heated controversies in Nigeria.

A. sufficiency   B. shortage   C. surplus   D. requirement

9. It adds that leaders need to agree on assistance to the poor, including food subsidies and cash transfers.

A. expenditures   B. provisions   C. allowances   D. supplies

10. But few days later, Ma roadside sidewalks, and he has adopted the construction nameplate.

A. flat plate   B. base plate   C. steel plate   D. data plate

III. Multiple choice: read the four suggested translations and choose the best answer.

1. The largest single refinery is the Skikda refinery in Algeria (300 million bpd), whereas the smallest operating refinery is the Solimar refinery in Madagascar, with a capacity of 14 million bpd.

A. 操作炼油厂　B. 运营炼油厂　　C. 合作炼油厂　　D. 纯炼油厂

2. Following the World Bank/IMF insistence on <u>market liberalization</u> in the early 1980s, many of the remaining refineries have faced significant challenges.

A. 市场经济　　B. 市场解放　　C. 市场开放　　D. 自由市场

3. Dubbed the 'Ayr Logistics Limited—Nacala', the project is <u>spearheaded</u> by a privately owned American company, Ayr Logistics, in partnership with one Mozambican and three South African investors.

A. 先锋　　　　B. 领导　　　　C. 牵头　　　　D. 控制

4. This is an approximately $4 billion project that represents <u>cash flow</u> at today's market rate of approximately $1.5 billion per annum.

A. 付现流　　　B. 现金兑现　　C. 现金流　　　D. 现金泛滥

5. However, this needs to be done in an <u>environment – friendly</u> manner.

A. 环境优美　　B. 环保　　　　C. 环境友好　　D. 环境好

Ⅳ. Put the following sentences into Chinese.

1. The downstream industry includes refining and retail activities. Oil refineries convert crude oil into fuel products, lubricating oils, bitumen, chemical feedstocks and other oil products.

2. Although installed capacity in Africa is higher than present consumption, the continent still faces high shortages in refined products that are balanced by imports.

3. The Mozambican Council of Ministers has approved the construction of an oil refinery, valued at more than $1.3 billion, in the northern province of Nampula.

4. Despite the illustration of the above plans and visions, the fact remains that very little global refining capacity has been added in the last three years, including in 2007.

5. It thus makes sense to increase refinery capacity in Africa as a way to reduce the costs of refined oil products.

Ⅴ. Put the following paragraphs into Chinese.

1. The Mozambican Council of Ministers has approved the construction of an oil refinery, valued at more than $1,3 – billion, in the northern province of Nampula, reports news agency Bloomberg. Dubbed the 'Ayr Logistics Limited – Nacala'. The project also has the responsibility of providing for humanitarian

assistance and support for the communities of Nacala, currently an impover-ished district owing to the infertility (贫瘠) of most of its soil, cyclical pests, and adverse (不利的) weather conditions.

2. Africa, an increasingly important oil exporter, is a major importer of re-fined products due to growing demand for fuel and a lack of refining capaci-ty. In Nigeria, the world's eight – biggest crude oil exporter, the government of former President Olusegun Obasanjo, issued 18 licenses to private investors in 2003 to build refineries but many have since been revoked (撤回,取消) as they have not been built.

2.3　Profile of Australian Oil

🔲 Guidance to Reading

In order to maintain the Australian petroleum industry's international competitiveness, west Australia has operated the upstream and downstream pe-troleum exploration and development projects. The petroleum sector and the rest of the resources industry, is contributing to Western Australia's current eco-nomic surge. Australia's current oil development focused on several major ba-sins, in many other unexplored waters, oil and gas reserves are considerable.

🔲 Text

Since oil was first discovered at **Rough Range**, a **distance** of about 1070km north from Perth, which is the capital of Western Australia in 1953, oil and gas have grown to become Western Australia's most **valuable** resource ex-ports. Over the past decade, Perth has become the centre of petroleum activities in Australia. Western Australia is currently the nation's largest petroleum pro-ducer and holds **approximately** 57 per cent of Australia's oil, 71 per cent of its **condensate** and 78 per cent of its gas **reserves**. The petroleum industry was the fastest growing economic **sector** in Western Australia during the 1990s and both national and international companies are being **attracted** to Perth.

Since the 1980s, petroleum production has increased **substantially** with the development of the **North West Shelf** (**NWS**) project. The **primary** focus of petroleum exploration continues to be the offshore **Northern Carnarvon Basin**.

The value of upstream and downstream petroleum projects being planned amounts to more than \$80 billion over the next few years. This will **boost** liquid production in the foreseeable future. Most of the future oil developments come from **Exmouth Sub – basin** fields, containing heavy oil, and as such, will decline rapidly. The current **boom** in the **liquefied** natural gas (LNG) market **underpins** a number of LNG developments, such as Gorgon, Jansz – Io and Ichthys, and it is expected that the industry will **apply to** develop other LNG projects in the near future. The **majority** of these oil and LNG developments are expected to come on stream during the coming decade.

These petroleum development projects will benefit Western Australians through an increase in **royalty** revenue for the Government, new employment, regional development, and **infrastructure** development. These projects are **crucial** to both State and nation as they provide Australia with a greater degree of self – sufficiency in liquid production, as well as **additional** security of supply.

However, there are **challenges** ahead. Both liquid production and the **associated** royalties from producing fields are **declining** fast. Australia's major producing basins have matured and to maintain oil production in Western Australia there is an **urgent** need to **promote** and **facilitate** exploration activities in the **Canning Basin** and facilitate and encourage industry's **efforts** for exploration in other frontier basins.

Australia needs to grow its **domestic** reserves base, particularly its liquids. Unless there are increased industry efforts, along with government assistance **in this respect**, Australia's self – sufficiency in liquid hydrocarbon production will drop from 75 per cent to 25 per cent by the year 2020, according to the **Australian Bureau of Agricultural and Resource Economics** (**ABARE**). This will have a **significant impact** on Australia's **balance** of payments and on Government taxation revenue.

In this current booming environment for the petroleum industry, more than ever before, **DoIR**'s **Petroleum and Royalties Division is conscious of** the priorities of companies **undertaking** exploration activities. The Division, therefore, **endeavors** to undertake approval processes with definite timelines in mind so as to **maximize potential** development opportunities presented to this key sector of the Western Australian economy.

Major Sedimentary Basins

There are seven **sedimentary** basins which cover an **estimated** 2. 1 million

km^2 (including the continental shelf) and in five there have been hydrocarbon shows. Economic production comes only from the **offshore** Northern Carnarvon Basin, the northern **Perth Basin**, and the **onshore** Canning Basin.

Western Australia is one of the least explored **territories** in the world with one exploration well per 3,124km^2 offshore and one well per 2,647km^2 onshore. On the NWS, well density is one well per 100 km^2. This **vast** resource region is one of the most attractive exploration targets in the world. Fifty to seventy per cent of the Australia's exploration expenditure was spent in Western Australia during the past decade.

The Northern Carnarvon Basin is the most productive basin in Western Australia and has been the focus of much exploration activity over the past 30 years. Presently 98 per cent of hydrocarbon production comes from the fields in the Northern Carnarvon Basin and this is likely to increase **considerably** in the near future with several fields to be brought **on stream** including Vincent, Van Gogh, Angel and Gorgon.

The offshore Perth Basin is a relatively old play **fairway** that is being revisited as of late by several companies with some excellent results. There are a number of oil and gas fields in production onshore and one offshore. **The Browse and Bonaparte basins** are relatively under – explored. Recently, activity has increased significantly in the offshore Browse Basin, and despite the Bonaparte only having one producing field, it is believed there is significant potential in these northern offshore basins.

Production and Reserves

Due to a combination of factors, including the State's oil and gas endowment and **comprehensive** infrastructure, the petroleum industry was the fastest growing economic sector during the 1990s. The number of developed and producing fields has almost doubled over the past decade. In 2007 there were 68 producing fields. During that year seven new fields came on stream: Apium, Doric, Eskdale, Lee, Searipple, Stybarrow, and West Cycad.

Western Australia's total estimated liquid and gas petroleum resources at the end of December 2007 were 2. 86 Bstb and 3704 Gm^3 (131 Tscf), respectively. Average liquid petroleum and gas production during 2007 were 328,000 bbl/d and 80 Mm^3/d **respectively**. A **cumulative** total of 228 Mm^3 (1,435 MMstb) crude, 92. 5 Mm^3 (582 MMstb) condensate and 448 Gm^3 (15. 8 Tscf) gas had been produced from Western Australian oil – and gas fields, to 31 December 2007.

Currently, the State's gas and petroleum liquid production **exceeds** that of Victoria's **Gippsland Basin.**

A peak in oil production was expected around 2008 – 09 mainly **attributable to** the development of heavy oilfields in the Exmouth Sub – basin and there would be a sharp decline after this point. Between 2010 and 2020, condensate production from gas condensate fields will play a key role in maintaining liquid hydrocarbon production in the future. Since condensate production comes principally from LNG developments, the **forecast** decline in condensate production is much slower than the decline in oil production.

Words and Expressions

rough	粗糙的,粗略的,粗暴的
range	范围,界限,区域
distance	距离,路程
valuable	贵重的,宝贵的
approximately	大约,近似地
condensate	浓缩物,冷凝物
reserve	储藏,保存
sector	部门,区域
attract	吸引;引诱,诱惑
substantially	充分地,丰富地;大量地
primary	第一的,最初的;主要的
boost	提高,增加;促进
boom	突然兴旺,景气,繁荣;暴涨,激增
liquefied	液化的
underpin	从下方支持;加固;支援,支持
majority	大多数,大部分
royalty	矿区土地使用费(由采矿或石油公司等付给土地所有人)
infrastructure	基础设施;基础建设
crucial	至关重要的,关键性的
additional	额外的,另外的

challenge	挑战
associated	相关的,有联系的
decline	下降,减少,衰退
urgent	急迫的,紧要的
promote	促进;推动;增进
facilitate	使便利,促进;促使
effort	努力,尽力;艰难的尝试,试图
domestic	国内的,国产的,家庭的
significant	有意义的,重大的
impact	影响,作用
balance	平衡,均衡
undertake	从事,着手
endeavor	尝试,试图
maximize	最大化;最大限度地利用
potential	潜在的,有可能的
sedimentary	沉积的,沉淀性的
estimate	估计,估量
offshore	近海的
onshore	海岸的;在岸上的
territory	领土,版图;(澳大利亚)区
vast	巨大的
considerably	相当,非常
fairway	航道;(高尔夫球场上的)平坦球道
comprehensive	综合的;全面的
respectively	分别;各自
cumulative	累积的,累计的;渐增的
exceed	超过;超越
forecast	预言,预报,预测

Phrases and Expressions

apply to	应用于
in this respect	在这方面,在这点上
be conscious of	慎重的,有意的
on stream	进行生产,投入生产

| be attributable to | 可归于……的 |

📖 Proper Names

NWS	西北大陆架
Northern Carnarvon Basin	卡那封盆地
Exmouth Sub – basin	埃克斯茅斯次盆
Canning Basin	坎宁盆地
ABARE	澳大利亚农业资源经济局
DoIR	工业资源部
Petroleum and Royalties Division	石油和特许权使用费司
Perth Basin	珀斯盆地
Browse Basin	布劳斯盆地
Bonaparte Basin	波拿巴盆地
Gippsland Basin	吉普斯兰盆地

📖 Language Focus

1. Since oil was first discovered at Rough Range, a distance of about 1070 km north from Perth, which is the capital of Western Australia in 1953, oil and gas have grown to become Western Australia's most valuable resource exports.

（参考译文：自从 1953 年首次在距离西澳大利亚州首府珀斯 1070 千米的拉夫·兰芝发现石油后，石油和天然气就发展成为西澳大利亚州最宝贵的出口资源性产品。）

本句 Rough Range, a distance of... 是同位语；其中 which 引导的非限制性定语从句，修饰 Perth。

2. The Division, therefore, endeavours to undertake approval processes with definite timelines in mind so as to maximise potential development opportunities presented to this key sector of the Western Australian economy.

（参考译文：为最大限度地利用出现在西澳大利亚经济这个主要部门的潜在发展机会，该司努力按确定的日程表进行审批程序。）

本句中的过去分词短语 presented to this key sector of the Western Australian economy 作后置定语，修饰 development opportunities；so as to maximise... 作目的状语。

3. The offshore Perth Basin is a relatively old play fairway that is being revisited as of late by several companies with some excellent results.

（参考译文：近海的珀斯盆地如同一个熟悉的球道，到目前为止，再次涉入的几家公司收益都不错。）

本句中的 that 从句修饰 play fairway；其中 as of late 表达时间关系，常译为：至今，截至，然后。如：

As of late April 2001, all loans in commercial banks, individual housing loans accounted for 5.54%; the annual growth rate is around 150%. （截至 2001 年 4 月末，在商业银行的全部贷款中，个人住房贷款余额占 5.54%，每年的增长速度都在 150% 左右。）

4. There are a number of oil and gas fields in production onshore and one offshore.

（参考译文：陆上有许多生产中的油气田，可近海却只有一个。）

本句中 "one offshore" 是个省略句，应为：there is only one oil and gas field in production on offshore.

Reinforced Learning

Ⅰ. Answer the following questions for a comprehension of the text.

1. What could Western Australians benefit from the petroleum development projects?

2. What will produce a material effect upon Australia's balance of payments and on government taxation revenue?

3. What is the most productive basin in Western Australia?

4. When did seven new fields, including Apium and so on, bring on stream?

5. What was the oil production around 2008 – 2009 peak attributed to?

Ⅱ. Multiple choice: choose the correct one from the alternative answers to give the exact meaning of the words.

1. Oil and gas have grown to become Western Australia's most <u>valuable</u> resource exports.

    A. very important   B. special   C. valid   D. effective

2. These projects are <u>crucial</u> to both state and nation as they provide Australia with a greater degree of self – sufficiency in liquid production.

    A. skeptical   B. very important

    C. deep   D. forecasting

3. There is an urgent need to promote and <u>facilitate</u> exploration activities in the Canning Basin.

　　A. organize　　　　B. assist　　　C. exchange　　D. develop

4. This will have a <u>significant</u> impact on Australia's balance of payments and on Government taxation revenue.

　　A. notable　　　　B. great　　　　C. immediate　D. definite

5. This will <u>boost</u> liquid production in the foreseeable future.

　　A. control　　　　B. release　　　C. encourage　D. increase

6. Australia needs to grow its <u>domestic</u> reserves base, particularly its liquids.

　　A. local　　　　B. regional　　　C. internal　　D. international

7. Both liquid production and the associated royalties from producing fields are <u>declining</u> fast.

　　A. decreasing　　　B. increasing　　C. ceasing　　D. leasing

8. Unless there are increased industry efforts, along with government assistance <u>in this respect</u>, Australia's self – sufficiency in liquid hydrocarbon production will drop from 75 per cent to 25 per cent by the year 2020.

　　A. in the regard　　B. in a way　　C. in the way　D. concerning

9. DoIR's Petroleum and Royalties Division <u>is conscious of</u> the priorities of companies undertaking exploration activities.

　　A. makes allowance for　　　　B. is allowing

　　C. takes action on　　　　　　D. is noticing

10. The Division <u>endeavours</u> to undertake approval processes with definite timelines in mind.

　　A. decides　　　　　　　　　B. promises

　　C. plans　　　　　　　　　　D. makes an attempt

Ⅲ. Multiple choice：read the four suggested translations and choose the best answer.

1. Western Australia is currently the nation's largest petroleum producer and holds <u>approximately</u> 57 per cent of Australia's oil, 71 per cent of its condensate and 78 per cent of its gas reserves.

　　A. 绝对性地　　　B. 广泛地　　　　C. 大约　　　　D. 分别地

2. The <u>primary</u> focus of petroleum exploration continues to be the offshore Northern Carnarvon Basin.

A. 首要的   B. 本来的   C. 核心的   D. 最初的

3. These projects are crucial to both State and nation as they provide Australia with a greater degree of self – sufficiency in liquid production, as well as additional security of supply.

A. 加法的   B. 额外的   C. 补充的   D. 上瘾的

4. This vast resource region is one of the most attractive exploration targets in the world.

A. 富饶的   B. 人迹罕至的   C. 种类繁多的   D. 广袤的

5. Between 2010 and 2020, condensate production from gas condensate fields will play a key role in maintaining liquid hydrocarbon production in the future.

A. 成为核心部分   B. 扮演着关键的角色
C. 不可或缺   D. 在……起重要作用

Ⅳ. Put the following sentences into Chinese.

1. Since the 1980s, petroleum production has increased substantially with the development of the North West Shelf (NWS) project.

2. These projects are crucial to both state and nation as they provide Australia with a greater degree of self – sufficiency in liquid production, as well as additional security of supply.

3. Unless there are increased industry efforts, along with government assistance in this respect, Australia's self – sufficiency in liquid hydrocarbon production will drop from 75 per cent to 25 per cent by the year 2020, according to the Australian Bureau of Agricultural and Resource Economics (ABARE).

4. Carnarvon Basin and this is likely to increase considerably in the near future with several fields to be brought on stream including Vincent, Van Gogh, Angel and Gorgon.

5. Due to a combination of factors, including the State's oil and gas endowment and comprehensive infrastructure, the petroleum industry was the fastest growing economic sector during the 1990s.

Ⅴ. Put the following paragraphs into Chinese.

1. The Australian oil refining industry is very important to the social and industrial stability of the nation. The local oil refining industry is critical in supplying and maintaining national social and industrial activities. The majority of

refinery output is used to supply the transport sector; however the agricultural industry, heavy industries, and general household activities are also reliant on locally produced oil products. If an Australian oil refinery were rendered unavailable for an extended period of time it would have significant consequences for the regional, and perhaps even national social and economic stability.

2. The upstream petroleum industry faces major challenges during the next two decades such as increased oil price and self – sufficiency, a widening gap between domestic supply and demand, maturity of current producing basins which requires enhanced onshore exploration, finding new frontier basins, diversification of Australian consumption, enhancing production from current fields and Government regulatory reforms to introduce a more competitive regulatory regime in Australia.

Chapter 3　Development of Oil Industry

3.1　Caspian Oil and Gas: Production and Prospects

⬚ Guidance to Reading

With higher output and large proven reserves of oil and gas, the Caspian Sea region appears the broad prospect, as a significant supplier of resource to world markets. Combined with much greater additional reserves of crude oil and natural gas, the Caspian Sea countries change the layout of the existing market operations, provide leverage in negotiating with Russia in terms of transit fees on shipments and expand the market including other potential markets, such as East Asian countries.

⬚ Text

Current Production and Proven Reserves

The Caspian Sea region presently is a significant, but not major, supplier of crude oil to world markets, **based upon** estimates by **BP** and **the Energy Information Administration** (**EIA**), U. S. Department of Energy. The Caspian region produced 1. 9 million barrels per day (bbls/day) including natural gas liquids in 2005, or 2 % of total world output. Thirteen non – Caspian region countries each produced more than 1. 9 million bbls/day in 2005. Caspian Sea region oil output has been higher, but suffered during the **dissolution** of the Soviet Union and the years following. Kazakhstan, whose production has risen rapidly since the late 1990s, **accounted for** 67 % and Azerbaijan for 22 % of regional crude oil output in 2005.

Based upon figures published by BP, Caspian Sea region oil production comes from proven reserves of 48 billion bbls. This **equals** about 4% of total world proven reserves, and much more than BP's figure for U. S. reserves (29 billion bbls). EIA estimates of much larger "possible" reserves suggest a potential for much greater production.

The Caspian Sea region's relative **contribution** to world natural gas supplies is larger than that for oil. Its gas production of 3.0 trillion cubic feet per year (tcf/yr) in 2005 was 3% of world output. As with oil, gas production has been higher, but suffered during the Soviet Union's **collapse** and the following years. Turkmenistan is the largest producer; with production of 2.0 tcf/yr, it accounts for almost two-thirds of the region's gas output.

Unlike oil, the region's proven reserves of natural gas are a higher **proportion** of the world total than its natural gas production. In some instances, exploration efforts hoping to find oil have found gas instead. The estimate of proven reserves of natural gas in the Caspian Sea region for the end of 2005 published by BP — 257 tcf — **represents** 4% of the world total. Increases in Caspian region gas production face **obstacles** are somewhat **similar** to those that challenge further oil development and production.

Resource and Production Prospects

There is a **likelihood** of much greater additional reserves of crude oil and natural gas being found in the Caspian Sea region. This is supported by the fact that a number of oil companies have large stakes there. Much of the known reserves have not been developed yet, and development usually leads to discovery that prospects are larger than originally estimated. Moreover, many areas **remain** unexplored. It is estimated that an additional 184 billion barrels of crude oil reserves are possible, which would raise the total to almost five times its present level. This level of proven reserves would nearly equal the **amount** now held by Saudi Arabia and could **come to** about 15% of total world reserves.

The prospective increase in natural gas proven reserves appears to be much smaller **in relative terms** than for oil, but still very large. It is estimated that there are nearly 300 tcf in additional natural gas reserves in the region. Should this be the case, total Caspian region proven reserves in 2010 would put the region's proven gas reserve total at more than twice its present level and far exceed present Saudi Arabian natural gas reserves. Given such expectations, it is estimated that annual Caspian region natural gas production would reach 5.4 tcf by 2010. Any **comparison** of the volumes of Caspian Sea region oil and natural gas reserves **versus** those of Saudi Arabia, however, must **be tempered by acknowledgment** of the considerable advantage of Saudi oil and gas in terms of much lower costs of production and much easier market access. Also, whatever the quantities and the production costs of their energy resources, Caspian countries' ability to develop and bring them to market could depend **to some extent** on the ability to establish and **maintain** relationships with international energy companies.

Present and Prospective Markets

In view of the above, Caspian Sea region countries potentially are large exporters of oil and gas. Caspian Sea oil and gas has several markets now and a wider **variety** of potential markets. These include nations trying to meet their economies' demand for energy and those that also wish to reduce their dependence on Persian Gulf energy.

Reflecting Soviet era **dictates** and infrastructure, nearly all Caspian region crude oil still goes north and/or west. It travels largely via pipeline to and/or through Russia to European markets, with refineries as part of the network. Some also goes by tanker through the Bosporus straits to Western European markets via the Mediterranean. Natural gas transportation, even more than oil, is tied to pipelines going mainly north and/or west through Russia and its monopoly pipeline system—**Transneft**. This, combined with the fact that Russia itself produces oil and gas, gives Russia the **market power** to **levy** transit fees **on** Caspian energy shipped through its transportation network, and to determine in some cases how much, if any, it is willing to transport. Also, because energy competes on a delivered – cost basis, reflecting transit fees, wellhead prices in the region suffer.

Caspian Sea countries thus have **incentives** to develop **alternatives** to routes through Russia – possibly a **consortia** of routes that would avoid long transits through Russia in reaching European and other markets and provide leverage in negotiating transit fees on shipments that do go through the Russian pipeline system. In addition, given Russia's early January 2006 cutting of natural gas supplies through Ukraine, it is likely that Western European countries— already seeking to **diversify** their sources of gas — will more actively seek non – Russian gas to reduce the effect of feared future **cut – offs**.

Caspian region energy sources are attractive to Turkey: they are close and offer Turkey an opportunity to **offset** part of its energy import bill through transit fees for shipments across its territory. Turkey's energy use is growing much faster than its economic output, making it a rapidly growing importer of both oil and gas; it already is a large importer of Russian gas. Also, Turkey has good relations with Caspian countries.

East Asian countries also are potentially attractive markets. Japan already imports a significant quantity of natural gas; and energy consumption in India and Pakistan is growing rapidly. Perhaps most significant, China's proven oil and gas reserves are small compared with the current and potential size of its economy, and the recent steep increases in its oil consumption. This has led, for example, to the building of an oil pipeline from Kazakhstan to China, which was completed and began to be filled in November 2005, and consideration of a Kazakhstan – to – China natural gas pipeline. The prospects of Caspian energy exports to the regions **identified** above, however, may be limited by newly **expanding** or developing non – Central Asian energy exports to those regions. These developments include **expansion** of North Africa's gas export capacity and discovery of a large natural gas province in and near Egypt.

Words and Expressions

proven	被证明的,已证实的
dissolution	分解,溶解;解散
equal	等于;比得上
contribution	捐献;贡献;促成作用
collapse	倒塌;瓦解;崩溃
proportion	比例
represent	等于,相当于
obstacle	障碍,干扰
similar	相似的
likelihood	可能性,可能
remain	保持;依然
amount	数量;总额
comparison	比较
versus	与……相对;与……相比
acknowledgment	承认
maintain	维持;继续
variety	多样;多样化/性
reflect	反射;表明
dictate	命令,规定,要求

incentive	动机;刺激
alternative	二中择一;供替代的选择
consortia	联盟;合作;公会
diversify	使多样化,使变化
cut – off	停止,中断
offset	抵消;弥补
identify	确定;认同
expand	扩张/大
expansion	扩张/大

◱ Phrases and Expressions

base upon	根据;以……基础;建立……之上
account for	(数量上、比例上)占
come to	共计,总共
in relative terms	相对而言
in terms of	依据;按照;在……方面
be tempered by	使缓和;使温和
to some extent	在一定程度上;在某种程度上
in view of	鉴于,考虑到
market power	市场权力
levy sth. on sb. / sth.	征收(税)

◱ Proper Names

BP	英国石油公司
EIA	美国能源资料协会
Transneft	俄罗斯国家石油运输公司

◱ Language Focus

1. The Caspian Sea region presently is a significant, but not major, supplier of crude oil to world markets, based upon estimates by BP and the Energy Information Administration (EIA), U. S. Department of Energy.

(参考译文:据英国石油公司和美国能源部的能源信息署(EIA)估计,目前里海地区是全球原油市场重要的供应商,但却不是主要的。)

本句中 based upon estimates by BP and the Energy Information Administration

（EIA），U. S. Department of Energy 为插入语。

2. Turkmenistan is the largest producer; with production of 2. 0 tcf/yr, it accounts for almost two – thirds of the region's gas output.

（参考译文：土库曼斯坦是最大的天然气生产国，年产 2 万亿立方英尺，占该地区天然气产量的近2/3。）

本句的 with production of 2. 0 tcf/yr 为独立主格，表示补充说明。

3. Any comparison of the volumes of Caspian Sea region oil and natural gas reserves versus those of Saudi Arabia, however, must be tempered by acknowledgment of the considerable advantage of Saudi oil and gas in terms of much lower costs of production and much easier market access.

（参考译文：里海地区大量的石油和天然气资源可与沙特阿拉伯相比，然而，也得承认沙特阿拉伯的石油和天然气生产成本较低以及市场就近等许多优势。）

本句中 those of Saudi Arabia 的 those 指代 the volumes of oil and natural gas reserves；谓语 must be tempered。

4. Reflecting Soviet era dictates and infrastructure, nearly all Caspian region crude oil still goes north and/or west.

（参考译文：几乎所有里海地区原油的北进和/或西行，都反映出苏联时期的规定和基础设施特征。）

句首分词短语为独立成分，表示说明。

5. This, combined with the fact that Russia itself produces oil and gas, gives Russia the market power to levy transit fees on Caspian energy shipped through its transportation network, and to determine in some cases how much, …

（参考译文：这一点，再加上俄罗斯本身也生产石油和天然气，使俄罗斯有市场权力对通过其交通网络的里海能源征收过境费，并在某些情况下由俄罗斯决定征收的费用，……）

本句过去分词短语 combined with… 作状语，表条件；后面的基本结构为：gives Russia the market power to levy… and to determine…。

Reinforced Learning

I. Answer the following questions for a comprehension of the text.

1. What do BP and the Energy Information Administration （EIA）, U. S. Department of Energy estimate?

2. What is the largest producer in the Caspian Sea region?

3. What are the advantages of Saudi oil and gas?

4. What entitles Russia to the market power to levy transit fees on Caspian energy shipped through its transportation network?

5. Why do Caspian Sea countries seek to develop alternatives to routes through Russia?

II. Multiple choice: choose the correct one from the alternative answers to give the exact meaning of the words.

1. This equals about 4% of total world <u>proven</u> reserves, and much more than BP's figure for U. S. reserves (29 billion bbls).

    A. drilled   B. tested   C. discovered   D. explored

2. It <u>accounts for</u> almost two – thirds of the region's gas output.

    A. explains   B. is equal to   C. destroys   D. reports

3. The region's proven reserves of natural gas are a higher <u>proportion</u> of the world total.

    A. dimension   B. measurement   C. part   D. quantity

4. Increases in Caspian region gas production face <u>obstacles</u> are somewhat similar to those that challenge further oil development and production.

    A. difficulties   B. poverty   C. alternatives   D. stuations

5. There is a <u>likelihood</u> of much greater additional reserves of crude oil and natural gas being found in the Caspian Sea region.

    A. number   B. vast   C. probability   D. a ray of hope

6. This level of proven reserves would nearly <u>equal</u> the amount now held by Saudi Arabia.

    A. figure out   B. reach   C. equate to   D. exceed

7. It must be tempered by <u>acknowledgment</u> of the considerable advantage of Saudi oil and gas in terms of much lower costs of production and much easier market access.

    A. acceptance   B. consideration   C. acquaintance   D. possession

8. Caspian Sea oil and gas has several markets now and a wider <u>variety</u> of potential markets.

    A. nature   B. area   C. species   D. number

9. Caspian Sea countries have <u>incentives</u> to develop alternatives to routes through Russia.

    A. stimulus   B. rewards   C. ambition   D. contiousness

10. They offer Turkey an opportunity to <u>offset</u> part of its energy import bill through transit fees for shipments across its territory.

    A. settle   B. balance out   C. pay   D. utilize

Ⅲ. Multiple choice：read the four suggested translations and choose the best answer.

1. Based upon figures published by <u>BP</u>, Caspian Sea region oil production comes from proven reserves of 48billion bbls.

    A. 巴格达条约   B. 英国石油公司

    C. 后台处理   D. 监狱管理局

2. The estimate of proven reserves of natural gas in the Caspian Sea region for the end of 2005 published by BP — 257 tcf — <u>represents</u> 4% of the world total.

    A. 表现   B. 展示   C. 相当于   D. 象征

3. These include nations trying to meet their economies' <u>demand</u> for energy and those that also wish to reduce their dependence on Persian Gulf energy.

    A. 发展   B. 过渡   C. 平稳   D. 需求

4. This gives Russia the <u>market power</u> to levy transit fees on Caspian energy shipped through its transportation network.

    A. 市场权力   B. 营销动力   C. 营销霸权   D. 市场能力

5. These developments include <u>expansion</u> of North Africa's gas export capacity and discovery of a large natural gas province in and near Egypt.

    A. 广阔   B. 扩张   C. 扩大   D. 膨胀

Ⅳ. Put the following sentences into Chinese.

1. Based upon figures published by BP, Caspian Sea region oil production comes from proven reserves of 48 billion bbls.

2. EIA estimates of much larger "possible" reserves suggest a potential for much greater production.

3. Much of the known reserves have not been developed yet, and development usually leads to discovery that prospects are larger than originally estimated.

4. This level of proven reserves would nearly equal the amount now held by Saudi Arabia and could come to about 15% of total world reserves.

5. These include nations trying to meet their economies' demand for energy

and those that also wish to reduce their dependence on Persian Gulf energy.

V. Put the following paragraphs into Chinese.

1. The Caspian Sea is a 700 – mile – long body of water in central Asia bordered by Azerbaijan, Iran, Kazakhstan, Russia, and Turkmenistan. Among the five nations, only Iran is a member of the Organization of Petroleum Exporting Countries. Azerbaijan, Kazakhstan, and Turkmenistan became independent when the Soviet Union dissolved in 1991. The Caspian Sea region historically has produced oil and natural gas, but the region is considered to have large resources of oil and gas capable of much greater production.

2. In addition, much of Caspian Sea energy resources are offshore, requiring special large drilling rigs（钻探设备）. Very limited rig production capacity in the relatively isolated region makes the acquisition of rigs expensive and logistically difficult, hampering development of Caspian energy resources.

3.2　Russian Oil and Gas Challenges

Guidance to Reading

Russia has more proven natural gas reserves than any other country, and it is among the top ten in proven oil reserves. Almost three fourths of Russian crude oil production is exported. Therefore, energy exports have been a major driver of Russia's economic growth over the last five years. However, Russia's ability to maintain and expand its capacity to produce and to export energy faces difficulties. In addition, the Russian government has moved to take control of the country's energy supplies through many ways.

Text

Russia is a major player in world energy markets. It has more proven natural gas **reserves** than any other country, is among the top ten in proven oil reserves, is the largest exporter of natural gas, the second largest oil exporter, and the third largest energy consumer.

Oil and Gas Reserves and Production

Most of Russia's 60 billion barrels of proven oil reserves are located in Western Siberia, between the Ural Mountains and the Central Siberian Plateau. This ample **endowment** of this region made the Soviet Union a major world oil producer in the 1980s, reaching production of 12.5 million barrels per day in 1988. Roughly 25% of Russia's oil reserves and 6% of its gas reserves are on Sakhalin Island in the far eastern region of the country, just north of Japan.

Russian oil production, which had begun to decline before the Soviet Union **dissolved** in 1991, fell more **steeply** afterward—to less than six million bbl/d in 1997 and 1998. State – mandated production surges had accelerated **depletion** of the large Western Siberian fields and the Soviet central planning system collapsed. Russian oil output started to recover in 1999. Many analysts attribute this to **privatization** of the industry, which **clarified incentives** and shifted activity to less expensive production. Increases in world oil prices, application of technology that was standard practice in the West, and **rejuvenation** of old oil fields helped boost output. After – effects of the 1998 financial crisis and subsequent **devaluation** of the ruble may well have contributed. After reaching about nine million bbl/d in 2004 depending upon the estimating source, Russian oil production continued to rise in the first several months of 2005, but only slightly. Potential growth of both oil and natural gas production in Russia is limited by the lack of full **introduction** of the most modern western oil and gas exploration, development, and production technology.

Oil and Gas Exports and Pipelines

Almost three fourths of Russian crude oil production is exported; the rest is refined in the country, with some refined products being exported. About two – thirds of Russia's 6.7 million bbl/d of crude oil exports in 2004 went to Belarus, Ukraine, Germany, Poland, and other destinations in Central and Eastern Europe. The remaining one – third of oil exports went to **maritime** ports and was sold in world markets. Recent high oil prices have enabled as much as 40% of Russia's oil exports to be shipped **via** more costly railroad and river **barge** routes. Most of Russia's exports of refined petroleum products to Europe are fuel oil and diesel fuel used for heating.

Energy exports have been a major driver of Russia's economic growth over the last five years, as Russian oil production has risen strongly and world oil prices have been very high. This type of growth has made the Russian economy dependent on oil and natural gas exports and vulnerable to fluctuations in oil prices. On average, a $1 per barrel change in oil prices **results in** a $1.4

billion change in Russian government revenues **in the same direction**.

Russia's ability to maintain and expand its capacity to produce and to export energy faces difficulties. Russia's oil and gas fields are **aging**. Modern western energy technology has not been fully implemented. There is **insufficient** export capacity in the crude oil pipeline system controlled by Russia's state – owned pipeline monopoly, **Transneft**. And, there is insufficient investment capital for improving and expanding Russian oil and gas production and pipeline systems.

Historically, most of Russia's natural gas exports went to Eastern Europe and to customers in countries that previously were part of the Soviet Union. But, in the mid – 1980s, Russia began trying to diversify its export options. By now, **Gazprom** has **shifted** some of its exports to meet the rising demand of Turkey, Japan, and other Asian countries. If Gazprom is to attain its long – term goal of increasing its European sales, it will have to boost its production, as well as secure more reliable export routes to the region.

The Russian government has moved to take control of the country's energy supplies. It **broke up** the previously large energy company Yukos and acquired its main oil production subsidiary. Yukos obtained majority control of a Lithuanian refinery by slowing oil supply to it, and buying it at a reduced price. Another example of Russian steps to have maximum control over energy supplies is routing of new and planned export pipelines. For example, it has agreed with Germany, with the support of the United Kingdom（UK）, to supply Germany and, eventually, the UK directly by building a natural gas pipeline under the Baltic Sea. Russia continues to maintain energy ties with Central Asian countries, as many transportation routes in that region are **oriented** toward European Russia. In East Asia, Russia is **contemplating** a pipeline destination that would allow it to decide to whom its oil gets sold. Also, Russia tried to cut off gas supply to Ukraine because the latter did not agree to greatly increase what it pays for the gas. Russia restored supply after other European countries complained. Much of Russia's gas exports to Europe pass through Ukraine.

In addition, a number of proposals would build new or expand existing Russian oil and natural gas export pipelines. Some are **contentious**, and although the Russian government is faced with a perceived need to expand its oil and gas export capacity, it also has limited resources.

Implications for the United States

Given that the United States, as well as Russia, is a major energy producer and user, Russian energy trends and policies affect U. S. energy markets and economic **welfare in general**. An increase in Russia's energy production and its ability to export that energy westward and eastward may tend to **ease** the supply situation in energy markets in the Atlantic and Pacific Basins. On the other hand, the Russian government's moves to take control of the country's energy supplies noted earlier may have the effect of making less oil available. Possibly as important as Russian oil and gas industry developments is the associated potential for U. S. suppliers of oil and gas field equipment and services to increase their sales and investment in Russia.

Similar to U. S. trade with Russia, U. S. investments there, especially direct investments, have increased since the dissolution of the Soviet Union, but the levels are far below their expected potential. Even so, as of the end of 2003, the United States was Russia's second largest source of foreign direct investment, largely concentrated in energy, communications, engineering, and transportation.

However, while they consider the climate to be improving, potential investors complain that the investment climate in Russia is **inhospitable** with respect to factors such as poor intellectual property rights protection, burden – some tax laws, and inefficient government **bureaucracy**.

Words and Expressions

reserves	（油气）储量
endowment	才能,天资
dissolve	解散;消失
steeply	陡峭地,急剧地
depletion	消耗;损耗
privatization	私有化
clarify	阐明,明确
incentive	激励的;刺激的
rejuvenation	复壮,复兴
devaluation	货币贬值
introduction	引进;采用
maritime	海事的;沿海的

via	通过
barge	驳船;游艇
aging	老化;陈化
insufficient	不足的,不充足的
shift	移动,转变
oriented	以……为方向的
contemplate	沉思,思忖
contentious	引起争论的
welfare	福利,福利事业
ease	减轻,缓和
inhospitable	荒凉的;不好客的
bureaucracy	官僚主义

Phrases and Expressions

result in	造成
in the same direction	向着同一方向
break up	解散
in general	一般而言

Proper Names

Transneft	俄罗斯国家石油运输公司
Gazprom	俄罗斯天然气工业股份公司

Language Focus

1. In East Asia, Russia is contemplating a pipeline destination that would allow it to decide to whom its oil gets sold.

(参考译文:俄罗斯正在考虑(寻找)在东亚的石油管道的目的地,允许俄罗斯来决定石油销售对象。)

本句是复合句,that 引导的定语从句修饰 destination,而 whom 作 to 的介词宾语。

2. An increase in Russia's energy production and its ability to export that energy westward and eastward may tend to ease the supply situation in energy markets in the Atlantic and Pacific Basins.

(参考译文:俄罗斯能源产量的提高,以及向西或向东的能源出口可能会缓和大西洋与太平洋地区能源市场的供求情况。)

本句是简单句,主语是由 and 连接的并列 An increase in Russia's energy production 和 its ability to export that energy westward and eastward 构成,谓语部分是 may tend to。

3. Possibly as important as Russian oil and gas industry developments is the associated potential for U. S. suppliers of oil and gas field equipment and services to increase their sales and investment in Russia.

(参考译文:可能同样重要的是,因为美国的石油和天然气设备及服务供应商努力提高其在俄罗斯的销售及投资,所以,俄罗斯石油和天然气工业的发展与美国存在潜在的联系。)

本句是简单句,谓语部分是 is the associated potential,for 是介词,表示"对于",to increase their sales and investment in Russia 是不定式作目的状语。

4. However, while they consider the climate to be improving, potential investors complain that the investment climate in Russia is inhospitable with respect to factors such as poor intellectual property rights protection, burden some tax laws, and inefficient government bureaucracy.

(参考译文:然而,尽管美国认为俄罗斯投资环境有所改善,但潜在的投资者抱怨俄罗斯不友好的投资环境,诸如缺乏知识产权保护、繁重的税收法、政府官僚效率低下等。)

本句是复合句,while 引导让步状语从句,主句的主谓部分是 potential investors complain,with respect to 是介词短语,表示"关于"。

▣ Reinforced Learning

I. Answer the following questions for a comprehension of the text.

1. Where are most of Russia's 60 billion barrels of proven oil reserves located?

2. Why did Russian oil output start to recover in 1999?

3. What kind of difficulties Russia has to maintain and expand its capacity to produce and to export energy?

4. Historically, who were Russia's natural gas exports customers according to the text?

5. For the potential investors of foreign countries, how is the investment climate in Russia?

II. Multiple choice: choose the correct one from the alternative answers to give the exact meaning of the words.

1. This <u>ample</u> endowment of this region made the Soviet Union a major world oil producer in the 1980s, reaching production of 12. 5 million barrels per day in 1988.

    A. tremendous   B. extraordinary   C. abundant   D. developed

2. Prices for basic foodstuffs have risen <u>steeply</u>, with sugar and maize meal costing double since the election.

    A. violently   B. hazardously   C. fleetly   D. sharply

3. State – mandated production surges had accelerated <u>depletion</u> of the large Western Siberian fields and the Soviet central planning system collapsed.

    A. corrupt   B. devour   C. consumption   D. sacrifice

4. The exact association between smoking and back pain will have to be <u>clarified</u> in appropriate studies.

    A. explained   B. involved   C. corresponded D. testified

5. In a society where the quest for happiness has never been more intense, there are powerful questions to <u>contemplate</u>.

    A. meditate   B. assume   C. accomplish   D. baffle

6. Officials say privately that the new policy emerged only after years of <u>contentious</u> internal debate.

    A. questionable B. ambiguous   C. controversial D. intense

7. The system is designed to <u>ease</u> traffic problems and add to family time as more women work.

    A. confront   B. recoil   C. alleviate   D. resolve

8. Since the Soviet Union <u>dissolved</u> in 1991, Kazakhstan has performed a delicate geopolitical balancing act, sharing its vast oil resources between Russia, China and the west.

    A. confronted   B. collapsed   C. disappeared D. resigned

9. The Russian government has moved to <u>take control of</u> the country's energy supplies.

    A. supervise   B. monopolize   C. dominate   D. confine

10. You're never afraid of a challenge and you see beauty even in the most <u>inhospitable</u> environments.

    A. predominant B. outrageous   C. desolate   D. nasty

III. Multiple choice : read the four suggested translations and choose the best answer.

1. Increases in world oil prices , application of technology that was standard practice in the West , and rejuvenation of old oil fields helped boost output.

    A. 恢复　　　　B. 振兴　　　　C. 改革　　　　D. 联合

2. After – effects of the 1998 financial crisis and subsequent devaluation of the ruble may well have contributed.

    A. 货币现象　　B. 货币替代　　C. 货币贬值　　D. 货币下滑

3. State – mandated production surges had accelerated depletion of the large Western Siberian fields and the Soviet central planning system collapsed. Russian oil output started to recover in 1999.

    A. 产量巨浪　　B. 激增产量　　C. 突破产量　　D. 产量需求

4. It broke up the previously large energy company Yukos and acquired its main oil production subsidiary.

    A. 附属物　　　B. 子公司　　　C. 辅助者　　　D. 分支

5. However , while they consider the climate to be improving , potential investors complain that the investment climate in Russia is inhospitable with respect to factors such as poor intellectual property rights protection , burden some tax laws , and inefficient government bureaucracy.

    A. 不适居住的　　B. 冷淡无情的　　C. 偏远荒凉的　　D. 不友好的

IV. Put the following sentences into Chinese.

1. Russian oil production , which had begun to decline before the Soviet Union dissolved in 1991 , fell more steeply afterward—to less than six million bbl/d in 1997 and 1998.

2. Potential growth of both oil and natural gas production in Russia is limited by the lack of full introduction of the most modern western oil and gas exploration , development , and production technology.

3. Energy exports have been a major driver of Russia's economic growth over the last five years , as Russian oil production has risen strongly and world oil prices have been very high.

4. Historically , most of Russia's natural gas exports went to Eastern Europe and to customers in countries that previously were part of the Soviet Union.

5. Given that the United States , as well as Russia , is a major energy producer

and user, Russian energy trends and policies affect U. S. energy markets and e-conomic welfare in general.

V. Put the following paragraphs into Chinese.

1. In East Asia, China, Japan, and South Korea, are trying to gain access to the undeveloped energy resources of eastern Siberia, as those countries strive to meet their increasing energy needs while reducing dependence on the Middle East. China and Japan appear to be engaged in a bidding (投标) war over Russian projects and are contesting access to Russian rival oil pipeline routes.

2. Also, as a major supplier of natural gas to European countries, Russia has some ability to set prices. For example, it could withhold (保留) supply and thereby affect customer country policies. In 2003, Russian gas accounted for 100% of Slovakia's gas consumption, 97% of Bulgaria's consumption, 79% of the Czech Republic's consumption, and 68% of Hungary's consumption.

3.3 Global Perspective and Status of Oil and Gas Resources in Africa

⌕ Guidance to Reading

As we all know, energy is an important guarantee for economic growth and social development, meanwhile, it has significant impact on the world economy and politics. The text points out Africa is playing a more and more important role in global energy utilization in the context of continued high demand toward world energy and the limited oil reserves in others continents. Furthermore, the governments of oil – producing countries in Africa have to solve the problems and meet the challenges regarding the governance of energy.

⌕ Text

Energy is an **indispensable** input for economic growth and social development. Two – thirds of global energy requirements are met with oil and gas supplies. Conventional wisdom holds that energy consumption **per capita** is strongly **correlated with** the level of economic and social progress. Remarkably, the three non – renewable fossil fuels, oil, natural gas, and coal, **constitute** almost 90 percent of commercial energy consumed globally.

The regional composition of global energy consumption reveals a wide

disparity in global use and **access to** commercial energy. Although Africa has about 15 percent of the world's population, it consumes only 3 percent of global commercial energy. The **paradox** is that Africa's share in global energy production is about 12 percent, and trending upwards.

The evolution of world energy markets in the post – 1970 period has been dramatic and its impact on the world economy and politics profound. This is illustrated by the worldwide economic **ripple effects** caused by price **volatility** and occasional spectacular spikes in the prices of the dominant global energy resources—oil and gas. World oil prices have trended ever higher since 2000, and natural gas prices have **tracked along**. Some of the reasons for the rise in oil prices include rising demand in **emerging economies**, especially in China and India, declining **spare capacity** in major producing countries, peaking of production in several important oil – producing areas, and lack of expansion in refinery capacity.

Driven by continued high demand in the Western world, **coupled with** signitcant and accelerating new demand from emerging economies, such as China, India, and Brazil, global energy consumption is expected to grow by more than 50 percent in the first quarter of this century. Oil and natural gas are expected to be in particularly high demand by 2025, with global oil consumption (demand) projected to rise by 57 percent.

It is very unlikely, even **taking into account** the massive investments in the energy sector around the world, that the oil and gas industry will be able to produce and **deliver** sufficient energy to meet global demand.

By some **projections**, the "**peak oil**" production has already been reached, or will be reached in a few years.

The **ensuing** shortages, coupled with **concomitant** rising energy prices, will place significant pressure on net oil – importing societies in Africa if not addressed strategically and aggressively.

Africa is **endowed** with vast quantities of both fossil and renewable energy resources. Furthermore, it is the main continent in the world with frequent and substantial new findings of oil and gas. In the past 20 years, oil reserves in Africa grew by over 25 percent, while gas grew by over 100 percent. Africa's rich oil fields and the prospects for discoveries have transformed it into an important player and a key "target" in global oil production and resource **extraction**. Oil production in the continent is expected to continue to rise at an average rate of 6 percent per year for the foreseeable future. The majority of oil reserves (and production) in Africa comes from Libya, Nigeria, Algeria, Angola, and Sudan, which together produce more than 90 percent of the continent's reserves. **Proved natural gas reserves** in Africa are mainly concentrated in four countries—Algeria, Egypt, Libya, and Nigeria—which possess 91.5 percent of the continent's proved reserves. In particular, Nigeria's undeveloped natural gas reserves are a logical target of the international giants in the sector. Furthermore, large deposits of natural gas have been identified in Tanzania; significant oil deposits are found in Albertine Graben in Uganda and in the western part of Ghana; and there are potential significant oil discoveries in South Africa, Mozambique, and Tanzania.

Considering the current uncertainties about energy supply, the key drivers of future demand, the policies of consumer countries (especially with respect to nuclear and other **alternatives** to oil and gas), and expected future global economic growth and technology development, there is need to clearly establish Africa's position and develop strategies for future supply adequacy. The energy crisis due to high oil prices, the environmental impacts of oil production, and the growing concern about the **viability** of oil – based fuels and products are leading to initiatives to find and develop alternative energy sources.

Maximizing the Benefits from Oil and Gas Resources

A key concern regarding the governance of oil and gas resources is that the governments of African oil – and gas – producing countries receive an inadequate share of the large rents from production. This may stem from a number of reasons, including contracts and **regimes** that are not designed to extract maximum rents; and oil and gas policies that are designed primarily to promote and attract investments and have not evolved with changing **global dynamics** and national interests. The sustainable development of oil and gas resources requires policies, principles, and practices that support the utilization of resources in a manner that does not prevent future generations from benefiting from the resources.

A great challenge, for oil – producing African countries, is to ensure sufficient, reliable, and environmentally responsible supplies of oil, at prices that reflect market fundamentals. To achieve this important goal, several challenges have to be addressed, including high and volatile oil prices; growing external and internal demand for oil; increasing import dependence of many African countries; and, most importantly, sustainable management of the continent's oil and gas resources. The regional nature of these challenges and the growing interdependence between net importing and net exporting African countries require a strengthened partnership among all **stakeholders** to enhance regional energy security.

The sustainable management of oil and gas also faces the challenge that large natural resource **revenues** tend to replace more stable and sustainable revenue streams, **exacerbating** existing problems related to development, **transparency**, and **accountability**. This tends to free natural resource – exporting governments from the types of citizen demands for **fiscal** transparency, and accountability that arise when people pay taxes directly to the government. Thus, natural resource export earnings actually **sever** important links between the people and their governments—links that are related to popular interests and control mechanisms. Governance indicators such as government effectiveness, voice and accountability, political instability and violence, the rule of law, regulatory quality, and control of **corruption** are correspondingly markedly weaker in oil – rich African countries.

Despite the challenges and issues involved, an oil and gas resource boom can, under the right circumstances, be an important **catalyst** for growth and development. The often – referred – to "natural resource curse" can be avoided with the right institutions and policies. Several countries in Africa have demonstrated this and there is some reason for cautious optimism that more countries have learned hard lessons from past resource booms, and, in future, will pursue strategies and policies that will allow them to fully reap the benefits of their natural resource wealth.

Words and Expressions

indispensable	不可缺少的
constitute	组成, 构成
disparity	不同, 不一致
paradox	自相矛盾的人或事
volatility	易变, 波动
deliver	传送, 传递

projection	预测,推测
ensuing	接着发生的
concomitant	附随的;相伴的
endow	天生具有;赋予
extraction	提取,抽出
alternative	替换物
viability	可行性
regimes	政体,管理体制
stakeholder	利益相关者
revenue	税收,收益
exacerbate	使恶化;使加剧
transparency	透明,透明度
accountability	有义务;有责任
fiscal	财政的
sever	割断,断绝
corruption	贪污,腐败
catalyst	催化剂

Phrases and Expressions

per capita	人均
be correlated with	与……有关
access to	有权使用
ripple effect	连锁反应
track along	追踪,沿着
emerging economies	新兴经济体（是指某一国家或地区经济蓬勃发展,成为新兴的经济实体）
spare capacity	储备能力
coupled with	加上,外加
take into account	考虑
peak oil	石油峰值

（一般认为,最晚到 2020 年全球石油产量将达到有史以来的最高点,此后,产量将不断下降,而开采成本将不断上升）

proved natural gas reserves	已探明天然气储量
global dynamics	全球动力学

Language Focus

1. Driven by continued high demand in the Western world, coupled with significant and accelerating new demand from emerging economies, such as China, India, and Brazil, global energy consumption is expected to grow by more than 50 percent in the first quarter of this century.

（参考译文：西方世界持续高需求，加上新兴经济体，如中国、印度、巴西对能源的迫切需求，本世纪的前 25 年，全球能源消费量预计增长 50%以上。）

本句是简单句，主谓部分是 global energy consumption is expected to；Driven... 是过去分词作原因状语，coupled with 表示"加上"。

2. It is very unlikely, even taking into account the massive investments in the energy sector around the world, that the oil and gas industry will be able to produce and deliver sufficient energy to meet global demand.

（参考译文：即使对全世界的能源行业进行大量投资，石油和天然气行业生产并输送足够的能源来满足全球需求不大可能。）

本句是简单句, even 表示让步，在句子中做插入成分；It 是形式主语，真正主语是 that 引导的句子。

3. The sustainable development of oil and gas resources requires policies, principles, and practices that support the utilization of resources in a manner that does not prevent future generations from benefiting from the resources.

（参考译文：石油和天然气的可持续发展要求利用资源的政策、原则和实践不妨碍后代受益。）

本句是复合句，谓语动词是 require，第一个 that 引导整个定语从句修饰 policies, principles, and practices，而第二个 that... 是前面的定语中套用的另外一个定语从句，修饰 manner。

4. The sustainable management of oil and gas also faces the challenge that large natural resource revenues tend to replace more stable and sustainable revenue streams, exacerbating existing problems related to development, transparency, and accountability.

（参考译文：石油和天然气的可持续管理也面临这样的挑战，大笔能源收入往往取代更稳定的可持续的收入来源，致使现存的发展问题、透明度和问责制更加恶化。）

本句是复合句，谓语动词 faces，其中 that 引导的定语从句修饰 challenge，

exacerbating 是现在分词作结果状语,而 related to 是过去分词,作定语修饰 problems。

Reinforced Learning

Ⅰ. Answer the following questions for a comprehension of the text.

1. In what position is Africa in energy consumption in the world?

2. Why have world oil prices trended ever higher since 2000?

3. Why is there need to clearly establish Africa's position and develop strategies for future supply adequacy?

4. What is the key concern regarding the governance of oil and gas resources?

5. What links do natural resource export earnings sever in rich oil counties in Africa according to the writer?

Ⅱ. Multiple choice: choose the correct one from the alternative answers to give the exact meaning of the words.

1. Remarkably, the three non‐renewable fossil fuels, oil, natural gas, and coal, constitute almost 90 percent of commercial energy consumed globally.

    A. non‐effective   B. non‐profit

    C. non‐regenerated   D. non‐conforming

2. The paradox is that Africa's share in global energy production is about 12 percent, and trending upwards.

    A. contradiction   B. contrary   C. opposition   D. adverseness

3. Driven by continued high demand in the Western world, coupled with significant and accelerating new demand from emerging economies, such as China, India, and Brazil, global energy consumption is expected to grow by more than 50 percent in the first quarter of this century.

    A. increasing in speed   B. decreasing in speed

    C. increasing in power   D. decreasing in power

4. It is very unlikely, even taking into account the massive investments in the energy sector around the world, that the oil and gas industry will be able to produce and deliver sufficient energy to meet global demand.

    A. extraordinary   B. remarkable   C. arrogant   D. enormous

5. The sustainable management of oil and gas also faces the challenge that

large natural resource revenues tend to replace more stable and sustainable revenue streams, <u>exacerbating</u> existing problems related to development, transparency, and accountability.

　　A. aggravating　　B. exaggerating　　C. emigrating　　D. indulging

　　6. Oil production in the continent is expected to continue to rise at an average rate of 6 percent per year for the <u>foreseeable</u> future.

　　A. incredible　　B. attainable　　C. predictable　　D. practicable

　　7. The ensuing shortages, coupled with <u>concomitant</u> rising energy prices, will place signitcant pressure on net oil – importing societies in Africa if not addressed strategically and aggressively.

　　A. accompanied　　　　　　　B. consolidated

　　C. stable　　　　　　　　　　D. diversed

　　8. I'd <u>take into account</u> his reputation with other farmers and business people in the community, and then make a decision about whether or not to approve a loan.

　　A. take into consideration　　　　B. account for

　　C. make up for　　　　　　　　D. make out

　　9. The other major requirement in a marketing program is assessing <u>access</u> to your target market.

　　A. refer to　　　　　　　　　B. take to

　　C. come close to　　　　　　　D. see to

　　10. In the Chinese household, grandparents and other relatives play <u>indispensable</u> roles in raising children.

　　A. sensible　　B. incapable　　C. necessary　　D. infinite

Ⅲ. Multiple choice: read the four suggested translations and choose the best answer.

　　1. To achieve this important goal, several challenges have to be <u>addressed</u>, including high and volatile oil prices; growing external and internal demand for oil; increasing import dependence of many African countries.

　　A. 面临　　　　B. 地址　　　　C. 处理　　　　D. 演讲

　　2. Despite the challenges and issues involved, an oil and gas resource boom can, under the right circumstances, be an important <u>catalyst</u> for growth and development.

　　A. 要素　　　　B. 化学制剂　　　C. 刺激物　　　　D. 催化剂

3. The regional nature of these challenges and the growing interdependence between net <u>importing and net exporting</u> African countries require a strengthened partnership among all stakeholders to enhance regional energy security.

    A. 纯进口和纯出口   B. 净进口和净出口

    C. 全进口和全出口   D. 实进口和实出口

4. This tends to free natural resource – exporting governments from the types of citizen demands for fiscal transparency, and <u>accountability</u> that arise when people pay taxes directly to the government.

    A. 所有制   B. 义务制   C. 问责制   D. 市用制

5. By some projections, the "<u>peak oil</u>" production has already been reached, or will be reached in a few years.

    A. 石油产量   B. 石油理论   C. 石油峰值   D. 石油价格

Ⅳ. Put the following sentences into Chinese.

1. The evolution of world energy markets in the post – 1970 period has been dramatic and its impact on the world economy and politics profound.

2. The ensuing shortages, coupled with concomitant rising energy prices, will place significant pressure on net oil – importing societies in Africa if not addressed strategically and aggressively.

3. Africa's rich oil fields and the prospects for more discoveries have transformed it into an important player and a key "target" in global oil production and resource extraction.

4. A key concern regarding the governance of oil and gas resources is that the governments of African oil – and gas – producing countries receive an inadequate share of the large rents from production.

5. Despite the challenges and issues involved, an oil and gas resource boom can, under the right circumstances, be an important catalyst for growth and development.

Ⅴ. Put the following paragraphs into Chinese.

1. Africa is a continent of 54 countries with an estimated mid – 2000 population of 805 million people. According to the 2008 Statistical Energy Survey, Africa had proven oil reserves of 117. 481 billion barrels at the end of 2007 or 9. 49 % of the world's reserves and in 2007 the region produced an average of 10317. 6 thousand barrels of crude oil per day, 12. 5% of the world total.

2. Five countries dominate Africa's upstream oil production. Together they account for 85% of the continent's oil production and are, in order of decreasing output, Nigeria, Libya, Algeria, Egypt and Angola. Other oil producing countries are Gabon, Congo, Cameroon, Tunisia, Equatorial Guinea, the Democratic Republic of the Congo, and Cote d'Ivoire. Exploration is taking place in a number of other countries that aim to increase their output.

Chapter 4　Oil, Politics and Economy

4.1　Oil and the International Relations of the Middle East

⌸ Guidance to Reading

Oil is a very important factor in shaping the relations between countries in the Middle East and the West. This text elaborates several diplomatic cases of how the western countries, including the United States, France and Italy deal with their relationship with the countries in the Middle East. These countries have been changing their diplomatic policies in order to get abundant and cheap oil. On the other hand, countries in Middle East also try to take advantages of oil resources to reap the benefit, indeed in order to sanction western countries, Arab countries used the "oil weapon" to implement an oil embargo against western countries which supported Israel.

⌸ Text

Oil is a very important factor in the international relations of the Middle Eastern states, both with respect to regional, or inter – Arab relations, and with respect to international relations **at large**—that is, relations with industrial and other developing countries.

The West and Arab Oil

It is quite evident, and amply documented in the historical literature, that **preoccupation** with oil has been **paramount** in shaping the attitude of the UK, and later the USA, towards the region. We have noted this already with respect to the formation of the state system in the region, but almost all policies of the key outside players towards the region were evaluated mainly with respect to their **implications** for oil. Consider, for example, the key episode of Iraq's independence, whose final granting **was subordinated to** the interests of the Iraq Petroleum Company; or the overthrow of the Mussadiq government in Iran, which was tied primarily, though not exclusively, to the nationalization of Anglo –

Iranian Oil Company. Similarly,the United States entered in very close **alliances** with Saudi Arabia—which was,and continues to be,problematic on most accounts,yet remains inescapable because of oil—and Iran. The latter developed following the **inclusion** of American companies in the Iranian **consortium**, which became possible after Mussadiq's **demise** and the return of Muhammad Reza Shah,and ended the **monopoly** of Anglo – Iranian on Iranian oil,forcing it to share its control with several others,primarily American,companies. (Anglo – Iranian also changed its name into British Petroleum.)

The **diplomacy** of other countries was also shaped by oil,**albeit** at a lower level of intensity,simply because they had far fewer assets,and were rather more interested in a **reshuffle** of the cards than in continuation of the existing order. Thus France attempted to hold on to Algeria,and did what was necessary to protect the interests of CFP in the **UAE**,but otherwise tried to **distinguish** itself **from** 'the Anglo – Saxons' by taking a line emphasizing 'cooperation' with the oil – producing countries. Other examples of this are France's immediate acceptance of the Iraqi nationalization in 1972; refusal to become member of the **IEA** when it was established,in Paris,in 1974; promotion of diplomatic initiatives for a "new international economic order" and later for the International Energy Forum; finally,the active **undermining** of US **sanctions** against Iran.

Italy too supported the creation of a national oil company,**ENI**,which became the prime mover of Italian diplomacy towards the Arab countries,leading to active support of the Algerian war of liberation (raising the suspicion that the bomb that downed Enrico Mattei's plane in 1962 might have been planted by the **French secret service**) as well as support for **Muhammad Reza Shah** when he fled Iran in conflict with Mussadiq,and the close relationship with Libya. More recently,ENI has **disregarded** the US embargo against Iran,and has, **imitating** the French,**flirted** with Saddam Hussein's Iraq—without getting much in return. In actual fact,however,none of these attempts was ever terribly successful: ENI got its best results from purchasing oil from the Soviet Union (a move that made the USA furious),and finding oil in the Sinai,in Egypt.

Oil has influenced diplomacy towards the region,but in most cases diplomacy has failed to yield the results that were expected of it,at least as far as oil is concerned. In more recent years,oil has more frequently been used as a tool, rather than as an objective: witness the American embargo against Iran, then

Libya, and the UN – imposed embargo against Iraq. In all cases, the major industrial powers have made their own access to oil more difficult, in order to pursue a political priority. Or is it the case that oil needs not only to be abundant and cheap, but also politically correct, in the sense of coming from a country whose government is friendly to us? Many seem to believe that this is indeed a priority or requirement, and rank suppliers in accordance to political **proximity**, although there is no **empirical** support to the belief that oil produced from a friend is either more reliable or cheaper.

Middle Eastern Oil Exporters and their International Relations

The oil – producing countries have naturally taken notice of the importance **attributed to** oil by the major powers, and attempted to take advantage of it, acquiring guarantees for their security against external and internal challenges, as well as access to sophisticated weapons systems. The guarantee against internal challenges was "lifted" from Iran by US President Jimmy Carter, who wanted to **uphold** basic human rights and **democracy**, and thus allowed the Pahlavi regime to collapse—with consequences that most observers would consider quite **disastrous**, to this date.

The less obvious point is that, in fact, oil does not appear to be a **prominent** preoccupation in shaping the foreign policy of the oil – producing countries. International oil policy is entrusted to a Minister of Petroleum or Energy, who is generally regarded as a technician; it is discussed in **OPEC** or other similar forums, which have a narrow, technical man – date. The only case in which there was an attempt to use oil as a weapon—in 1973—was a short – lived affair and oil never truly became physically scarce.

At the outbreak of war between Israel and its Arab neighbours in October 1973, the Organization of Arab Oil Exporting Countries imposed an embargo against the United States and the Netherlands. Prices increased rapidly on oil markets, **precipitating** the first "energy crises". In fact, the embargo was **fictional**: Middle Eastern oil production increased steadily and rapidly until 1974. It declined the following year because of the recession and decrease in oil demand **triggered** by the increase in prices. In fact, oil was never used as a weapon. Nevertheless, commentators still refer to **OAPEC**'s decision as a dangerous **precedent** and proof of the unreliability of Gulf oil supplies.

That episode was a success from the point of view of **provoking** an increase in prices, but politically a disastrous failure, which the Gulf oil producers still regret today. In fact, the **perception** that Gulf oil supplies are insecure and unreliable is still based essentially on just that one decision, and since that time Gulf producers have demonstrated more than once that they are able to deliver all the oil that is required even in the presence of conflict in the region.

Words and Expressions

preoccupation	当务之急；关注的事物
paramount	最重要的，主要的
implication	牵连，卷入
alliance	联盟，联合
inclusion	包含，内含物
consortium	联合，联盟
demise	终止；死亡
monopoly	垄断，垄断者
diplomacy	外交；外交手腕
albeit	即使，虽然
reshuffle	改组，重新安排
undermine	逐渐损害
sanction	制裁；处罚
disregard	忽视，漠视
imitate	仿效，模仿
flirt	调情；轻率地对待
proximity	亲近，接近
empirical	经验主义的
uphold	赞成，支撑
democracy	民主，民主主义
disastrous	灾难性的
prominent	突出的，显著的
precipitate	突如其来的
fictional	虚构的
trigger	引发，引起
precedent	先例
provoke	驱使；惹起
perception	感觉；看法

🏠 Phrases and Expressions

at large	整个的
be subordinated to	从属于
distinguish from	区别,辨别
attributed to	归因于
French secret service	法国特工

🏠 Proper Names

UAE	阿拉伯联合酋长国(United Arab Emirates)
IEA	国际能源机构 (International Energy Association)
ENI	埃尼集团(公司名)
Muhammad Reza Shah	穆罕默德·礼萨·巴列维(伊朗孔雀王座上 最后一位国王)
OPEC	石油输出国家组织
OAPEC	阿拉伯石油输出国组织

🏠 Language Focus

1. It is quite evident, and amply documented in the historical literature, that preoccupation with oil has been paramount in shaping the attitude of the UK, and later the USA, towards the region.

(参考译文:很明显,从大量的历史文献中可知,对石油的攫取是英国及随后的美国对中东地区态度变化的关键。)

本句是简单句,It 是形式主语,that 后引导的句子是真正的主语,第一个 and 与 that 后的从句并列,本句子可以这样改写 It is quite evident that preoccupation with oil has been paramount in shaping the attitude of the UK, and later the USA, towards the region and amply documented in the historical literature.

2. Consider, for example, the key episode of Iraq's independence, whose final granting was subordinated to the interests of the Iraq Petroleum Company; or the overthrow of the Mussadiq government in Iran, which was tied primarily, though not exclusively, to the nationalization of Anglo – Iranian Oil Company.

(参考译文:例如,伊拉克独立这一重要事件,最终是以服从伊拉克石油公司的利益达成，还有伊朗摩萨台政府的瓦解虽然不完全是，但最初却与其对盎格鲁—伊朗石油公司的国有化有关。）

本句是简单句，是祈使句，consider 是谓语动词，or 连接两个名词短语作宾语，其中 whose、which 分别引导的非限定性定语从句修饰两个并列宾语。

3. The oil – producing countries have naturally taken notice of the importance attributed to oil by the major powers, and attempted to take advantage of it, acquiring guarantees for their security against external and internal challenges, as well as access to sophisticated weapons systems.

（参考译文：中东石油生产国自然地注意到石油对于大国的重要性，并尝试利用这一优势获得安全保证和先进的武器装备，以应付内外挑战。）

本句是简单句，and 连接的是两个并列的谓语部分，即 taken notice of... 和 attempted to...，acquiring 是现在分词作目的状语。

Reinforced Learning

Ⅰ. Answer the following questions for a comprehension of the text.

1. What kind of role did oil play in the international relations of the Middle Eastern states?

2. What was the diplomacy of France towards Middle Eastern according to the text?

3. What reasons have made the major industrial powers more difficult in accessing to oil from the point view of the writer?

4. What happened in the region of Middle Eastern in 1973 and what's the bad result of the event?

5. What did internal challenges refer to for the oil – producing countries?

Ⅱ. Multiple choice：choose the correct one from the alternative answers to give the exact meaning of the words.

1. Similarly, the United States entered in very close alliances with Saudi Arabia—which was, and continues to be, problematic on most accounts, yet remains inescapable because of oil—and Iran.

A. inevitable　　B. unstable　　C. inexhaustible　D. inflexible

2. They made an alliance against the common enemy.

A. league　　　B. team　　　C. group　　　　D. class

3. More recently, ENI has disregarded the US embargo against Iran, and

has, imitating the French, flirted with Saddam Hussein's Iraq—without getting much in return.

    A. detrain   B. block   C. ban   D. sanction

    4. In fact, the embargo was fictional: Middle Eastern oil production increased steadily and rapidly until 1974. It declined the following year because of the <u>recession</u> and decrease in oil demand triggered by the increase in prices. In fact, oil was never used as a weapon.

    A. crisis   B. depression   C. restrain   D. disappointment

    5. The guarantee against internal challenges was "lifted" from Iran by US President Jimmy Carter, who wanted to <u>uphold</u> basic human rights and democracy, and thus allowed the Pahlavi regime to collapse—with consequences that most observers would consider quite disastrous, to this date.

    A. erect   B. insist   C. stimulate   D. encourage

    6. <u>Perception</u> and attitudes to Product Placement are diverse and complex.

    A. Concept   B. Observation   C. Idea   D. Insight

    7. If people <u>disregard</u> the great works of the past, it is because these works no longer answer the needs of the present.

    A. emphasize   B. compliment   C. ignore   D. engage

    8. It would be <u>disastrous</u> if they sought to do so by pandering to the more populist elements of their constituency.

    A. unfortunate   B. catastrophic   C. horrible   D. awful

    9. The pursuit of information has been a human <u>preoccupation</u> since knowledge was first recorded.

    A. stress   B. combat   C. absorption   D. enhance

    10. Yet he has shaped two <u>prominent</u> careers for himself, as an economist and a politician.

    A. fantastic   B. remarkable   C. grateful   D. hostile

III. Multiple choice: read the four suggested translations and choose the best answer.

    1. The latter developed following the inclusion of American companies in the Iranian consortium, which became possible after Mussadiq's demise and the return of Muhammad Reza Shah, and ended the <u>monopoly</u> of Anglo – Iranian on Iranian oil, forcing it to share its control with several other, primarily American, companies.

    A. 垄断   B. 控制   C. 禁止   D. 支配

2. Italy too supported the creation of a national oil company, ENI, which became the <u>prime mover</u> of Italian diplomacy towards the Arab countries.

A. 最初行动者　B. 最初发动机　C. 主要推动者　D. 主要鼓动者

3. More recently, ENI has disregarded the US embargo against Iran, and has, imitating the French, <u>flirted</u> with Saddam Hussein's Iraq – without getting much in return.

A. 调情地挑逗　B. 挥动告别　　C. 关系密切　　D. 轻易地抛弃

4. Many seem to believe that this is indeed a priority or requirement, and rank suppliers in accordance to political <u>proximity</u>, although there is no empirical support to the belief that oil produced from a friend is either more reliable or cheaper.

A. 相似性　　　B. 同化性　　　C. 亲疏性　　　D. 优先性

5. International oil policy <u>is entrusted to</u> a Minister of Petroleum or Energy, who is generally regarded as a technician; it is discussed in OPEC or other similar forums, which have a narrow, technical man – date.

A. 授权给　　　B. 转交给　　　C. 承诺给　　　D. 委托给

Ⅳ. Put the following sentences into Chinese.

1. We have noted this already with respect to the formation of the state system in the region, but almost all policies of the key outside players towards the region were evaluated mainly with respect to their implications for oil.

2. The diplomacy of other countries was also shaped by oil, albeit at a lower level of intensity, simply because they had far fewer assets, and were rather more interested in a reshuffle of the cards than in continuation of the existing order.

3. Oil has influenced diplomacy towards the region, but in most cases diplomacy has failed to yield the results that were expected of it, at least as far as oil is concerned.

4. The less obvious point is that, in fact, oil does not appear to be a prominent preoccupation in shaping the foreign policy of the oil – producing countries.

5. That episode was a success from the point of view of provoking an increase in prices, but politically a disastrous failure, which the Gulf oil producers still regret today.

V. Put the following paragraphs into Chinese.

1. In despite of postwar plans to break up Agip, administrator Enrico Mattei converted it to a state monopoly, renamed Eni. The name derives from the initials of the company's original full title Ente Nazionale Idrocarburi. The Italian Government authorized (批准,认可) its establishment on February 10,1953 in order to implement a national energy strategy based on the concentration of all the activities in the energy sector into one group. Eni was to supply energy to Italy and contribute to the country's industrial development.

2. The Organization of Arab Petroleum Exporting Countries (OAPEC) is a multi – governmental organization headquartered in Kuwait which coordinates energy policies between oil – producing Arab nations, and whose main purpose is developmental.

4. 2   The Main Diplomatic Policies of the United States and Britain in the Middle East

Guidance to Reading

From the angle of history, western powers have been trying to control the Middle East in order to gain cheap and plentiful flow of energy resource – oil. After the First World War, Britain and France tried to make the Middle East divided to ensure their interests in the region and to avoid seeing a powerful independent Arab state. And then the United States became the dominant world power in the world. In 1957 , Eisenhower Doctrine declared outlining U. S. policy in the Middle East to resist Soviet power.

Text

Since the Second World War, the United States has been the **dominant** world power in the Middle East. Every U. S. policy shift, every military intervention, every CIA plot has been **carried out** to secure one main aim: to ensure the cheap and plentiful flow of the world's most important energy resource— oil. Despite new discoveries of oil reserves in Central Asia, the Middle East still has two – thirds of the world's proven oil reserves, and its oil is still the cheapest to pump and produce. As Lawrence Korb's statement about Kuwait and carrots makes clear, nothing that takes place in the Middle East today can be understood without first understanding the strategic and economic importance of "black gold. "

The U. S. has relied on **brutal, repressive** regimes—Iran under the Shah, Saudi Arabia, Israel—to do its dirty work. It has used the CIA to **foment coups** against "unfriendly" regimes. When necessary, it has **intervened** directly to punish regimes that have challenged its dominance in the region—as it did to Iraq in 1991.

After the collapse of the Ottoman Empire, Britain and France drew the boundaries of the new states in the Middle East with absolutely no input from the people of the region. All promises of Arab independence the British had made to various local leaders during the First World War were **scrapped**. At the 1919 peace conference, when the victorious powers sat down to **divvy up** the spoils, foremost in their minds was the need to keep the region divided and thereby easier to control.

Private oil concerns pushed their governments to **renounce** all wartime promises to the Arabs. For the oilmen saw only too well that oil concessions and royalties would be easier to negotiate with a series of rival Arab states lacking any sense of unity, than with a powerful independent Arab state in the Middle East.

Britain took the areas that became Iraq, Kuwait, and Saudi Arabia. France took Syria and Lebanon. Each state was then handed to local kings and **sheiks** who owed their position to British **tutelage**. Kuwait was handed to the al – Sabah family. After he was promised a United Arab Republic, the **Hashemite King Hussein** was awarded Jordan. Britain gave **Ibn Saud Saudi Arabia**—the only country in the world **named after** its ruling family. France put **Lebanon** in the hands of the Christian minority.

Journalist Glenn Frankel describes how British High **Commissioner** Sir Percy Cox settled boundaries between Iraq, Kuwait, and Saudi Arabia at a 1922 conference in Baghdad.

The meeting had gone on for five **grueling** days with no **compromise** in sight. So one night in late November 1922, Cox, Britain's representative in **Baghdad, summoned** to his tent Sheik Abdul – Aziz Ibn Saud, soon to become ruler of Saudi Arabia, to explain the facts of life as the British **carved up** the **remnants** of the defeated Ottoman Empire.

The modern borders of Iraq, Saudi Arabia, and Kuwait were established by

British **Imperial** fiat at what became known as the Uqauir Conference.

There was one unique exception to this arrangement. The 1917 **Balfour Declaration** had committed Britain to supporting the formation of a "national home for the Jewish people" in Palestine. When the postwar settlement made the country a British **protectorate**, Britain backed Jewish **immigration** to Palestine, hoping to create a "secure strategic **outpost** in an Arab world." Though Lord Arthur Balfour was an anti – Semite, he and other members of the British ruling class could see the value of creating a colonial – settler outpost that, dependent on British support, could become a loyal protector of British interests in the area. The full significance of the role of such an outpost would not become apparent, or fully **taken advantage of** by the U. S. , until several years after the formation of the state of Israel in 1948.

In the aftermath of the Second World War, the U. S. moved in quickly to establish itself as the number – one power in the Middle East. American policy in this period was chiefly concerned that countries in the region did not come under the control of nationalist regimes. They had their first taste of that threat in Iran, when the democratically elected president Mohammed Mossadeq, with mass popular support, nationalized the British – owned Anglo – Iranian Oil Company. In a coup engineered by CIA operative Kermit Roosevelt, Mossadeq was **toppled** and replaced by the Shah. The Shah's power was **underwritten** by massive **infusions** of American aid and upheld by the **notoriously** savage secret police, **Savak**.

The U. S. worried that Egypt, under **Gamal Abdel Nasser**—a nationalist military officer who had come to power, ironically, with the CIA's blessing after a 1952 coup—might become a **pole** of attraction for pan – Arab movements. U. S. interests in the region were **couched** in the Cold War terms of preventing Soviet domination, though it was clear that any regime attempting to leave the orbit of the U. S. , whether it had ties to Russia or not, was considered a threat. In 1957 Eisenhower **Doctrine** declared that the United States was "prepared to use armed forces to assist" any Middle Eastern country "requesting assistance against armed aggression from any country controlled by international communism. "

The Eisenhower Doctrine reflected Washington's anger over Nasser's turn to the Eastern Bloc for weapons. The U. S. refused to arm Egypt unless it agreed to join the U. S. – sponsored Baghdad Pact, a regional security agreement under U. S. **auspices**. The doctrine was quickly put to the test as a series of developments in the region seemed to **augur** a wave of nationalism. In Jordan, King Hussein was threatened by a newly elected pro – Nasser parliament. In 1958, Egypt and **Syria** joined together to form the United Arab Republic. In Lebanon, Muslim Arab nationalists led a struggle against the minority Christian regime led by Camille Chamoun. More importantly to the U. S. , a nationalist military coup in Iraq that same year overthrew pro – British **dictator** Nuri Said. This event was **perceived** as a severe blow to U. S. **prestige** in the region and as a threat to American oil interests.

U. S. officials feared that the new Iraqi regime might **reassert** its historical claim on Kuwait, a tiny country created by British fiat in order to prevent any larger state from controlling what was then the biggest oil – producing area in the Gulf. A **memorandum** based on an emergency meeting between **Secretary of State** John Foster Dulles, Chair of the Joint Chiefs of Staff Nathan Twining, and CIA director Allen Dulles asserted that unless the United States intervened, "the U. S. would lose influence," its "bases" would be "threatened," and U. S. credibility would be "brought into question throughout the world. " The U. S. was also concerned about the nationalist threat to what were very profitable oil concessions in Kuwait and Iraq.

Fearing that he was on the brink of losing power, Lebanon's Chamoun asked the U. S. for assistance under the Eisenhower Doctrine. With its eye on Iraq, the U. S. seized this opportunity and declared a nuclear alert. When the new Iraqi regime announced its commitment to "respect its **obligations**," the U. S. withdrew its forces.

Words and Expressions

dominan	支配的;统治的
brutal	残忍的;野蛮的
repressive	镇压的,抑制的
foment	煽动;挑起
coup	政变
intervene	干涉;调停
scrap	废弃;拆毁

renounce	宣布放弃
sheik	酋长,族长
tutelage	监护,指导
commissioner	委员,专员
grueling	折磨人的
compromise	妥协,和解
summon	召唤,召集
remnant	剩余
imperial	帝国的
protectorate	保护国
immigration	移居,外来移民
outpost	前哨
topple	推翻,颠覆
underwrite	给……保证
infusion	援助,注入物
notoriously	众所周知地;恶名昭著地
pole	极点
couch	使躺下,弯下
doctrine	学说,主义
auspice	主办,赞助
augur	是……的预兆
dictator	独裁者
perceive	认知,感到,察觉
prestige	声誉,威望
reassert	重复主张
memorandum	备忘录
obligation	义务,职责

Phrases and Expressions

carry out	执行,实行
divvy up	分配,瓜分
named after	以……命名
carve up	瓜分;划分
take advantage of	利用

Proper Names

Hashemite King Hussein	侯赛因国王
Ibn Saud Saudi Arabia	伊本沙特阿拉伯
Lebanon	黎巴嫩
Baghdad	巴格达(伊拉克首都)
Balfour Declaration	贝尔福宣言
Savak	萨瓦克(伊朗国家安全情报组织)
Gamal Abdel Nasser	加麦尔·阿卜杜勒·纳赛尔
Syria	叙利亚共和国
Secretary of State	国务卿

Language Focus

1. As Lawrence Korb's statement about Kuwait and carrots makes clear, nothing that takes place in the Middle East today can be understood without first understanding the strategic and economic importance of "black gold."

(参考译文:正如劳伦斯考伯关于科威特和胡萝卜的论述明确指出,不先理解"黑色黄金"在战略上和经济中的重要性,就不理解今天中东地区发生的一切。)

本句是复合句,主语是 nothing,谓语动词是 can be understood,that 引导的定语从句修饰 nothing,as 是介词,表示"正如"。

2. For the oilmen saw only too well that oil concessions and royalties would be easier to negotiate with a series of rival Arab states lacking any sense of unity,than with a powerful independent Arab state in the Middle East.

(参考译文:因为石油商看得很清楚,关于石油开采权和特许权使用费的谈判,与中东地区一个强大的独立的阿拉伯国家相比,一群缺乏团结意识的对手会更容易对付。)

本句是复合句,For 是连词表示"因为",that 引导宾语从句,lacking any sense of unity 是现在分词作定语修饰 a series of rival Arab states,than with 是比较结构,与前一个 with 进行比较。

3. Though Lord Arthur Balfour was an anti–Semite,he and other members of the British ruling class could see the value of creating a colonial–settler outpost that,dependent on British support,could become a loyal protector of British interests in the area.

（参考译文：尽管亚瑟·贝尔福勋爵是反犹太主义者，但他和英国统治阶级其他成员认识到建立一个殖民定居地前哨的价值，殖民地定居者依赖英国的支持，可能成为英国在该地区利益的忠实保护者。）

本句是复合，Though 引导让步状语从句，that 引导定语从句被逗号隔开，that could become a loyal protector of British interests in the area 修饰 a colonial – settler outpost，而 dependent on British support 是插入语，对 a colonial – settler outpost 进行说明。

4. The U. S. worried that Egypt, under Gamal Abdel Nasser—a nationalist military officer who had come to power, ironically, with the CIA's blessing after a 1952 coup—might become a pole of attraction for pan – Arab movements.

（参考译文：具有讽刺意味的是，在美国中央情报局的默许下，1952 年埃及发生了政变，民族主义军官贾迈勒·阿卜杜纳赛尔上台，美国担心埃及可能成为一个泛阿拉伯民主运动的中心。）

本句为复合句，句子的主干是 The U. S. worried that Egypt might become a pole of attraction for pan – Arab movements，中间的逗号隔开的部分做插入语，其中"——"后面的部分是对 Gamal Abdel Nasser 的解释说明，who 引导的定语从句修饰 a nationalist military officer。

🔲 Reinforced Learning

Ⅰ. Answer the following questions for a comprehension of the text.

1. What does "black gold" refer to in the text?

2. Why did the British scrap all promises of Arab independence to various local leaders during the First World War?

3. Which country supported the formation of a "national home for the Jewish people" in Palestine?

4. What was specific content of "Eisenhower Doctrine" mentioned in the text?

5. What did U. S. officials fear in the issue of the new Iraqi regime?

Ⅱ. Multiple choice：choose the correct one from the alternative answers to give the exact meaning of the words.

1. The U. S. has relied on brutal, repressive regimes—Iran under the Shah, Saudi Arabia, Israel—to do its dirty work.

A. tremendous   B. substantial   C. cruel   D. incredible

2. All promises of Arab independence the British had made to various local leaders during the First World War were scrapped.

　A. wasted　　　B. broken　　　C. fulfilled　　　D. sustained

3. Private oil concerns pushed their governments (in the national interest, of course) to renounce all wartime promises to the Arabs.

　A. withdraw　　　B. violate　　　C. promise　　　D. cancel

4. Some clashes are still taking place and the situation is extremely tense.

　A. shock　　　B. awesome　　　C. stressed　　　D. failing

5. We can't reach our strategic goal unless we carry out the reform and adhere to the open policy.

　A. scheme　　　B. project　　　C. implement　　　D. persevere

6. Each state was then handed to local kings and sheiks who owed their position to British tutelage.

　A. grant　　　B. custody　　　C. guidance　　　D. hindrance

7. While being executive chef at the White House is prestigious, the job also can be grueling .

　A. catastrophic　　B. gracious　　　C. superior　　　D. torturous

8. The Shah's power was underwritten by massive infusions of American aid and upheld by the notoriously savage secret police, Savak.

　A. supported　　B. opposed　　　C. exploited　　　D. threatened

9. Most members in "Three Orange" have to take the role of being actors, play writers and even run about to attract auspices.

　A. protections　　B. concern　　　C. investments　　D. sponsorships

10. Recognizing that men and women may perceive situations differently may help the genders to get along.

　A. come to mind　　　　　　B. come to hand

　C. come to realize　　　　　　D. come to light

Ⅲ. Multiple choice : read the four suggested translations and choose the best answer.

1. So one night in late November 1922, Cox, Britain's representative in Baghdad, summoned to his tent Sheik Abdul – Aziz Ibn Saud, soon to become ruler of Saudi Arabia, to explain the facts of life as the British carved up the remnants of the defeated Ottoman empire.

　A. 通知　　　B. 命令　　　C. 召集　　　D. 要求

2. U. S. officials feared that the new Iraqi regime might <u>reassert</u> its historical claim on Kuwait, a tiny country created by British fiat in order to prevent any larger state from controlling what was then the biggest oil – producing area in the Gulf.

    A. 再次证明   B. 再次断言   C. 再次重申   D. 再次振作

3. U. S. interests in the region were <u>couched</u> in the Cold War terms of preventing Soviet domination, though it was clear that any regime attempting to leave the orbit of the U. S. , whether it had ties to Russia or not, was considered a threat.

    A. 限制   B. 压制   C. 影响   D. 损害

4. Journalist Glenn Frankel describes how British High Commissioner Sir Percy Cox <u>settled</u> boundaries between Iraq, Kuwait, and Saudi Arabia at a 1922 conference in Baghdad.

    A. 解决   B. 建立   C. 划分   D. 定居

5. <u>With its eye on</u> Iraq, the U. S. seized this opportunity and declared a nuclear alert. When the new Iraqi regime announced its commitment to "respect its obligations," the U. S. withdrew its forces.

    A. 关注伊拉克 B. 盯着伊拉克 C. 对付伊拉克 D. 注视伊拉克

Ⅳ. Put the following sentences into Chinese.

1. Every U. S. policy shift, every military intervention, every CIA plot has been carried out to secure one main aim: to ensure the cheap and plentiful flow of the world's most important energy resource—oil.

2. After the collapse of the Ottoman Empire, Britain and France drew the boundaries of the new states in the Middle East with absolutely no input from the people of the region.

3. In the aftermath of the Second World War, the U. S. moved in quickly to establish itself as the number – one power in the Middle East.

4. U. S. interests in the region were couched in the Cold War terms of preventing Soviet domination, though it was clear that any regime attempting to leave the orbit of the U. S. , whether it had ties to Russia or not, was considered a threat.

5. This event was perceived as a severe blow to U. S. prestige in the region and as a threat to American oil interests.

V. Put the following paragraphs into Chinese.

1. The term Eisenhower Doctrine refers to a speech by President Dwight David Eisenhower on 5 January 1957, within a "Special Message to the Congress on the Situation in the Middle East". Under the Eisenhower Doctrine, a country could request American economic assistance and/or aid from U. S. military forces if it was being threatened by armed aggression from another state.

2. Balfour declared his support for the establishment of a Jewish homeland in the area known as Palestine – though there had to be safeguards for the "rights of non – Jewish communities in Palestine". Other nations that fought for the Allies offered their support for the declaration.

4.3　China Oil Demand and the Geopolitics of Oil in the Asian Pacific Region

Guidance to Reading

With the rapid development of China's economy, China's demand for oil has increased very significantly and there is potential for further increases. Therefore, a large amount of oil import is a solution to meet the increasing demand. On the other hand, China's attempt to diversify its oil supply and transport routes could lead to serious conflict with Japan and other Asian countries. Although there is a risk of conflict with its most important neighbors (Japan, South Korea and India), there could also be cooperation in joint, coordinated access to resources.

Text

In the words of a leading specialist in international energy affairs: "Rapid energy growth in China is leading to dramatic impacts throughout the world **in terms of** commodity markets and prices, and within China, growing thirst for energy is creating a new sense of urgency and energy insecurity. Indeed, the means by which Beijing chooses to deal with its energy security will not only affect the Chinese economy, but the global economy as well. China's energy needs have global **implications** today, as was witnessed last year through competition with Japan for imported oil from Russia. Ultimately the US, China, and

Japan will be **vying** for the same Middle Eastern crude oil. Over the next two decades, China will play a larger and larger role in the Middle East since the country is so dependent on foreign oil imports, as well as Central Asia, West Africa, and other parts of the world which could help meet China's growing energy requirements. "

Energy in China: a voracious appetite

China's strong economic growth in recent years has led to a very significant increase in its oil consumption. For example, oil demand doubled between 1995 and 2005, reaching 6. 8 million barrels per day (bbl/d). China has been consuming more oil than Japan since 2003, the year it became the world's second biggest consumer. In 2004, China consumed 6. 6 million bbl/d, still only a third of US consumption (20. 5 million bbl/d), but **nonetheless** a 16% increase over the previous year.

Since it became a net oil importer in 1993, China has greatly increased its foreign purchases. In 2004, **gross** oil imports (crude and oil products) rose to 3. 4 million bbl/d, representing more than half the country's consumption. In 2000, imports accounted for barely 1. 9 million bbl/d, equivalent to 38% of consumption.

Forecasts for the coming decades all point to strong growth in demand and, above all, a great increase in oil imports. Consumption could reach 12 million bbl/d in 2020 and 16 million bbl/d in 2030, while imports could increase even more quickly, reaching 7 million bbl/d in 2020 and 11 million bbl/d in 2030. In short, according to the vast majority of forecasts, China could more than double its consumption of crude and **treble** its oil imports over the next quarter of a century. China could increase its oil consumption by an average of about 4. 5% a year over the next two decades, more than **quadrupling** the consumption increases forecast for developed western countries.

This rise in consumption and in oil imports will be the result of several factors, including rapid GDP growth of about 6% − 7% a year over the next two or three decades, compared with a rate of 9. 5% between 1980 and 2004. Other important factors are the **energy − intensive industrial sector**, a sharp increase in the number of vehicles on the country's roads (rising from 20 million in 2004 to at least 130 million in 2020), and the need to reduce the relative weight in energy consumption of inefficient and extremely polluting coal.

If Chinese oil imports increase from 4 million bbl/d today to 7 million bbl/d in 2020, to 8 million bbl/d in 2025, and to 11 million bbl/d in 2030, the global effects of such a rise will significantly affect both the **availability** and the price of crude. China is already actively seeking oil (and natural gas) beyond its borders. This search will undoubtedly **accelerate** in the coming years, with the effect of altering the geopolitics of energy and oil in the Asian Pacific region and around the world.

China's growing demand for oil is significantly changing the international **geopolitics** of energy, especially in the Asian Pacific region. The recent growth in oil consumption **combined with** forecasts of increased oil imports (especially from the Middle East), have led to deep concern among Chinese leaders regarding their country's energy security. They are responding in a number of different ways. In particular, they **are determined to** increase the security and **reliability** of oil imports by searching for new sources of supply, and to control purchases and transport **lanes**, while **boosting** national production at any cost. This is already causing **tension** and could lead to further disputes with the US and other big oil consumers, such as Japan and India, as well as with other Asian Pacific countries. However, enhanced cooperation among the big East Asian economies (China, Japan and South Korea) is also a possibility.

China and the geopolitics of oil in the Asian Pacific region: the Chinese factor

These geopolitical effects will be particularly intense because of China's growing concern regarding increasing US **hegemony** in the Middle East (the source of a projected 70% of China's oil imports in 2025 – double the current proportion –) and the **vulnerability** of transported oil, most of which reaches China by sea, through the straits of Hormuz and Malacca. In particular, China intends to diversify its supply sources, importing more oil from Russia, Central Asia, West Africa and Latin America, and doing everything possible to secure transport lanes for its crude imports.

China's efforts to control and develop its oil supply will have a **considerable** impact on the geopolitics of energy in Asia and around the world. China will also become a key and very active player in the international geopolitics of energy. Its energy trade with producing countries will bring with it a greater economic, political and military influence in these countries, and its territorial claims in the East China and South China seas may lead to conflict with some of its neighbours. For example, the construction of oil and gas pipelines from Russian and central Asia could also lead to conflict with Japan. The search for land and sea alternatives to the **chokepoint** formed by the Strait of Malacca (now the route for three quarters of China's oil imports) could lead to a strategic **rapprochement** with Thailand, Myanmar and Indonesia. Naval protection of lanes in the Indian Ocean and the South China Sea could cause tension with India, Vietnam and the US. Moreover, the desire to increase national production **at any cost** has led – and will continue to lead – China to take a firmer stance on territorial issues, including its **sovereignty** in the East China Sea (especially the Diaoyu islands, known as the Senkaku islands to the Japanese) and in the South China Sea (especially the Spratly islands). A stronger stance on this issue could lead to major tension with Japan and other east Asian countries.

However, although it is true that there are several trends towards **heightened** geopolitical tension in the Asia Pacific region as a result of competition for oil, the possibility exists that the **pragmatic** countries of the region may reach enhanced cooperation agreements on energy issues. At the end of the day, China, Japan, South Korea and even India all share common interests, high among which is the desire to reduce their dependence on the Middle East and to **proportionally** increase their consumption of natural gas.

It is still early to determine whether the Asia Pacific region is headed towards an **era** of increasing rivalries or, on the contrary, towards an era of greater cooperation on energy issues, particularly those involving the consumption and importation of oil. In any case, a move towards one scenario or the other will largely depend on China's strategic decisions in the coming years.

Words and Expressions

implication	暗示,含义
vying	竞争的
voracious	贪婪的;贪吃的
nonetheless	但是,尽管如此
gross	总额,总数
treble	变成三倍
quadruple	使成四倍

availability	可用性；实用性
accelerate	加速，促进
geopolitics	地缘政治学
reliability	可靠性
lanes	线路；跑道
boost	促进；增加
tension	紧张；不安
hegemony	霸权；领导权
vulnerability	易损性；弱点
considerable	重要的；大量的
chokepoint	阻塞点
rapprochement	友善关系的建立
sovereignty	主权，主权国家
heighten	提高；加强
pragmatic	实用主义的，务实的
proportionally	成比例地
era	时代，年代

Phrases and Expressions

in terms of	在……方面
energy – intensive industrial sector	能源密集型行业
combined with	联合；连同
be determined to	下决心做……
at any cost	不惜任何代价

Language Focus

1. Rapid energy growth in China is leading to dramatic impacts throughout the world in terms of commodity markets and prices, and within China, growing thirst for energy is creating a new sense of urgency and energy insecurity.

（参考译文：中国能源需求的快速增长对全球商品市场和商品价格产生了重大影响，在中国，日益增长的能源需求造成了新的能源危机和能源紧张。）

本句是并列句，and 连接并列成分，growing thirst for energy 为第二个句子的主语部分。

2. Other important factors are the energy – intensive industrial sector, a sharp increase in the number of vehicles on the country's roads (rising from 20 million in 2004 to at least 130 million in 2020), and the need to reduce the relative weight in energy consumption of inefficient and extremely polluting coal.

(参考译文:其他重要因素包括能源密集型工业产业的发展,中国车辆数目急剧增加(从 2004 年两千万辆增至 2020 年一亿三千万辆),及减少相对低效及污染极大的煤能源使用的需求。)

本句是简单句,主谓部分是 Other important factors are,表语是三个并列的名词 the energy – intensive industrial sector, a sharp increase 及后面的 and the need,句子后部的 to reduce the relative... 是不定式作定语,修饰 the need。

3. These geopolitical effects will be particularly intense because of China's growing concern regarding increasing US hegemony in the Middle East (the source of a projected 70% of China's oil imports in 2025 – double the current proportion –) and the vulnerability of transported oil, most of which reaches China by sea, through the straits of Hormuz and Malacca.

(参考译文:因为中国日益关注美国在中东的霸权(预计到 2025 年中国 70% 的石油进口来源于中东——是目前比例的两倍),因此地缘政治的影响将尤为激烈,中国也十分关注脆弱的石油运输,石油运输大部分要通过霍尔木兹海峡和马六甲海峡由海路到达中国。)

本句是简单句,because of 表示原因状语,and 连接并列两部分 increasing US hegemony in the Middle East and the vulnerability of transported oil 作 regarding 的介词宾语,most of which reaches China by sea, through the straits of Hormuz and Malacca 是定语从句修饰 the vulnerability of transported oil。

4. However, although it is true that there are several significant trends towards heightened geopolitical tension in the Asia Pacific region as a result of competition for oil, the possibility exists that the pragmatic countries of the region may reach enhanced cooperation agreements on energy issues.

(参考译文:然而,尽管因为石油竞争,亚太地区地缘政治紧张局势确实有加剧的趋势,但该地区务实的国家就能源问题有可能达成加强合作的协议。)

本句是复合句,although 引导让步状语从句,状语从句中 it 是形式主语,that 引导的句子是真正主语;主句的主语 the possibility 由 that 引导的同位语从句修饰,由于谓语动词 exists 太短,同位语从句放在后面,这种现象称为分割式同位结构。

Reinforced Learning

I . Answer the following questions for a comprehension of the text.

1. In 2004,how much crude oil was consumed in China compared with US consumption?

2. In the next few years,what's the status of China's oil imports in the world?

3. What factors cause the rise in consumption and oil imports in China according to text?

4. What reasons led to conflict between China and Japan?

5. What tendency will be formed in the Asia Pacific region?

II . Multiple choice:choose the correct one from the alternative answers to give the exact meaning of the words.

1. Theory,only when combined with practice,can play the best role.

A. associate with　B. together with　C. related with　D. connect with

2. Equally important is a more explicit agenda to boost growth in the medium term.

A. promote　　　B. foster　　　C. change　　　D. increase

3. Barack Obama said America's "voracious" economy should no longer be relied upon as the sole engine of global growth.

A. prosperous　　B. accursed　　C. ridiculous　　D. greedy

4. In particular,they are determined to increase the security and reliability of oil imports by searching for new sources of supply,and to control purchases and transport lanes.

A. feasibility　　B. dependence　　C. dependability　D. facticity

5. China could increase more than quadrupling the consumption increases forecast for developed western countries.

A. increasing by a factor of four　　B. increasing by a factor of three

C. increasing by a factor of two　　D. increasing by a factor of five

6. As well as the west,India,Brazil and Russia are also vying for business.

A. expanding　　B. evolving　　C. competitive　D. representative

7. It is still early to determine whether the Asia Pacific region is headed towards an era of increasing rivalries or,on the contrary,towards an era of greater

cooperation on energy issues, particularly those involving the consumption and importation of oil.

    A. cooperations   B. neighbours   C. partners   D. opponents

    8. Even in a negative <u>scenario</u>, such voices would struggle to win all their arguments: enlargement has given the newcomers a big say, and they are not about to harmonize away all their advantages.

    A. morale   B. background   C. situation   D. effect

    9. As befits a former businessman, he is <u>pragmatic</u> rather than ideological.

    A. practical   B. predictive   C. calculated   D. adaptive

    10. <u>Nonetheless</u>, it appears that the number of "irregular" migrants in Britain has been growing fast.

    A. while   B. yet   C. although   D. then

III. Multiple choice: read the four suggested translations and choose the best answer.

    1. These geopolitical effects will be particularly intense because of China's growing concern regarding increasing US <u>hegemony</u> in the Middle East and the vulnerability of transported oil, most of which reaches China by sea, through the straits of Hormuz and Malacca.

    A. 权力   B. 霸权   C. 宣传   D. 制衡

    2. Ultimately the US, China, and Japan will be <u>vying</u> for the same Middle Eastern crude oil.

    A. 制衡的   B. 合作的   C. 占领的   D. 竞争的

    3. The search for land and sea alternatives to the chokepoint formed by the Strait of Malacca could lead to a strategic <u>rapprochement</u> with Thailand, Myanmar and Indonesia.

    A. 加强合作   B. 保持联系   C. 友好关系   D. 经贸往来

    4. Rapid energy growth in China is leading to dramatic impacts throughout the world <u>in terms of</u> commodity markets and prices, and within China, growing thirst for energy is creating a new sense of urgency and energy insecurity.

    A. 以……措词   B. 依据   C. 在……方面   D. 按照

    5. The desire to increase national production at any cost has led – and will continue to lead – China to take a firmer <u>stance</u> on territorial issues, including its sovereignty in the East China Sea and in the South China Sea.

    A. 立场   B. 态度   C. 位置   D. 姿态

IV. Put the following sentences into Chinese.

1. China's growing demand for oil is significantly changing the international geopolitics of energy, especially in the Asian Pacific region.

2. Over the next two decades, China will play a larger and larger role in the Middle East since the country is so dependent on foreign oil imports, as well as Central Asia, West Africa, and other parts of the world which could help meet China's growing energy requirements.

3. Indeed, the means by which Beijing chooses to deal with its energy security will not only affect the Chinese economy, but the global economy as well.

4. In particular, China intends to diversify its supply sources, importing more oil from Russia, Central Asia, West Africa and Latin America, and doing everything possible to secure transport lanes for its crude imports.

5. China's efforts to control and develop its oil supply will have a considerable impact on the geopolitics of energy in Asia and around the world.

V. Put the following paragraphs into Chinese.

1. Increased energy production will not be sufficient, although China is self – sufficient in coal and natural gas, it is not self – sufficient in oil. Although coal supplies nearly 70% of primary energy consumption in China, the relative weight of oil has increased significantly in recent years, though remaining well below corresponding levels in other Asian countries.

2. In the late nineties, a study noted that the growing demand for oil and China's ever – increasing crude imports would have serious strategic implications, especially in terms of the country's relations with the Middle East, central Asia, Russia and the rest of East Asia.

Chapter 5　Petroleum Supervision

5. 1　Fiscal Rules and Fiscal Responsibility Legislation in Oil – Producing Countries

⊡ Guidance to Reading

In OPCs, fiscal rules and FRL have a more critical role, as both of them are intended to constrain overall fiscal policy. In general, the design of appropriate fiscal rules in OPCs is more challenging than in other countries, the experience of OPCs with fiscal rules and FRL has been relatively limited, but a growing number of OPCs are starting to implement them.

⊡ Text

Fiscal rules are defined, in a **macroeconomic** context, as **institutional mechanisms** that are intended to **permanently** shape fiscal policy design and **implementation**. They **are** often **enshrined in constitutional** or legal provisions, such as fiscal responsibility legislation (FRL). Some countries opt for more informal fiscal guidelines. The design of fiscal rules and FRL varies considerably across countries, with important differences among numerical rules, which guide and **benchmark** performance against **quantitative indicators** (such as the fiscal balance or debt), and **procedural** rules that establish **transparency**, coverage, and **accountability** requirements.

Use of fiscal rules and FRL in oil – producing countries

In OPCs, fiscal rules and FRL often enshrine a desire to reduce the **procyclicality** of fiscal policy and/or to promote long – term savings and **sustainability** objectives. While oil **funds** are more **common**, fiscal rules and FRL can have a more critical role, as they **are intended to constrain** overall fiscal policy.

The design of **appropriate** fiscal rules in OPCs is more challenging than in other countries. This is due to the characteristics of oil revenue — highly volatile, uncertain, and dependent on a non – renewable resource. As such, the applicability in OPCs of fiscal rules frequently used in other countries would be questionable. For instance, rules that target specific overall or primary balances or particular debt ratios to GDP could be highly procyclical—as they would **transmit** oil **fluctuations** to expenditure and the non – oil balance.

The past experience of OPCs with fiscal rules and FRL has been relatively limited, but a growing number of countries are starting to implement them. There are only a few cases of FRL in OPCs. One of the first and more comprehensive was in Alberta in the early 1990s. Ecuador introduced FRL in 2002, but the main focus was on numerical fiscal rules. Venezuela passed an organic budget law in 1999 as a step toward improving fiscal policy and accountability. Mexico also passed FRL in 2006. In cases where countries have set numerical fiscal rules or guidelines, targets have typically been set on the non – oil balance (Norway and Timor – Leste), the overall balance (Alberta and Mexico), expenditures (Equatorial Guinea), or on several fiscal variables (Ecuador).

Norway and Alberta have adopted different institutional **frameworks** that have been relatively successful in managing fiscal policy—although both face challenges. While Norway implemented a relatively flexible framework, using the non – oil **deficit** as an **anchor**, Alberta introduced comprehensive FRL. Both cases have in common strong institutions and a **broad consensus** in favor of fiscal discipline.

● Under the fiscal guidelines that Norway introduced in 2001, the central government's structural non – oil deficit should not exceed 4 percent of the oil fund's total financial assets, **equivalent** to the expected long – run real rate of return of the fund's accumulated financial **assets**. The guidelines, which allow **deviations** for **countercyclical** fiscal policy and shocks to the value of the oil fund, were seen as a tool to help set a long – term benchmark for fiscal policy, reduce expenditure pressures, and **insulate** the budget from oil price **volatility**. While Norway has maintained **moderate** spending growth during the oil boom, the framework allows some degree of procyclicality—higher oil prices lead to a larger accumulation of financial assets, which **in turn** could lead to rising non – oil deficits. In addition, the fiscal guideline has not been met **so far**, which could reduce its **credibility** over time and **intensify** spending pressures.

● Following the **deterioration** of its fiscal position in the late 1980s, Alberta undertook a significant fiscal **adjustment** in the early 1990s. The province adopted comprehensive FRL (1993 – 1995) to strengthen fiscal policy, prevent future deficits, and **eliminate** provincial debt by 2025. The rules under the FRL have been **tightened** over time, requiring a balanced budget every year (since 1999) and no net debt (since 2005). The focus in recent years has **shifted** to how best to manage the additional oil revenues, given rising public pressures for investment spending, and how to avoid an excessively **expansionary** fiscal policy. This partly reflects the focus of Alberta's framework on the overall fiscal balance, which could lead to procyclical policies.

The experience of other OPCs, mainly with fiscal rules, has highlighted the difficulties in implementing effective and durable rules — largely due to design problems and political economy factors. In particular, fiscal policy concerns have been mostly focused on short – term constraints, resulting in fiscal rules that are too **rigid** to adjust to economic fluctuations and lack **robust** political support. This has become more evident during the recent oil boom, which has reduced liquidity constraints and made it more difficult for some governments to contain spending pressures.

In several cases, the fiscal rules or frameworks have been weakened over time or ignored. In particular:

● Ecuador introduced FRL in 2002, which included three fiscal rules focused on the central government's non – oil balance, primary expenditure growth in real terms, and the public debt ratio to GDP. The legislation was intended to help improve the fiscal position, manage higher oil revenues, and reduce the procyclicality of expenditures. However, fiscal outcomes have often **breached** the deficit and spending rules. The limit on the public debt ratio has been met, partly due to the large rise in oil prices in recent years (and associated increases in **nominal** GDP). Eventually, as **liquidity** constraints **diminished**, growing political and social pressures led to the revision of the FRL in 2005 and a relaxation of the constraints on spending.

● **Equatorial Guinea**'s expenditure rule, under which current spending should not exceed non – oil revenue, has been consistently breached in recent years. The rule is being **re – interpreted** as a medium – term objective, and expenditure has been growing substantially faster than non – oil revenue. Given the dramatic increase in the oil sector in Equatorial Guinea in recent years (to more than 80 percent of GDP), the rule no longer provides a realistic benchmark for fiscal policy.

　　● Venezuela approved an organic law for public finances in 1999, intended to strengthen fiscal policy and reduce expenditure volatility. The law focused on improving the budget process, including by using a **multiyear** framework, and introduced fiscal rules for the current balance, expenditure growth, and the public debt. Implementation of the law, however, has been **postponed**, while expenditures have continued to be highly **correlated** to oil revenue. In addition, the quality of **budgetary** institutions has deteriorated, in part due to a **proliferation** of extra budgetary funds and **quasi – fiscal** activities.

🔲 **Words and Expressions**

macroeconomic	宏观经济的
institutional	制度的,体制的
mechanisms	机制;机构(mechanism 的复数)
permanently	永久地
implementation	履行,落实
constitutional	宪法的
benchmark	基准;标准检查程序
quantitative	数量的,定量的
indicator	指示器,指示剂
procedural	程序的
transparency	透明度
accountability	有责任,有义务
procyclical	顺周期的,顺循环的
sustainable	可持续的,合理利用的
funds	资金
common	普通的,平常的
constrain	强迫,限制
appropriate	适当的,相称的
transmit	传达,传染,传送
fluctuation	波动,起伏现象
framework	框架,体系,结构
deficit	赤字,逆差
anchor	锚,锚状物,依靠

broad	宽广的,清楚无误的,明显的
consensus	一致,同意,共识
equivalent	相等的,等价的
asset	资产
deviation	偏差
countercyclical	反周期的
insulate	使绝缘,隔离
volatility	易变状态
moderate	适度的,温和的
credibility	可信,确实性
intensify	增强,强化,加剧
deterioration	恶化,退化,变坏
adjustment	调整,调节
eliminate	除去,剔除,忽略,淘汰
tighten	勒紧,固定
shift	移动,改变
expansionary	扩张性的
rigid	严格的,固执的,僵硬的,刻板的
robust	强健的,稳固的
breach	违反,突破
nominal	名义上的,象征性的,名词性的
liquidity	液态,流动性,流动资产,资产折现力
diminish	减少,减损,贬低
equatorial	赤道的
re – interpret	再解释,再诠释
multiyear	需好几年的
postpone	延期,推迟
correlate	使相互关联
budgetary	预算的
proliferation	增殖,扩散
quasi – fiscal	准财政

🔲 Phrases and Expressions

be enshrined in	庄严载入
be intended to	意图,是用来

| in turn | 依次,轮流,反之,反过来 |
| so far | 迄今为止,到某个程度 |

Proper Names

| Equatorial Guinea | 赤道几内亚(西非国家) |

Language Focus

1. The design of fiscal rules and FRL varies considerably across countries, with important differences among numerical rules, which guide and benchmark performance against quantitative indicators (such as the fiscal balance or debt), and procedural rules that establish transparency, coverage, and accountability requirements.

(参考译文:不同国家的财政规则和财政责任立法设计差异很大,其中主要的差别在于以量化指标为标准数值规则之间的差异,这一差异指导绩效并以绩效为基准(如财政平衡或债务);以及因为程序规则建立透明度、适用范围和问责制的要求不同。)

本句中关键性短语 vary with(随……发生变化),with 后 3 个名词性短语,情况分别为:非限制性定语 which guide,修饰 important differences among numerical rules;后置介词短语 against quantitative indicators (such as the fiscal balance or debt) 修饰 benchmark performance;that 从句修饰 procedural rules。

2. While oil funds are more common, fiscal rules and FRL can have a more critical role, as they are intended to constrain overall fiscal policy.

(参考译文:虽然石油基金是比较常见的,财政规则和财政责任立法却有更重要的作用,因为它们的目的是约束整体的财政政策。)

本句中的 while,作并列连词用,译为"而,然而",表示前后意义上的对比或转折。如:Some people waste food while others haven't enough. (有些人浪费粮食,然而有些人却食不果腹。)

3. The guidelines, which allow deviations for countercyclical fiscal policy and shocks to the value of the oil fund, were seen as a tool to help set a long-term benchmark for fiscal policy, reduce expenditure pressures, and insulate the budget from oil price volatility.

(参考译文:准则允许反周期财政政策的偏差和对石油基金价值的冲击,准则被视为一种工具,这种工具有助于建立财政政策的长期基准,削减开支的压力,并使预算免受石油价格波动的影响。)

本句中 which 引导的非限制性定语从句,修饰 The guidelines;不定式短语 to help set a long – term benchmark for fiscal policy, reduce expenditure pressures, and insulate the budget from oil price volatility 为后置定语,修饰限定 a tool;句子的基本结构是 The guidelines were seen as. . .。

4. In addition, the fiscal guideline has not been met so far, which could reduce its credibility over time and intensify spending pressures.

(参考译文:此外,到目前为止尚不符合财政准则,随着时间的推移,这可能会减少财政准则的信誉和加大支出压力。)

本句中的 which 引导的是限制性定语从句。

⤷ Reinforced Learning

I. Answer the following questions for a comprehension of the text.

1. Why are fiscal rules and FRL of significance in OPCs?

2. What are the differences between institutional frameworks of Norway and Alberta in managing fiscal policy?

3. What changes have there been in fiscal adjustment in Alberta in recent years?

4. What did Ecuadorian FRL contain in 2002?

5. In part, the deterioration of the quality of Venezuelan budgetary institutions can be attributed to _____.

II. Multiple choice: choose the correct one from the alternative answers to give the exact meaning of the words.

1. The design of <u>appropriate</u> fiscal rules in OPCs is more challenging than in other countries.

    A. absolute   B. suitable   C. excessive   D. flexible

2. Norway and Alberta have adopted different institutional <u>frameworks</u> that have been relatively successful in managing fiscal policy.

    A. shapes and supports   B. structure

    C. orders   D. principles or ideas

3. The central government's structural non – oil deficit should not exceed 4 percent of the oil fund's total financial assets, <u>equivalent</u> to the expected long – run real rate of return of the fund's accumulated financial assets.

    A. continue   B. amounts   C. equal   D. add up

4. Alberta undertook a significant fiscal <u>adjustment</u> in the early 1990s.

A. accommodation　B. residence　　C. allowance　　D. alteration

5. The province adopted comprehensive FRL（1993 – 1995）to strengthen fiscal policy, prevent future deficits, and <u>eliminate</u> provincial debt by 2025.

A. remove from　B. dismiss　　C. pay off　　D. put out

6. The focus in recent years has <u>shifted</u> to how best to manage the additional oil revenues.

A. changed　　B. attributed　C. managed　　D. promoted

7. In particular, fiscal policy concerns have been mostly focused on short – term constraints, resulting in fiscal rules that are too <u>rigid</u> to adjust to economic fluctuations and lack robust political support.

A. gross　　　B. healthy　　C. strong　　D. rough and crude

8. Eventually, as liquidity constraints <u>diminished</u>, growing political and social pressures led to the revision of the FRL in 2005 and a relaxation of the constraints on spending.

A. departed　　B. decreased　C. disappeared　D. attended

9. Implementation of the law has been <u>postponed</u>.

A. delayed　　　B. launched　　C. prohibited　D. allowed

10. Expenditures have continued to be highly <u>correlated</u> to oil revenue.

A. manifested　B. related　　　C. interpreted　D. correspond

III. Multiple choice: read the four suggested translations and choose the best answer.

1. Fiscal rules are defined, in a macroeconomic context, as institutional mechanisms that are intended to <u>permanently</u> shape fiscal policy design and implementation.

A. 迫切地　　B. 突出地　　C. 永久地　　D. 暂时地

2. In OPCs, fiscal rules and FRL often enshrine a desire to reduce the pro-cyclicality of fiscal policy and/or to promote long – term savings and <u>sustainability</u> objectives.

A. 持续性　　B. 准确性　　C. 保护性　　D. 抑制力

3. In addition, the fiscal guideline has not been met so far, which could reduce its <u>credibility</u> over time and intensify spending pressures.

A. 威力　　　B. 知名度　　C. 可信性　　D. 说服力

4. The rules under the FRL have been <u>tightened</u> over time, requiring a

balanced budget every year (since 1999) and no net debt (since 2005).

    A. 废除   B. 恐惧   C. 实施   D. 加紧

5. In addition, the quality of <u>budgetary</u> institutions has deteriorated, in part due to a proliferation of extra budgetary funds and quasi – fiscal activities.

    A. 目标的   B. 预算的   C. 计划的   D. 税收的

Ⅳ. Put the following sentences into Chinese.

1. In OPCs, fiscal rules and FRL often enshrine a desire to reduce the procyclicality of fiscal policy and/or to promote long – term savings and sustainability objectives.

2. The guidelines, which allow deviations for countercyclical fiscal policy and shocks to the value of the oil fund, were seen as a tool to help set a long – term benchmark for fiscal policy, reduce expenditure pressures, and insulate the budget from oil price volatility.

3. The legislation was intended to help improve the fiscal position, manage higher oil revenues, and reduce the procyclicality of expenditures.

4. Given the dramatic increase in the oil sector in Equatorial Guinea in recent years (to more than 80 percent of GDP), the rule no longer provides a realistic benchmark for fiscal policy.

5. In addition, the quality of budgetary institutions has deteriorated, in part due to a proliferation of extra budgetary funds and quasi – fiscal activities.

Ⅴ. Put the following paragraphs into Chinese.

1. Alberta's capital city, Edmonton, is located approximately in the geographic centre of the province. It is the most northerly major city in Canada, and serves as a gateway and hub for resource development in northern Canada. The region, with its proximity to Canada's largest oil fields, has most of western Canada's oil refinery capacity. Alberta is the largest producer of conventional crude oil, synthetic crude, natural gas and gas products in the country.

2. Fiscal rules have attracted increasing attention and many countries have adopted some rules. Present fiscal policy rules are fairly diverse in both design and implementation. Whereas Anglo – Saxon countries place primary emphasis on transparency, in continental Europe (EMU) Stability and Growth Pact, Switzerland's proposal and emerging market economies rely far more on a set of numerical reference values (targets, limits) on performance indicators.

5.2 Oil Production and Oil policy of the Middle East

Guidance to Reading

The Middle East oil production is playing a key role in the world energy supply. The text introduces the oil production history of four major Gulf producers and ups and downs they experienced in oil production. In addition, ethnic tension between Arab nations and Israel is a key factor affecting the oil producer's foreign policy with major powers of the world. Therefore, it is necessary to adjust the relations with other countries of the world for the countries in Middle East, especially to enhance the closer ties with the emerging Asian economies in order to promote the development of oil industry in the region.

Text

The Middle East plays a special role in the international oil industry. Five Gulf producers possess 65 per cent of the world's proven oil reserves. Their oil is by far cheapest to produce and, if oil were a competitive industry, they would probably be the almost **exclusive** source of world oil. However, because oil is not a competitive industry, the Middle Eastern producers' share of global production has been kept low, well below their share in global reserves. Over the years, this has been especially true of Iraq—this being both cause and consequence of Iraq's difficult relations with the rest of the world.

Iran was the first country in the Gulf to become an oil exporter, and kept the pride of first place until 1950. In that year, the **controversy** between the company controlling all Iranian production—Anglo – Iranian—and the nationalist government of Iranian Prime Minister Muhammad Mussadiq erupted. Following the nationalization of Anglo – Iranian, all international oil companies **boycotted** Iranian oil; production collapsed to almost nothing in 1952 and 1953, and recovered only after the coup that overthrew Mussadiq and the formation of the Iranian Consortium, in which Anglo – Iranian's role was reduced to 40 percent.

Production in Iraq started in 1928 but remained at a low level because of an **ongoing** controversy between the Iraq Petroleum Company (IPC) and the Iraqi government. Saudi Arabia began producing in 1938, but production there was **constrained** during the war, and **took off** only after 1945. Kuwaiti production began only in 1946 but grew very rapidly, and in 1953 had already overtaken Saudi production. The production of all three countries—Iraq, Saudi Arabia, and Kuwait—increased rapidly to compensate for the collapse of Iranian production in 1951; but Saudi and Kuwaiti production remained high, while Iraq's was reduced. Kuwaiti production reached a maximum of 3 million barrels per day in 1973, and has since declined. It was reduced to almost zero by the Iraqi invasion in 1991, but has since recovered. Iranian production reached a peak in 1974, and declined **precipitously** after the revolution in 1979. It continued to decline after the **onset** of the Iran – Iraq War in 1980 but recovered after the war ended in 1988. Iraqi production peaked in 1979, before the war with Iran. It recovered in the final stages of the war, but collapsed again when Kuwait was invaded in 1990. It recovered once more under the UN **oil – for – food programme** only to collapse again in 2003, when the **coalition** invaded and occupied the country. Saudi Arabia's production peaked in 1980, when it had to compensate for the loss of Iranian and Iraqi oil. It has since been constrained primarily by OPEC **quotas**.

In discussing the Middle East, oil is inescapable. It has influenced the region's relations with the rest of the world, **notably** the major powers. Although the US – led forces still denied repeatedly their invading Iraq in order to liberate the oil sector and secure their oil interest in the Middle East. From a corporate point of view, major US and UK energy and engineering companies will benefit from great opportunities and leverage to access the Iraq market. As with the politics of UN **sanction** lifting on Iraq——which would have allowed for investments——oil interests are likely to play significant role. **In this respect**, the French threat of UN **veto** against the US – led war has been linked to that fact the **French oil company Total** had the highest stake in Iraq. Access to the Iraq oil fields is also of major importance to Russian and Chinese companies. It has influenced relations within the region, because it is not **uniformly distributed**; on the contrary it is highly concentrated, creating a very distinctive **polarization** between oil – haves and oil – have – nots. And it has influenced the domestic politics of the Arab countries, allowing the **consolidation** of regimes that, in the absence of the oil rent, would probably not have survived to the twenty – first century.

Mostly, the diplomacy of the oil – producing countries has been busy pursuing objectives that are either **irrelevant** to their position as major exporters of oil—be it the promotion of Islam or the fight against Israel, pan – Arabism, or some milder form of pan – Africanism, or sheer military expansionism. Indeed, most oil – producing countries should blame their ill – advised foreign – policy initiatives for most of the problems they find themselves **mired** in. Even the Gulf countries, which have a record of less **pernicious adventurism** than Iraq, Libya (the Lockerbie bombing), or even Algeria (still mired in conflict with Morocco on southern Sahara, a **heritage** of its Third Worldism), still bear the consequences of their support for Arafat, the Afghan mujahidin, and Islamist tendencies everywhere. The advantage of Norway, one is tempted to say, is that it has no "Great Cause" that it should sponsor—although the cases of Nigeria, Venezuela, and others are there to demonstrate that it is possible to create a disaster out of oil even in the absence of a Great Cause.

It is remarkable how little attention the oil – exporting countries have otherwise devoted to oil in international relations. OPEC members meet to discuss production and prices, but otherwise limited resources have been devoted to shaping a **full – fledged**, well – structured oil diplomacy. Since 2000 the major Arab Gulf producers have considerably **diversified** their diplomatic initiative, notably engaging in dialogue with their most important clients to reassure them about the reliability of supplies. In particular, closer ties have been shaped with some of the emerging Asian economies, which are the most rapidly growing markets for Gulf oil. Saudi Arabia has also considerably increased public diplomacy **with respect to** oil affairs, with frequent speeches and presentations in international forums.

Words and Expressions

exclusive	独有的;排外的
controversy	论战;争论
boycott	联合抵制
ongoing	不间断的
constrain	束缚
precipitously	陡然地;出乎意料地
onset	开始,着手

coalition	联合,结合
quota	配额,定额
notably	显著地,尤其
sanction	制裁,处罚
veto	否决权
uniformly	一致地
distributed	分布式的,分散式的
polarization	两极分化
consolidation	巩固,坚固
irrelevant	不相干的
mire	使陷入困境
pernicious	有害的;恶性的
adventurism	冒险主义
heritage	遗产,传统
full – fledged	发育完全的
diversify	使多样化

Phrases and Expressions

take off	腾飞
in this respec	在这方面
with respect to	关于

Proper Names

| oil – for – food programme | 石油换食品计划(联合国为解决美国对伊拉克的经济封锁使其国内物资短缺而进行的"人道主义"援助) |
| French oil company Total | 法国石油公司道达尔 |

Language Focus

1. Following the nationalization of Anglo – Iranian, all international oil companies boycotted Iranian oil; production collapsed to almost nothing in 1952 and 1953, only recovered after the coup that overthrew Mussadiq and the formation of the Iranian Consortium, in which Anglo – Iranian's role was reduced to 40 percent.

（参考译文：随后，盎格鲁·伊朗公司国有化，所有的国际石油企业抵制伊朗石油；伊朗石油产量暴跌，到 1952 年和 1953 年其产量几乎为零，直到推翻摩萨台的政变发生及伊朗联盟形成后，生产才得以恢复，而盎格鲁—伊朗公司的产量减少到 40% 。）

本句是由两个句子构成的并列句，其标志是"；"，第一个句子的主谓分别是 international oil companies boycotted，第二个句子中有两个并列的谓语动词 production collapsed and recovered，that 引导定语从句修饰 coup，in which 是非限定定语从句。

2. In this respect, the French threat of UN veto against the US – led war has been linked to that fact the French oil company Total had the highest stake in Iraq.

（参考译文：在这一问题上，法国威胁联合国否决美国为首的战争，这与法国石油公司道达尔在伊拉克股份总额最多的事实相关。）

本句是复合句，主语部分是 the French threat of UN veto against the US – led war，注意 threat，veto 这里都是名词，谓语是 has been linked to，the French oil company Total had the highest stake in Iraq 是省略 that 的同位语从句说明 fact 的内容。

3. And it has influenced the domestic politics of the Arab countries, allowing the consolidation of regimes that, in the absence of the oil rent, would probably not have survived to the twenty – first century.

（参考译文：此政策对阿拉伯国家的国内政治产生了影响，在没有石油租金的情况下，阿拉伯国家稳定的政权也不可能存活到 21 世纪。）

本句是简单句，其中 and 是连词，表示"而且"，主句是 it has influenced the domestic politics of the Arab countries，allowing 是现在分词做整个句子的结果状语，in the absence of the oil rent 是插入语，allowing the consolidation of regimes that would probably not have survived to the twenty – first century 中的 that 引导定语从句，修饰 regimes。

4. Even the Gulf countries, which have a record of less pernicious adventurism than Iraq, Libya (in the Lockerbie bombing), or even Algeria (still mired in conflict with Morocco on southern Sahara, a heritage of its Third Worldism), still bear the consequences of their support for Arafat, the Afghan mujahidin, and Islamist tendencies everywhere.

（参考译文：即使在海湾国家，其中有比伊拉克冒险行为更为有害的事件,利比亚(洛克比空难),阿尔及利亚(仍然与摩洛哥在撒哈拉沙漠的南部发生的第三世界遗产冲突),海湾国家一直承担着支持阿拉法特、阿富汗圣战者和随处可见的伊斯兰倾向所造成的后果。)

本句是复合句,主语是 Even the Gulf countries,or even Algeria 谓语部分是 still bear the consequences of...,which 引导非限定性定语从句,修饰 the Gulf countries。

Reinforced Learning

I. Answer the following questions for a comprehension of the text.

1. What was the oil production history of Iran according to the text?

2. What benefits did US and UK energy and engineering companies reap from their invading Iraq?

3. What attitude did French government take towards US – led war of Iraq?

4. What objectives has the diplomacy of the oil – producing countries been busy pursuing according to the text?

5. Since 2000 what initiatives have the major Arab Gulf producers taken to improve the relations with others of world?

II. Multiple choice:choose the correct one from the alternative answers to give the exact meaning of the words.

1. There are good reasons to believe that emerging markets' share of world growth will continue to climb.

    A. banlence   B. lot   C. percent   D. scale

2. Their oil is by far cheapest to produce and,if oil were a competitive industry,they would probably be the almost exclusive source of world oil.

    A. antiforeign   B. shared   C. coexisted   D. subsistent

3. IVF(人工授精) has been a source of moral,ethical,and religious controversy since its development.

    A. worship   B. diversity   C. debate   D. contradiction

4. To provide a range of learning and knowledge sharing opportunities to city officials and their supporting staff in order to assist them in their ongoing professional development.

    A. pursuing   B. industrious   C. perpetual   D. advancing

5. For this part, please don't feel <u>constrained</u> to the settings and colors that I choose——feel free to follow your own ideas.

　　A. unexpected　　B. unfortunate　　C. uncomfortable　D. unreasonable

6. Maintaining content more, we need to seriously build, on the other hand, may have our own <u>distinctive</u> features.

　　A. prominent　　B. unusual　　C. extraordinary　D. distinguishable

7. Love is not an <u>irrelevant</u> emotion; it is the blood of life, the power of re-union of the separated.

　　A. unrelated　　B. irregular　　C. irresponsible　D. irrational

8. It's not the <u>heritage</u>, it's the design decisions and what we think is best for our players.

　　A. tendency　　B. tradition　　C. prescription　　D. instruction

9. Saudi Arabia has also considerably increased public diplomacy <u>with respect to</u> oil affairs, with frequent speeches and presentations in international forums.

　　A. repect for　　B. reflect upon　C. think of　　D. regard to

10. He tried to increase his income by gambling only to plunge more deeply into the <u>mire</u>.

　　A. marsh　　B. lack　　C. difficulty　　D. poverty

Ⅲ. Multiple choice：read the four suggested translations and choose the best answer.

1. Following the nationalization of Anglo – Iranian, all international oil companies <u>boycotted</u> Iranian oil and recovered only after the coup.

　　A. 联合倾销　　B. 联合限制　　C. 联合抵制　　D. 联合开采

2. Iranian production reached a peak in 1974, and declined <u>precipitously</u> after the revolution in 1979.

　　A. 过早地　　B. 陡峭地　　C. 迅速地　　D. 急剧地

3. It has influenced relations within the region, because it is not uniformly distributed; on the contrary it is highly concentrated, creating a very distinctive <u>polarization</u> between oil – haves and oil – have – nots.

　　A. 巨大差异　　B. 偏离振态　C. 两极分化　　D. 极化效应

4. As with the politics of UN <u>sanction lifting</u> on Iraq – which would have allowed for investments – oil interests are likely to play significant role.

A. 提升制裁　　B. 升级制裁　　C. 反对制裁　　D. 解除制裁

5. OPEC members meet to discuss production and prices, but otherwise limited resources have been devoted to shaping a <u>full – fledged</u>, well – structured oil diplomacy.

A. 稳定的　　　B. 丰满的　　　C. 有效的　　　D. 完整的

IV. Put the following sentences into Chinese.

1. However, because oil is not a competitive industry, the Middle Eastern producers' share of global production has been kept low, well below their share in global reserves.

2. In that year, the controversy between the company controlling all Iranian production—Anglo – Iranian—and the nationalist government of Iranian Prime Minister Muhammad Mussadiq erupted.

3. Although the US – led forces still denied repeatedly their invading Iraq in order to liberate the oil sector and secure their oil interest in the Middle East.

4. Access to the Iraq oil fields is also of major importance to Russian and Chinese companies.

5. It is remarkable how little attention the oil – exporting countries have otherwise devoted to oil in international relations.

V. Put the following paragraphs into Chinese.

1. On December 21, 1988, Pan Am Flight 103, a U. S. registered Boeing 747 en route from London, Heathrow Airport, to JFK Airport in New York, was destroyed when an improvised explosive device, concealed (隐藏) in an item of luggage, detonated (引爆) in the cargo hold of the aircraft. This explosion resulted in the deaths of all 259 passengers and crew aboard, including 189 Americans, as well as 11 residents of the Scottish town of Lockerbie.

2. OPEC (Organization of Petroleum Exporting Countries) is an intergovernmental organization of 12 oil – producing countries made up of Algeria, Angola, Ecuador, Iran, Iraq, Kuwait, Libya, Nigeria, Qatar, Saudi Arabia, the United Arab Emirates, and Venezuela. OPEC has maintained its headquarters in Vienna since 1965, and hosts regular meetings among the oil ministers of its Member Countries. It is considered to be one of the most effective organizations in the world.

5.3　Legal Grounds for Resolving the Issues over Oil and Oil Management of the Caspian Sea

🔲 Guidance to Reading

With proper help from the International Court of Justice (ICJ) and the United Nations (UN), similar issues over oil and oil management in the Caspian Sea can be mitigated and the oil can be used by the rest of the world. Under normal circumstances, the ICJ and International Tribunal on the Law of the Sea (ITLOS) would broker an agreement between these two nations based on the UNCLOS. The Timor Gap Treaty and the Timor Sea Treaty have helped to ease the Timor regional tension and promoted the economic development of the relevant countries and regions.

🔲 Text

The Caspian Sea region possesses large oil reserves that, when properly exported, can help many countries worldwide. The main issues **impeding** the exportation of this oil are the legal status of the Sea, the political instability within the region and the countries that contain pipelines for the oil, and environmental issues. Azerbaijan, Iran, Kazakhstan, Russia and Turkmenistan —the five countries bordering the Sea—have differing views on dividing the Sea; this is a cause of **unrest** in the region. Additionally, the surrounding area through which many current and future pipelines would run is **wrought** with a variety of problems. The US war on terrorism has **wreaked havoc** in Afghanistan, India and Pakistan often argue over the border of the Kashmir region, and Turkey has claimed that environmental issues in the Bosporus Strait will impede increased oil exportation from the region. With proper help from the International Court of Justice (ICJ) and the United Nations (UN), these issues can be **mitigated** and the oil can be used by the rest of the world.

Similar issues over oil and oil management have been brought before the ICJ, namely a **dispute** between Cameroon and Nigeria over the ownership of oil in the Bakassi Peninsula. The court has decided the case in favor of Cameroon and the UN has helped implement the decision of the court by taking into account the regional issues that the Court could not. One of the laws used to decide this case was the UN Convention on the Law of the Sea (UNCLOS), which governs international **waterways**. Another oil management issue of interest to the ICJ is the East Timor and Australia dispute over majority ownership of the Timor Gap. Though the Court has not yet intervened, it is widely accepted that the Court would **invoke** the UNCLOS and **award** most of the oil in this region to East Timor. In addition, this ruling would **invalidate** a previous treaty signed between two countries (Indonesia and Australia) that no longer share the border in dispute. The precedents set in these cases can be applied to the Caspian Sea region. Although this situation in the Caspian Sea region is more **complex** because of the number of countries **involved**, an ICJ decision and UN help to implement the decision would bring much – needed stability to the region.

In 1989, Indonesia and Australia signed the Timor Gap Treaty, which **stipulated** that Australia and Indonesia would jointly develop the oil fields within the Timor Gap **in return for** Australian recognition of East Timor as a part of Indonesia. The Timor Gap is part of the Indian Ocean between East Timor and Australia. The Gap was split into three regions: one that would be **mutually** developed by both Indonesia and Australia, one that would be primarily developed by Indonesia and one that would be primarily developed by Australia. In 1999, East Timor **declared** its independence from Indonesia and with the help of UN forces (a majority of which came from Australia), East Timor was able to **hold off** the Indonesian opposition. Upon formal international recognition of this independence, East Timor negotiated the Timor Sea Treaty with Australia, which was **merely** a **revision** of the Timor Gap Treaty. Under the Timor Sea Treaty, the three zones previously **demarcated** by the Timor Gap Treaty would remain **intact**, and East Timor would receive ninety percent of the profits from the oil in the jointly developed zone. On paper, this agreement looks to favor East Timor, but in reality, the treaty is less beneficial for East Timor. With this arrangement, the East Timorese would **yield** more **to** Australia in oil revenues than Australia would give East Timor in foreign aid. Additionally, East Timor would prefer that the boundary in this oil rich region be determined by the UN **Convention** on the Law of the Sea, which would give East Timor a larger share of the oil in the region. Despite these shortcomings of the Timor Sea Treaty, the newly independent government of East Timor signed the treaty in May 2002 **in an effort to jump – start** the young economy.

Under normal circumstances, the ICJ and International Tribunal on the Law of the Sea (ITLOS) would **broker** an agreement between these two nations based on the UNCLOS.

UN Secretary General Kofi Annan created a **commission** to broker a workable agreement between the two sides. The UN appointed Special Representative Ahmedou Ould – Adballah to chair the commission that would **oversee** this agreement. Among the measures taken to ensure a working agreement would be met were regularly scheduled meetings between local authorities and the Heads of State to discuss the border arrangement and confidence building measures.

This commission would **take into account** the **relevant sentiments** between the two countries and their relative **stakes** in the area. These situations highlight the importance of both the ICJ and the UN in brokering working agreements between differing **factions**, especially over oil. The ICJ can objectively decide a case based on the **merits** presented and the UN can work out the details to implement that decision, based on the sentiments present in the region. This is the best approach to be taken in determining how oil in the Caspian Sea region should be divided.

Words and Expressions

resolve	解决;分析
impede	阻碍;妨碍;阻止
unrest	不安;动荡的局面
wrought	锻造的;加工的;精细的;工作
wreak	发泄;报仇
havoc	大破坏;浩劫;蹂躏;损毁
mitigate	使缓和,使减轻
dispute	辩论;争论
waterway	航道;水路
invoke	调用;祈求;引起;恳求
award	授予;判定
invalidate	使无效;使无价值
complex	复杂的;合成的
involve	包含;牵涉;使陷于;潜心于
stipulate	规定;保证

mutually	互相地；互助
declare	宣布，声明；断言，宣称
merely	仅仅，只不过；只是
revision	修正；修订本
demarcate	划分界线；区别
intact	完整的；原封不动的；未受损伤的
convention	惯例；约定；协定；习俗；大会
jump – start	启动；发动
broker	安排；协商，磋商
commission	委员会
oversee	监督；审查
relevant	有关的；中肯的；有重大作用的
sentiment	观点，态度
stake	赌注；风险；利益
faction	派系
merits	值得称赞或奖励的事情、品质等

Phrases and Expressions

in return for	作为……的报答
hold off	阻止；挡住
yield to	屈服；让步
in an effort to	企图（努力想）；试图要
take into account	考虑；重视；体谅

Language Focus

1. The main issues impeding the exportation of this oil are the legal status of the Sea, the political instability within the region and the countries that contain pipelines for the oil, and environmental issues.

（参考译文：妨碍石油出口的主要问题是里海的法律地位，以及有石油管道的国家和地区因石油和环保问题而导致的政治不稳定因素。）

本句分词短语 impeding the exportation of this oil 为后置定语，修饰主语 The main issues；within 引导的介宾短语为后置定语，修饰名词性短语 the political instability；that 从句修饰名词性短语 the region and the countries，为后置定语。

2. In addition, this ruling would invalidate a previous treaty signed between two countries (Indonesia and Australia) that no longer share the border in dispute.

(参考译文:此外,这一裁决将会废除先前两国之间(印度尼西亚和澳大利亚)签署的条约:不再分别拥有争端中边界的归属权。)

本句中的过去分词短语 signed between two countries 和 that 从句都为后置定语,分别修饰 a previous treaty 和 two countries。

3. In 1989, Indonesia and Australia signed the Timor Gap Treaty, which stipulated that Australia and Indonesia would jointly develop the oil fields within the Timor Gap in return for Australian recognition of East Timor as a part of Indonesia.

(参考译文:1989 年,印度尼西亚和澳大利亚签署了《帝汶沟条约》,其中规定:澳大利亚和印度尼西亚将共同开发在东帝汶内的帝汶沟,以换取澳大利亚承认东帝汶作为印度尼西亚的一部分。)

本句中的 which 引导的非限制性定语从句修饰 the Timor Gap Treaty。

4. East Timor would prefer that the boundary in this oil rich region be determined by the UN Convention on the Law of the Sea, which would give East Timor a larger share of the oil in the region.

(参考译文:此外,东帝汶希望在这个石油丰富的边界地区按《联合国海洋法公约》来决议,这将使东帝汶在该地区占有较大的石油份额。)

本句中 that 从句为宾语从句,其中 which 引导的非限制性定语从句修饰 the UN Convention on the Law of the Sea。

5. Among the measures taken to ensure a working agreement would be met were regularly scheduled meetings between local authorities and the Heads of State to discuss the border arrangement and confidence building measures.

(参考译文:采取措施确保可行性协议能让当地政府和国家元首定期会晤,讨论边界问题和建立信心的措施。)

本句为倒装句,结构复杂,基本结构应为:regularly scheduled meetings were among....。主语应为 regularly scheduled meetings,其中 the border arrangement and confidence building measures 为 discuss 的宾语,to discuss...不定式为后置定语修饰 local authorities and the Heads of State, between 引导的介宾短语为后置定语,修饰 regularly scheduled meetings; a working agreement would be met 为 ensure 的宾语从句, to ensure...不定式为后置定语修饰 the measures,分词 taken 也是 the measures 的定语。

🔲 Reinforced Learning

I. Answer the following questions for a comprehension of the text.

1. What are the five countries bordering the Caspian Sea?

2. How to deal with the similar issues over oil and oil management?

3. Why did Indonesia agree to sign the Timor Gap Treaty in 1989?

4. Why did the newly independent government of East Timor sign the Timor Sea Treaty in May 2002?

5. Under normal circumstances, what would the ICJ and International Tribunal on the Law of the Sea (ITLOS) broker an agreement between these two nations based on?

II. Multiple choice: choose the correct one from the alternative answers to give the exact meaning of the words.

1. The main issue impeding the exportation of this oil is the legal status of the Caspian Sea.

　　A. presenting　　B. promoting　　C. hindering　　D. encountering

2. With proper help from the International Court of Justice (ICJ) and the United Nations (UN), these issues can be mitigated and the oil can be used by the rest of the world.

　　A. strengthened　B. disappeared　　C. tackled　　　D. lessened

3. It is widely accepted that the Court would invoke the UNCLOS and award most of the oil in this region to East Timor.

　　A. prize　　　　B. reward　　　C. allow　　　D. grant

4. This ruling would invalidate a previous treaty signed between two countries that no longer share the border in dispute.

　　A. recognize legally　　　　B. disagree

　　C. agree　　　　　　　　　D. not recognize legally

5. This situation in the Caspian Sea region is more complex because of the number of countries involved.

　　A. complicated　B. apparent　　　C. intense　　D. definite

6. The Timor Gap Treaty stipulated that Australia and Indonesia would jointly develop the oil fields within the Timor Gap.

　　A. obliged　　　B. addressed　　C. regulated　　D. illustrated

7. East Timor was able to hold off the Indonesian opposition.

　　A. restrain　　　B. ignore　　　C. resist　　　D. delay

8. The newly independent government of East Timor signed the treaty in May 2002 in an effort to jump – start the young economy.

　　A. start　　　B. revive　　　C. improve　　　D. encourage

9. Under normal circumstances, the ICJ and International Tribunal on the Law of the Sea (ITLOS) would broker an agreement between these two nations based on the UNCLOS.

　　A. establish　　　B. confirm　　　C. conclude　　　D. negotiate

10. UN Secretary General Kofi Annan created a commission to broker a workable agreement between the two sides.

　　A. mission　　　B. committee　　　C. delegation　　　D. unit

Ⅲ. Multiple choice：read the four suggested translations and choose the best answer.

1. Azerbaijan , Iran , Kazakhstan , Russia and Turkmenistan —the five countries bordering the Sea—have differing views on dividing the Sea；this is a cause of unrest in the region.

　　A. 失控　　　B. 动荡　　　C. 暴乱　　　D. 恶化

2. The court has decided the case in favor of Cameroon and the UN has helped implement the decision of the court by taking into account the regional issues that the Court could not.

　　A. 管理　　　B. 负责　　　C. 解释　　　D. 考虑

3. Although this situation in the Caspian Sea region is more complex because of the number of countries involved , an ICJ decision and UN help to implement the decision would bring much – needed stability to the region.

　　A. 投资的　　　B. 反复考虑的　　C. 涉及的　　　D. 分析的

4. Upon formal international recognition of this independence , East Timor negotiated the Timor Sea Treaty with Australia , which was merely a revision of the Timor Gap Treaty.

　　A. 撰写　　　B. 修订　　　C. 补充　　　D. 再版

5. This commission would take into account the relevant sentiments between the two countries.

　　A. 态度　　　B. 感情　　　C. 利益　　　D. 关系

IV. Put the following sentences into Chinese.

1. Additionally, the surrounding area through which many current and future pipelines would run is wrought with a variety of problems.

2. With proper help from the International Court of Justice (ICJ) and the United Nations (UN), these issues can be mitigated and the oil can be used by the rest of the world.

3. Though the Court has not yet intervened, it is widely accepted that the Court would invoke the UNCLOS and award most of the oil in this region to East Timor.

4. Although this situation in the Caspian Sea region is more complex because of the number of countries involved, an ICJ decision and UN help to implement the decision would bring much – needed stability to the region.

5. Upon formal international recognition of this independence, East Timor negotiated the Timor Sea Treaty with Australia, which was merely a revision of the Timor Gap Treaty.

V. Put the following paragraphs into Chinese.

1. The ICJ and UN have not yet become involved in this dispute because East Timor has yet to ask for international help; instead, the East Timorese are waiting for Australia to approve the treaty. However, if the ICJ were to get involved, it is expected that the Court would invoke the UNCLOS and rule in favor of East Timor. This would invalidate the Timor Gap Treaty, which was signed by Indonesia and Australia, two countries that no longer share a border along the Timor Gap because East Timor declared its independence from Indonesia.

2. Another international dispute over oil is in the Bakassi Peninsula, which juts out into the Gulf of Guinea in Africa. This area borders both Nigeria and Cameroon and both have laid claims to the oil rich land, despite the fact that it is inhabited mostly by Nigerians.

Chapter 6　Oil Funds

6.1　Oil Funds

🔳 Guidance to Reading

Many oil exporters have set up oil funds to utilize their massive and growing oil revenues. Most oil funds focus on stablization and saving objectives during the proliferation and have relatively rigid operational rules for the deposit and withdrawal of resources. Provisions for the use of oil funds' resources have also been used to moderate the effects of rigid accumulation rules.

🔳 Text

Soaring oil prices since the early 2000s has led to a historic **transformation** of wealth from consuming regions to major oil exporters. In recent years many of these exporters have set up oil funds to **utilize** their **massive** and growing oil revenues.

The basic framework of oil funds can be **summarized** as follows:

• The **overarching** policy objectives of oil funds include macroeconomic stabilization (**smoothing** government expenditure in view of volatile and **unpredictable** oil revenue); financial saving (**intergenerational equity**); and/or enhancing transparency in the management of oil revenue and fiscal policy.

• The operational objectives of oil funds are typically **formulated** in terms of smoothing the net flow of oil revenue into the **budget**, **depositing** a share of revenue into the fund, and providing information about oil revenue **inflows** and changes in **gross financial assets**. Operational rules cover specific principles for the **accumulation** and **withdrawal** of resources; asset management principles; and **governance**, transparency, and accountability **provisions**.

There has been a recent proliferation of oil funds. 21 OPCs have established funds, 16 of which were created after 1995. Two funds were **abolished** in 2005 – 2006. Ten funds focus on stabilization, and eight have both stabilization and saving objectives.

While the newer oil funds **predominantly** focus on stabilization objectives, the recent increase in oil prices has added emphasis to saving objectives, and in some cases enhanced asset management. Following a period of the lowest oil price levels in real terms since the early 1970s, several funds created in 1999 – 2000 included as a key objective the stabilization of oil revenue **accruing to** the budget. Nevertheless, as oil prices have risen, countries are now focusing more on long – term saving objectives. For example, Russia is now considering establishing a separate savings fund. Legislation has been **drafted** in **Trinidad** and **Tobago** to establish a savings and stabilization fund. In addition, some countries that increased production substantially in recent years (e. g. , **Azerbaijan**, **Chad**, and **Ecuador**) created funds to help improve the management of additional oil revenue.

The performance of funds is looked at mainly from an operational perspective, focusing on operational rules; integration with the budget; asset and liability management; and transparency.

Many oil funds have relatively rigid operational rules for the deposit and withdrawal of resources.

- Many oil stabilization funds have or have had price – or revenue – **contingent** deposit and/or withdrawal rules (e. g. , **Algeria**, Iran, Libya, Mexico, Russia, Trinidad and Tobago, and Venezuela).

- Most saving funds are revenue – share funds, where a pre – determined share of oil or total revenues is deposited in the fund (e. g. , Equatorial Guinea's Fund for Future Generations, **Gabon**, and **Kuwait**).

- By contrast, only a few are financing funds, where the operations of the fund **are linked** directly **to** the budget's non – oil deficit (**Norway** and **Timor – Leste**).

The introduction of funds with rigid rules has been mostly based on the expectation that removing "high" oil revenues from the budget would help **moderate** and/or make expenditures more stable, and as a means of reducing policy **discretion**. However, rigid operational rules could **be inconsistent with** actual fiscal policy (if the government is not liquidity **constrained**). The **specification** of proper and financially and politically sustainable operational rules has often been complicated by difficulties in identifying **permanent** and **temporary** **components** of oil price changes and by political economy factors. In addition, an emphasis on oil fund gross assets should not **detract attention from** assessing the government's overall net financial position.

A number of countries have dealt with rigid accumulation rules by changing, bypassing, or eliminating them. **Tensions** have often surfaced in the operation of rigid rules, particularly in situations of significant **exogenous** changes, shifting policy priorities or increased spending pressures, or because of broader asset and liability management objectives. In the 1980s and 1990s, the operating rules of funds in **Alaska**, Alberta, **Oman**, **Papua New Guinea**, and other countries were changed, in some cases several times. Some countries have adjusted upward the reference oil prices that govern deposits to, and withdrawals from, the oil funds, or changed the revenue base, in response to the recent sustained increase in international oil prices (e. g. , Kazakhstan, Russia, and **Trinidad and Tobago**). Mexico's legislature authorized the depletion of the oil fund in 2002. Venezuela has changed the operating rules of its stabilization fund several times since its creation and suspended its operation for an extended period. Gabon has yet to **comply** fully **with** provisions to **set aside** part of its oil revenue in its Fund for Future Generations. Chad, Ecuador, and Papua New Guinea found their funds operationally or politically **unworkable** and abolished them.

Provisions for the use of oil funds' resources have also been used to moderate the effects of rigid accumulation rules. In several countries, the rules allow **discretionary** transfers from the oil fund to the budget (e. g. , **Bahrain** and Libya). In Algeria, while the oil fund's deposit and withdrawal rules were based on a conservative reference oil price of US19 per barrel between 2000 and 2005, the authorities simultaneously issued debt to finance the budget, which was then serviced by the oil fund (the spread between the higher interest rate paid on debt and the returns on oil fund assets representing a cost to the government).

The resources of some oil funds are earmarked for specific purposes. Some **earmarking** provisions are based on political economy considerations, such as creating a **constituency** supportive of the oil fund (e. g. , Alaska), making it easier to resist political pressures to use oil revenues inappropriately, or prioritizing the use of resources for special purposes, such as poverty – reduction or debt service (e. g. , Azerbaijan, Chad, and Ecuador). Earmarking would, in principle, help limit the discretionary powers of governments to reallocate spending inappropriately. However, it results in resources being placed outside the **allocative** budget process and can reduce **flexibility**, **complicate** liquidity management, and affect the efficiency of government spending. **In the absence of** liquidity constraints, the impact of earmarking is also uncertain, as resources are **fungible**.

Words and Expressions

transformation	转化;转换
utilize	利用
massive	大量的;巨大的
summarize	总结;概述
overarching	首要的
smooth	使……光滑;变平滑
unpredictable	不可预知的;不定的;出乎意料的
formulate	明确地表达;制订;规定
budget	预算
deposit	存放,储蓄,储备
inflow	流入
accumulation	积聚,累积
withdrawal	收回;取消
governance	管理;统治;支配
provision	规定;条款
abolish	废除,废止;取消
predominantly	主要地;显著地
accrue (to)	增长,增加
draft	起草
contingent	因情况而异的;不一定的;偶然发生的
moderate	变缓和
discretion	任意决定权;自由裁决;自由裁量
constrained	约束的,抑制的,被强迫的
specification	规格;说明书;详述
permanent	永久的,永恒的
temporary	暂时的,临时的

component	成分;组件
tension	紧张,不安
exogenous	外生的;外因的;
unworkable	不能实行的;难运转的;不切实际的
discretionary	任意的;自由决定的
earmark	(为某一目的)指定或安排
constituency	选民,选(民)区
allocative	配置的,分配的
flexibility	灵活性;弹性
complicate	使复杂化;使恶化;使卷入
fungible	代替的;可取代的

Phrases and Expressions

by contrast	相比之下;与之相比
be linked to	与……有关联,与……有联系
be inconsistent with	不符合,相违背
detract attention from	转移注意力
comply with	照做,遵守
set aside	储蓄
in the absence of	缺乏,没有

Proper Names

intergenerational equity	代际公平
gross financial assets	总金融资产
Trinidad	特立尼达(古巴最有名的古城)
Tobago	多巴哥岛(南美洲特立尼达和多巴哥的第二大岛,哥伦布第二次航行美洲,命名了现在的多巴哥岛)
Azerbaijan	阿塞拜疆
Chad	乍得
Ecuador	厄瓜多尔
Algeria	阿尔及利亚
Gabon	加蓬
Kuwait	科威特

Norway	挪威
Timor – Leste	东帝汶
Barnett	巴尼特
Alaska	阿拉斯加(加拿大的能源大省)
Oman	阿曼(位于亚洲西南部的阿拉伯半岛东南部,它扼守着世界上最重要的石油输出通道——波斯湾的霍尔木兹海峡)
Papua New Guinea	巴布亚新几内亚
Trinidad and Tobago	特立尼达和多巴哥共和国(加勒比地区最大的石油和天然气生产国以及最重要的石油输出国)
Bahrain	巴林(位于阿拉伯半岛)

Language Focus

1. The operational objectives of oil funds are typically formulated in terms of smoothing the net flow of oil revenue into the budget, depositing a share of revenue into the fund, and providing information about oil revenue inflows and changes in gross financial assets.

(参考译文:一般石油基金的经营目标,是根据平滑石油收入的预算而制定的,将部分收入存入基金,并提供石油现金和金融资产总额变化的信息。)

本句中分词性短语 smoothing..., depositing..., and providing... 为 in terms of 的宾语。

2. Operational rules cover specific principles for the accumulation and withdrawal of resources; asset management principles; and governance, transparency, and accountability provisions..

(参考译文:操作规则,包括资源的积累和撤出的具体规则、资产管理原则和治理、透明度和问责制的规定。)

本句中 for 后所有的名词性短语为其宾语,for 引导的介词宾语为 specific principles 的后置定语。

3. The introduction of funds with rigid rules has been mostly based on the expectation that removing "high" oil revenues from the budget would help moderate and/or make expenditures more stable, and as a means of reducing policy discretion.

（参考译文：创建有硬性规定的基金主要根据这样的期望，从预算中删除"高"的石油收入，将有助于缓和和（或）使支出更加稳定，并作为一种减少政策的自由裁量权的手段。）

本句中 that 从句为 the expectation 的同位语从句，该从句中 and as a means of reducing policy discretion，为省略句，完整结构可为：and removing "high" oil revenues from the budget would. . . 。

4. Some countries have adjusted upward the reference oil prices that govern deposits to, and withdrawals from, the oil funds, or changed the revenue base, in response to the recent sustained increase in international oil prices (e. g. , Kazakhstan, Russia, and Trinidad and Tobago).

（参考译文：一些国家针对近期国际油价的持续上涨已向上调整控制石油基金储备和取消石油基金的参考油价，或改变收入基数（例如，哈萨克斯坦、俄罗斯、特立尼达和多巴哥）。）

本句中 the oil funds 分别为 deposits to 与 withdrawals from 的介词宾语，govern 的宾语有 deposits 与 withdrawals；句子主干成分为 Some countries have adjusted. . . , or changed. . . 。

Reinforced Learning

Ⅰ. Answer the following questions for a comprehension of the text.

1. Why are there many exporters to introduce oil funds nowadays?
2. When did the oil price levels fall to the lowest?
3. What are financing funds related to? Give examples.
4. What has the creation of funds with rigid rules been largely based on?
5. What measures did Mexico's legislature take in 2002?

Ⅱ. Multiple choice: choose the correct one from the alternative answers to give the exact meaning of the words.

1. In recent years many of these exporters have set up oil funds to utilize their massive and growing oil revenues.

A. manage   B. raise   C. make use of   D. distribute

2. The operational objectives of oil funds are typically formulated in terms of smoothing the net flow of oil revenue into the budget.

A. attained   B. expressed   C. adjusted   D. made

3. Rigid operational rules could be inconsistent with actual fiscal policy.

A. be for   B. be against   C. be based upon   D. be prone to

4. A number of countries have dealt with rigid <u>accumulation</u> rules by changing, bypassing, or eliminating them.

A. calculation   B. valuation

C. administrative   D. getting together

5. Operational rules cover specific principles for <u>governance</u>, transparency, and accountability provisions.

A. defence   B. guidance   C. supervision   D. integrity

6. Mexico's legislature authorized the <u>depletion</u> of the oil fund in 2002.

A. distribution   B. compensation

C. appropriation   D. considerable reduction

7. Gabon has yet to comply fully with provisions to <u>set aside</u> part of its oil revenue in its Fund for Future Generations.

A. reject   B. save   C. not consider   D. place aside

8. Ecuador and Papua New Guinea found their funds operationally or politically <u>unworkable</u> and abolished them.

A. unsuitable   B. insufficient   C. impractical   D. invalid

9. In several countries, the rules allow <u>discretionary</u> transfers from the oil fund to the budget.

A. leagal   B. financial   C. administrative   D. free

10. The resources of some oil funds are <u>earmarked</u> for specific purposes.

A. donated   B. raised   C. designated   D. misappropriated

Ⅲ. Multiple choice：read the four suggested translations and choose the best answer.

1. The overarching policy objectives of oil funds include <u>macroeconomic</u> stabilization, financial saving and/or enhancing transparency in the management of oil revenue and fiscal policy.

A. 宏观经济的   B. 宏观调控的

C. 微观经济的   D. 微观调控的

2. Most saving funds are <u>revenue – share</u> funds, where a pre – determined share of oil or total revenues is deposited in the fund.

A. 赋税均摊   B. 税收份额   C. 收入份额   D. 收入分成

3. It results in resources being placed outside the <u>allocative</u> budget process.

A. 修订的   B. 提交的   C. 平衡的   D. 分配的

4. It can reduce flexibility, complicate liquidity management, and affect the efficiency of government spending.

    A. 适应性   B. 灵活性   C. 柔韧性   D. 敏感性

5. In the absence of liquidity constraints, the impact of earmarking is also uncertain, as resources are fungible.

    A. 没有   B. 缺席   C. 失效   D. 解除

Ⅳ. Put the following sentences into Chinese.

1. Soaring oil prices since the early 2000s has led to a historic transformation of wealth from consuming regions to major oil exporters.

2. The performance of funds is looked at mainly from an operational perspective, focusing on operational rules; integration with the budget; asset and liability management; and transparency.

3. Venezuela has changed the operating rules of its stabilization fund several times since its creation and suspended its operation for an extended period.

4. Gabon has yet to comply fully with provisions to set aside part of its oil revenue in its Fund for Future Generations.

5. Provisions for the use of oil funds' resources have also been used to moderate the effects of rigid accumulation rules.

Ⅴ. Put the following paragraphs into Chinese.

1. Oil funds should be well integrated with the budget to enhance both the coordination of fiscal policy—including integrated asset and liability management—and the efficiency of public spending. This is best achieved by ensuring that the fund operates as a government account rather than a separate institution.

2. Oil funds can play a useful role in asset management, provided they are properly integrated with other government financing operations. The resources in the oil fund should be managed to support the government's overall asset and liability management strategy with a medium – to long – term horizon, taking account of the major risks. This requires the development of a clear, comprehensive, and transparent investment and risk management framework. Macroeconomic stabilization, competitiveness, and liquidity considerations suggest the advisability of placing oil fund resources abroad.

6. 2   Integration with Budget Systems and Asset Management on Oil Funds

Guidance to Reading

The assessment of oil funds is generally based on a qualitative analysis of country cases, the performance of funds is embodied in integration with the budget systems, asset management and the others from an operational perspective.

Text

Integration with Budget Systems

The operation of an oil fund may be assessed in terms of how well it helps (or hinders) the budget system in meeting its basic objectives. The experience with oil funds points to several key issues, in addition to earmarking and transparency:

- Extrabudgetary spending **authority**. This may lead to **fragmentation** of **policymaking**, a loss in control over expenditure, and reduced efficiency in the allocation of resources. Around half of the oil funds **have the authority to** spend or invest assets domestically separate from the budget system. For example, the resources in the oil funds in Azerbaijan and **Kazakhstan** can be spent **off – budget** through **presidential directives**. The Libyan oil fund has also financed substantial extrabudgetary spending. The oil funds in Iran and Kuwait may invest or lend to the **private** domestic economy outside the budget process.

- Creation of "islands of excellence". When **public financial management** (**PFM**) systems are perceived to be weak, as in many developing countries, it is sometimes argued that the creation of a fund with **separate procedures** and controls might **yield** better results than the budget. There is little **tangible evidence**, however, to support the creation of such "islands of excellence." Moreover, such an **approach** would also have to consider the potentially negative impact on the development of a national public financial management system.

- Cash management. Some countries have experienced difficulties in asset and liability management **associated with** rigid oil fund rules and fragmentation of cash management. In Chad, **given** concerns about institutional capacity and governance and the objective of **putting** oil resources **to good use**, separate cash management systems were established to support a complex arrangement of **multiple** budgets and an oil fund, with revenues earmarked for specific purposes. Spending pressures in the country's main operating budget resulted in **arrears** and costly borrowing, while **low – yield** assets were being accumulated in the oil fund. In early 2006, the government abolished the oil fund to ease liquidity constraints on its operating budget. In Venezuela, the government could only make deposits into the oil fund (that were mandated by law) in 1999 – 2000 with recourse to expensive financing, as the budget remained in deficit. In late 2000, the operation of the oil fund was temporarily suspended. In Ecuador, extensive oil revenue earmarking (including to the oil funds) and cash fragmentation contributed to the accumulation of domestic arrears despite large deposit **holdings**.

Financing funds are integrated with the budget process. These funds provide an **explicit** link between fiscal policy and the accumulation of financial assets, and address **fungibility** issues. They do not **attempt to** "discipline" expenditure through the **removal** of some resources from the budget—the flows in and out of the fund depend on oil revenue and policy decisions **embodied** in the non – oil fiscal **stance**. Their **establishment** has been linked to the desire to **enhance** transparency and promote public **awareness** of **intertemporal** constraints.

- The overarching policy objectives of oil funds include macroeconomic stabilization (smoothing government expenditure in view of volatile and unpredictable oil revenue); financial saving (intergenerational equity); and/or enhancing transparency in the management of oil revenue and fiscal policy.

- Norway's oil fund is formally a government account at the central bank that receives **the net central government receipts** from petroleum activities and transfers to the budget the amounts needed to finance the non – oil deficit. The oil fund has no authority to spend and the decisions on spending and the fiscal policy stance are made within the budget process. In addition, the fund is ruled by stringent transparency and accountability provisions.

The oil fund in Timor – Leste was designed along the lines of Norway's fund. It is fully integrated into the central government budget and managed with a high standard of transparency and accountability.

A number of countries have made or are **making efforts to** better integrate their oil funds with budget systems. This reflects growing awareness of the potential loss in fiscal control and the importance to public spending efficiency of **unifying** expenditure policy and **subjecting approval** and **execution** of **outlays** to the same budgetary standards, and of enhancing the efficiency of asset/liability management. For instance, since 2005, Azerbaijan has reported the operations of the oil fund in the annual budget presented to parliament (although parliament does not **approve** the oil fund's budget). In Libya, the government has indicated its **intention** to eliminate the practice of using the oil fund to finance extrabudgetary spending. The rules of the Kazakhstani oil fund have recently been **amended** to provide better integration with the budget. Alberta **discontinued** the extrabudgetary operations undertaken by its **original** oil savings fund **in light of** their disappointing performance. The Algerian authorities are moving towards implementing oil fund rules that will increase integration with the budget and **transform** the existing oil fund into a financing fund.

Asset management

Oil funds' financial balances have increased substantially in recent years. A simultaneous build up of deposits and debt, which partially resulted from rigidities in fund accumulation rules, was **observed** in some countries (e. g. , Azerbaijan, Chad, and Iran). Other countries **were active in** reducing debt (e. g. , Algeria, Kuwait, Libya, and Russia), and some **explicitly** tried to avoid the impact on domestic liquidity that would have resulted from **repaying** domestic debt more rapidly (e. g. , Norway), or **sought to** issue debt to develop the domestic debt markets.

Only a few of the oil funds examined have a clear, comprehensive, and transparent investment strategy. In particular:

• There is a general preference to place funds assets abroad, mainly to **allay** fears about appreciation of the domestic **currency**. Many governments place their deposits at the central bank (e. g. , almost all of African and western **hemisphere** countries, Algeria, Kazakhstan, and Russia), which in some cases acts as the government's investment agent. Funds in Kuwait and Oman are believed to have some domestic investments, while the oil fund in Iran is **allowed** to invest up to 50 percent of its balance in foreign currency **loans** to the domestic private sector.

● Returns on the assets held by oil funds vary, but are generally low. Average real returns were below 2 percent in relatively active funds in the first few years of this decade (e. g. , Alaska, Alberta, and Azerbaijan). This was partly **due to** the sharp fall in return in international capital markets at the beginning of the **decade**. **CEMAC** countries, including those with oil funds, have expressed concerns about the **remuneration** of their deposits at **BEAC**, the regional central bank. In a few countries, oil fund deposits with the central bank do not earn interest, although the government may **nonetheless** receive income indirectly from central bank **dividend payments**.

Words and Expressions

integration	集成;综合;融合
authority	权威;权力;当局
fragmentation	破碎;分裂
policymaking	决策;制定政策
off – budget	预算外的,非预算的
presidential	总统的
directive	指示;指令
private	私人的;私有的
separate	单独的;分开的
procedure	程序,手续;步骤
yield	产生或提供(结果、利润等)
tangible	有形的;切实的;看得见的
evidence	证据,证明
approach	方法;途径;接近
given	考虑到
multiple	多重的;多样的;许多的
arrear	欠款,逾期债款
low – yield	低产量的;产量很低的
holdings	占有的财产;所持股份;控股
explicit	明确的;清楚的
fungibility	可替代性;可互换
discipline	训练,训导;惩戒
removal	移动;排除

embody	体现,使具体化;具体表达
stance	立场
establishment	确立,制定
enhance	提高;加强;增加
awareness	意识,认识
intertemporal	跨时期的
unify	统一;使相同,使一致
subject	使臣服,使顺从,压服
approval	批准;认可;赞成;核准
execution	执行,实行;完成
outlay	经费;支出
approve	批准;认可;赞成;核准
intention	意图;目的;意向
amend	修改;改善,改进
discontinue	停止;使中止
original	原始的;最初的
transform	改变,使……变形;转换
observe	观察;注意到
explicitly	明确地;明白地
repay	偿还;回报
allay	减轻;使缓和
currency	货币
hemisphere	半球
allow	允许;认可
loan	贷款;借款
decade	十年
remuneration	报酬;酬劳,赔偿
nonetheless	尽管如此,但是
dividend	股息,红利
payment	支付

Phrases and Expressions

have the authority to do sth.	有权做
be associated with	与……联系在一起;与……有关

put sth. to good use	使……充分发挥作用,好好利用
attempt to do sth.	尝试做某事
make efforts to do sth.	努力做
in light of	根据;鉴于
be active in	对(于)……很积极;热心于
seek to	力图,寻求
due to	由于;应归于

Proper Names

Kazakhstan	哈萨克斯坦
public financial management（PFM）	公共财政管理
the net central government receipts	中央政府净收入
CEMAC	中非经济与货币共同体
BEAC	中非国家银行

Language Focus

1. Around half of the oil funds have the authority to spend or invest assets domestically separate from the budget system.

（参考译文:大约有一半的石油基金有权在国内消费或者投资预算系统外的资产。）

本句中 separate from the budget system 是形容词短语,充当 assets 的后置定语。

2. ..., the resources in the oil funds in Azerbaijan and Kazakhstan can be spent off – budget through presidential directives.

（参考译文:在阿塞拜疆和哈萨克斯坦,根据总统的指示,石油基金可进行预算外的支出。）

本句的 off – budget 是形容词用作副词,作状语,表示说明。

3. In Chad, given concerns about institutional capacity and governance and the objective of putting oil resources to good use, separate cash management systems were established to support a complex arrangement of multiple budgets and an oil fund, with revenues earmarked for specific purposes.

（参考译文:鉴于对机构能力和治理与善加利用石油资源目标的关注,乍得设立了独立的现金管理系统,支持多个预算和石油基金的复杂安排,并设立了专项财政收入。）

本句中 institutional capacity... to good use 都是 about 的介词宾语,with revenues earmarked for specific purposes,独立主格,表示补充说明。

4. In Venezuela, the government could only make deposits into the oil fund (that were mandated by law) in 1999 – 2000 with recourse to expensive financing, as the budget remained in deficit.

(参考译文:1999—2000 年,委内瑞拉依然是预算赤字,政府只会把存款放入对高昂的融资有追索权的石油基金(由法律规定)。)

本句中介宾短语 with recourse to expensive financing 为后置定语,修饰 the oil fund;as 引导原因状语从句。

5. A simultaneous build up of deposits and debt, which partially resulted from rigidities in fund accumulation rules, was observed in some countries.

(参考译文:对一些国家进行观察后发现,基金积累原则的刚性规定一定程度上造成了储蓄和债务共存。)

本句 which 引导的非限制定语从句,修饰 build up。

🔲 Reinforced Learning

I . Answer the following questions for a comprehension of the text.

1. What are the critical issues concerning oil funds?

2. In early 2006, why did Chad's government abolish the oil fund?

3. What is the oil fund in Timor – Leste characterized by?

4. Why do many oil funds prefer inverstment abroad to domestic investment?

5. There is a sharp fall in return in international capital markets at the beginning of the decade. What happened as a result of it?

II . Multiple choice:choose the correct one from the alternative answers to give the exact meaning of the words.

1. This may lead to fragmentation of policymaking.

A. split   B. unbalance   C. mistakes   D. out of control

2. There is little tangible evidence to support the creation of such "islands of excellence. "

A. experimental B. material   C. accurate   D. firsthand

3. They were established to support a complex arrangement of multiple budgets and an oil fund.

A. excessive　　B. many　　　C. different　　D. adequate

4. In Ecuador, extensive oil revenue earmarking (including to the oil funds) and cash fragmentation <u>contributed</u> to the accumulation of domestic arrears despite large deposit holdings.

　　A. added to　　B. prevented　　C. delayed　　D. led to

5. These funds provide an <u>explicit</u> link between fiscal policy and the accumulation of financial assets.

　　A. slight　　　B. connecting　　C. direct　　　D. clear

6. They do not attempt to "<u>discipline</u>" expenditure through the removal of some resources from the budget.

　　A. extend　　　B. raise　　　C. punish　　　D. stimulate

7. The Algerian authorities are moving towards <u>implementing</u> oil fund rules.

　　A. applying　　B. working out　　C. formulating　　D. carrying out

8. The impact on domestic liquidity resulted from <u>repaying</u> domestic debt more rapidly.

　　A. recovering　　B. arrears　　　C. paying again　　D. paying back

9. To place funds assets abroad is mainly to <u>allay</u> fears about appreciation of the domestic currency.

　　A. conquer　　　B. moderate　　　C. throw away　　D. confrim

10. The oil fund in Iran is allowed to invest up to 50 percent of its balance in foreign currency <u>loans</u> to the domestic private sector.

　　A. costs　　　B. lending　　　C. deposits　　　D. savings

Ⅲ. Multiple choice：read the four suggested translations and choose the best answer.

1. Spending pressures in the country's main operating budget resulted in <u>arrears</u> and costly borrowing.

　　A. 经济低迷　　B. 欠款　　　C. 破产　　　D. 通货膨胀

2. Their establishment has been linked to the desire to enhance transparency and promote public awareness of <u>intertemporal</u> constraints.

　　A. 暂时的　　　B. 跨时的　　　C. 相互的　　　D. 内部的

3. It receives the net central government <u>receipts</u> from petroleum activities and transfers to the budget the amounts needed to finance the non – oil deficit.

　　A. 净利　　　B. 毛利　　　C. 收入　　　D. 收据

4. This reflects growing awareness of the importance to public spending efficiency of unifying expenditure policy and subjecting approval and execution of outlays to the same budgetary standards.

　　A. 外流　　　　B. 摊派　　　　C. 回报　　　　D. 支出

5. CEMAC countries, including those with oil funds, have expressed concerns about the remuneration of their deposits at BEAC.

　　A. 报酬　　　　B. 冻结　　　　C. 回报　　　　D. 增加

Ⅳ. Put the following sentences into Chinese.

1. The operation of an oil fund may be assessed in terms of how well it helps (or hinders) the budget system in meeting its basic objectives.

2. Moreover, such an approach would also have to consider the potentially negative impact on the development of a national public financial management system.

3. Some countries have experienced difficulties in asset and liability management associated with rigid oil fund rules and fragmentation of cash management.

4. In early 2006, the government abolished the oil fund to ease liquidity constraints on its operating budget.

5. Alberta discontinued the extrabudgetary operations undertaken by its original oil savings fund in light of their disappointing performance.

Ⅴ. Put the following paragraphs into Chinese.

1. The sheer volumes of assets—even the smallest SWF (Sovereign Wealth Fund 主权财富基金), the Timor – Leste Petroleum Fund is above $ 1 billion and the speed with which they have grown—the East Timorese fund was set up just three years ago—means the agencies established to manage the funds have to look for external help.

2. Transparency and accountability practices for oil funds differ substantially across OPCs. The oversight of oil funds takes several different forms, in particular regarding provisions for compliance by governments and national oil companies with stated deposit and withdrawal rules, audit of the accounts of the fund, whether investment decisions are taken in compliance with an agreed investment framework, and standards for the disclosure (披露) of information. The approach to disclosure of oil fund's assets and investments often mirrors

general attitudes to public sector Transparency.

6.3 Norwegian Oil Fund

Guidance to Reading

Norway's Government Pension Fund – Global (GPF) is one of the largest and fastest – growing SWFs in the world, has a number of exemplary features that could serve as a model for other SWFs, which in many ways are considered best practices by international standards. The Norwegian GPF could help design a set of successful voluntary principles for SWFs, which helps countries where SWFs are located to both strengthen their domestic policy frameworks and institutions and facilitate their macroeconomic and financial interests. Further on it will also help ease concerns in countries receiving SWF investments and promote an open global monetary and financial system.

Text

The Norwegian Oil Fund—recently renamed "the Government Pension Fund – Global"—is often **cited** as an **exemplary sovereign wealth fund** (SWF).

This **uniquely positions** the fund as a model for and potentially important **contributor** to the new set of **voluntary principles** being developed for SWFs.

SWFs have been receiving increased **scrutiny** due to their growing presence in global financial markets. Their **total assets** are currently estimated at about $ 3 **trillion**. Experts are expecting that their assets will increase rapidly to over $ 10 trillion in the next 5 – 10 years.

The growing importance and active investment strategies of SWFs are expected to affect the structure of international financial markets and **asset pricing**. On the one hand, their long horizons, lack of **leverage**, and absence of claims for **imminent withdrawal** of funds could help **stabilize** international financial markets by enhancing market **liquidity** and **dampening** asset price volatility.

On the other hand, their sheer size, rapid growth, and potential to **abruptly** change investment strategies, **coupled with**—in some cases—a lack of transparency and uncertainty surrounding the purpose of their investments, could **exacerbate** market uncertainty and thus increase volatility.

Voluntary Code of Conduct

In light of the concerns about SWFs, the **IMF** has been given a new mandate to facilitate the development of a set of voluntary principles for these funds. These principles would cover issues of public governance, transparency, and accountability. **To this end**, an **International Working Group of SWFs** (**IWG**) was formed at end – April 2008 and began work on the set of principles.

The new set of principles should help countries where SWFs are located to both strengthen their domestic policy frameworks and **institutions** and **facilitate** their macroeconomic and financial interests. The principles will also help **ease** concerns in countries receiving SWF investments and promote an open global monetary and financial system.

Lessons from Norway's Experience

Norway's Government Pension Fund – Global (**GPF**) has a number of exemplary features that could serve as a model for other SWFs. The GPF is one of the largest and fastest – growing SWFs in the world, with total assets amounting to ＄373 billion at end – 2007, or close to 100 percent of Norway's GDP. But size aside, the Norwegian GPF is mostly known for its features, which in many ways are considered best practices by international standards:

• The GPF's stated aim is to support government saving and promote an **intergenerational transfer** of resources. The fund facilitates the long – term management of the government's petroleum revenues. Given the expected population aging in Norway, it serves to pre – fund public pension expenditures.

• The GPF functions as a fiscal policy tool, which, **together with** the fiscal guideline, serves to limit government spending. The fund's capital **consists of** revenues from petroleum activities. The fund's **expenditure** is a transfer to the fiscal budget to finance the non – oil budget deficit. The fiscal guideline, introduced in 2001, **calls for** a limit on the non – oil structural central government deficit of around 4 percent of the assets of the GPF. Since 4 percent is the estimated long – run real rate of return, this rule amounts to saving the real capital of the fund and spending only its return (**akin** to an **endowment** fund).

• The fund is fully integrated into the budget. The net allocation to the fund forms part of an integrated budgetary process. This process makes transparent the actual surplus of the fiscal budget and the state's use of petroleum revenues.

● It pursues a highly transparent investment strategy. **The Ministry of Finance—the fund's owner—reports regularly on the governance framework**, the fund's goals, investment strategy and results, and **ethical** guidelines. The Central Bank—the fund's operational manager—**publishes quarterly** and **annual** reports on the management of the fund, including its performance and an annual listing of all investments. **Detailed** information on the fund's **voting in shareholders'** meetings is also published.

● Its assets are invested **exclusively** abroad. This strategy ensures risk **diversification** and good financial returns. Moreover, it helps to **shield** the non – oil economy **from** shocks in the oil sector, which can put pressure on **the exchange rate** (so – called "Dutch disease" effects). The GPF has small ownership shares in over 7,000 individual companies worldwide (the average ownership stake at end – 2007 was 0.6 percent, against a maximum allowed of 5 percent).

● Its high – return, moderate – risk investment strategy has been hitting the mark. Currently, the fund is adjusting its **portfolio** to its new strategic benchmark of 60 percent of assets in equities and 40 percent in **fixed income**. There are plans to move gradually into real estate, to improve the **risk – return tradeoff**. The investment strategy has produced a healthy 4.3 percent average annual **real return** during the past decade.

● Its asset management is governed by a set of ethical guidelines. These guidelines, established by the Ministry of Finance, are based on internationally accepted principles developed by the United Nations and **the Organization for Economic Cooperation and Development**(OECD). Two policy **instruments** are used to promote the fund's ethical **commitments**. First, the fund exercises ownership rights in companies in which it invests **with a view to** promoting good and responsible **conduct** and respecting human rights and the environment when this **is consistent with** the fund's financial interests. Second, the Ministry of Finance can decide to avoid fund investments in specific companies whose practices constitute an unacceptable risk that the fund could become **complicit** in **grossly** unethical activities.

A Role for Norway

The Norwegian GPF brings to the table several elements that could help design a set of successful voluntary principles for SWFs. The fund's role as a fiscal policy tool could guide other countries with **nonrenewable** resources in managing their policies in a **sustainable** way over the long run.

The GPF's highly transparent, yet competitive and successful asset management strategy—buying in markets whose **values** are falling to **rebalance** its portfolios—can serve as an example that open strategies not only produce financial results, but also enhance market liquidity and financial resource allocation and act as a stabilizing influence. Its experience with ethical guidelines provides further proof that commitment to the common good is not necessarily **antagonistic** to high returns.

Given their experience with managing the GPF, the Norwegian authorities have been openly supporting the IMF's work on SWFs and firmly **back** equal treatment of investors. They do not think that the investment activities of SWFs need to be more restricted than the activities of other investors, especially since, in contrast to hedge funds, SWFs have yet to be proven to be **disruptive** to markets. The Norwegians also **caution** that restricting investments of oil - related SWFs may reduce extraction, which could have a **destabilizing** effect on oil markets.

▯ **Words and Expressions**

cite	引证,引用
exemplary	典范的,可做模范的
uniquely	独特地;唯一地
position	安置;把……放在适当位置
contributor	出资人
scrutiny	详细审查
trillion	万亿
leverage	(AmE)资产与负载比率
imminent	即将来临的;迫近的
withdrawal	收回;取消;退股
stabilize	使稳固,使安定
liquidity	流动性
dampen	抑制
abruptly	突然地
exacerbate	使加剧;使恶化;激怒

institution	（社会或宗教等）公共机构
facilitate	促进;帮助;使容易
ease	减轻,缓和
intergenerational	代间的,代际的
transfer	转让;转移
expenditure	支出,花费;经费
akin	类似的;同类的;同族的
endowment	养老金,专项基金
ethical	伦理的;道德的
publish	发表;公布
quarterly	季度的
annual	年度的
detailed	详细的,精细的;复杂的,详尽的
voting	投票;表决
shareholder	股东;股票持有人
exclusively	唯一地;专有地
diversification	多样化;变化;分散投资
portfolio	投资组合
risk－return	风险收益;风险收益
tradeoff	权衡;折中;(公平)交易
instrument	工具;手段
commitment	承诺,保证;投入;使用
conduct	行为;实施
complicit	有同谋关系的,串通一气的
grossly	很;非常
nonrenewable	不可再生的;不可更新的
sustainble	可持续的,可忍受的
value	价格
rebalance	再平衡;调整
antagonistic	敌对的;对抗性的;反对的
back	支持
disruptive	破坏的;分裂性的;制造混乱的
caution	警告
destabilizing	不安定的,动摇的

Phrases and Expressions

coupled with	加上,外加;与……相结合
voluntary principles	自愿原则
total assets	总资产
asset pricing	资产定价
to this end	为了达到这个目的,为此
together with	和;连同
consist of	包含;由……组成
call for	要求;需要;提倡
shield. . . from	保护……免受
The Ministry of Finance	财政部
the exchange rate	汇率
fixed income	固定收益;固定收入
real return	真实回报,实际收益
with a view to	着眼于;考虑到;以……为目的
be consistent with	与……一致

Proper Names

SWF	主权财富基金
IMF	国际货币基金组织
IWG	主权财富基金国际工作小组
GPF	挪威政府全球养老基金
OECD	经济合作与发展组织

Language Focus

1. This uniquely positions the fund as a model for and potentially important contributor to the new set of voluntary principles being developed for SWFs.

（参考译文：它独特地将基金定位为新的一套自愿性原则的模式和潜在的重要出资方,专为主权财富基金而制定。)

本句基本结构为 position sth. as, a model for and potentially important contributor 为 as 的并列宾语,the new set of voluntary principles being developed for SWFs 为二者的定语。

2. On the one hand, their long horizons, lack of leverage, and absence of claims for imminent withdrawal of funds could help stabilize international financial markets by enhancing market liquidity and dampening asset price volatility.

（参考译文：一方面，他们的长期规划、无资产负债比率和对即将撤出的资金不索赔的情况，可以帮助稳定国际金融市场，提高市场的流动性和抑制资产价格的波动。）

本句的 their long horizons, lack of leverage, and absence of claims for imminent withdrawal of funds 为并列主语，后面的 enhancing... and dampening... 为 by 的并列介词宾语。

3. On the other hand, their sheer size, rapid growth, and potential to abruptly change investment strategies, coupled with—in some cases—a lack of transparency and uncertainty surrounding the purpose of their investments, could exacerbate market uncertainty and thus increase volatility.

（参考译文：另一方面，其庞大的规模、快速的增幅、投资策略突然改变的可能性，再加上在某些情况下，围绕着其投资的目的还存在缺乏透明度和不确定性的问题，都可能会加剧市场的不确定性，从而增加波动。）

本句中主语较长：their sheer size, rapid growth, and potential to abruptly change investment strategies；再者 coupled with... surrounding the purpose of their investments 为插入语，补充说明主语，其中分词短语 surrounding the purpose of their investments 为后置定语；谓语为 could exacerbate... and thus increase...。

4. The new set of principles should help countries where SWFs are located to both strengthen their domestic policy frameworks and institutions and facilitate their macroeconomic and financial interests.

（参考译文：这套新原则应有助于主权财富基金所在的国家来强化国内政策框架和机构，并促进他们的宏观经济利益和金融利益。）

本句基本结构为 help countries to both strengthen ... and facilitate...，从句 where SWFs are located 修饰限定 countries，strengthen 的宾语为 their domestic policy frameworks and institutions。

5. First, the fund exercises ownership rights in companies in which it invests with a view to promoting good and responsible conduct and respecting human rights and the environment when this is consistent with the fund's financial interests.

（参考译文：首先，当与基金的经济利益一致时，鉴于强化良好的、负责的行为，尊重人权和环境，该基金在投资的企业行使所有权。）

本句中定语从句 in which it invests 修饰限定 companies，with a view to promoting ... and respecting ... 这一复合介词短语作状语，when 引导条件状语从句。

Reinforced Learning

Ⅰ. Answer the following questions for a comprehension of the text.

1. Why have SWFs been receiving critical scrutiny?

2. Please briefly elaborate on that the growing importance and active investment strategies of SWFs are expected to affect the structure of international financial markets and asset pricing.

3. What does an International Working Group of SWFs largely work on?

4. How is Norway's Government Pension Fund – Global (GPF) adjusting its portfolio?

5. What could those countries with nonrenewable resources derive any significance from GPF?

Ⅱ. Multiple choice：choose the correct one from the alternative answers to give the exact meaning of the words.

1. It could help stabilize international financial markets by enhancing market liquidity and dampening asset price volatility.

    A. steady   B. enlarge   C. affect   D. corner

2. The countries where SWFs are located strengthen their domestic policy frameworks and institutions.

    A. traditions   B. foundations   C. organizations D. establishment

3. The principles will also help ease concerns in countries receiving SWF investments.

    A. manage   B. relieve   C. control   D. loosen

4. The Central Bank publishes quarterly and annual reports on the management of the fund.

    A. draws up   B. presents   C. reveals   D. issues

5. Detailed information on the fund's voting in shareholders' meetings is also published.

    A. owners'   B. investors'   C. shareowners' D. bondholders'

6. Its assets are invested underline{exclusively} abroad.

A. singularly   B. entirely   C. only   D. exceedingly

7. It helps to underline{shield} the non – oil economy from shocks in the oil sector.

A. protect. . . from   B. prevent. . . from

C. prohibit. . . from   D. part. . . from

8. The fund's role as a fiscal policy tool could guide other countries with nonrenewable resources in managing their policies in a underline{sustainable} way over the long run.

A. reasonable   B. continuous   C. persistent   D. unreasonable

9. SWFs have yet to be proven to be underline{disruptive} to markets.

A. constructive   B. disturbing   C. upsetting   D. destructive

10. The Norwegians also caution that restricting investments of oil – related SWFs may reduce extraction, which could have a underline{destabilizing} effect on oil markets.

A. destroying   B. unsteady   C. unhealthy   D. stimulating

Ⅲ. Multiple choice: read the four suggested translations and choose the best answer.

1. Norway's Government Pension Fund – Global is often cited as an exemplary sovereign wealth underline{fund (SWF)}.

A. 稳定型主权财富基金   B. 冲销型主权财富基金
C. 战略型主权财富基金   D. 主权财富基金

2. Their underline{total assets} are currently estimated at about $ 3 trillion.

A. 全部财富   B. 所有宝物
C. 总资产   D. 所有的有利条件

3. It can put pressure on underline{the exchange rate}.

A. 套汇   B. 汇率   C. 汇兑   D. 基准价

4. There are plans to move gradually into real estate, to improve the underline{risk – return tradeoff}.

A. 风险收益交易   B. 风险收益权衡
C. 风险收益率   D. 套利交易

5. Two policy instruments are used to promote the fund's ethical underline{commitments}.

A. 承诺   B. 委托   C. 投入   D. 奉献

IV. Put the following sentences into Chinese.

1. The growing importance and active investment strategies of SWFs are expected to affect the structure of international financial markets and asset pricing.

2. But size aside, the Norwegian GPF is mostly known for its features, which in many ways are considered best practices by international standards.

3. The GPF functions as a fiscal policy tool, which, together with the fiscal guideline, serves to limit government spending.

4. The fund's expenditure is a transfer to the fiscal budget to finance the non – oil budget deficit.

5. Its experience with ethical guidelines provides further proof that commitment to the common good is not necessarily antagonistic to high returns.

V. Put the following paragraphs into Chinese.

1. The Government Pension Fund was established in 2006 and consists of two parts: "The Government Pension Fund Global", which is a continuation of the Petroleum Fund, and "The Government Pension Fund Norway", which was previously known as the National Insurance Scheme Fund. Revenues in the Government Pension Fund Global consist of the Government's total income from petroleum activities, and the return on the Fund's investments. The Ministry of Finance is responsible for the management of the Fund. The operational management of the Government Pension Fund Global is delegated to（授权）Norges Bank. The operational management of the Government Pension Fund Norway is delegated to the National Insurance Scheme Fund. The management is carried out in accordance with regulations laid down by the Ministry of Finance.

2. Over the past few years, with the aggressive development of sovereign wealth funds in emerging economies, Western countries have attempted to intervene in such funds using both administrative and legislative means. They have erected many protectionist barriers obstructing investment in sovereign funds, creating great difficulties for investors, even rendering some investments impossible.

Chapter 7 Oil Transportation

7.1 Central Asian Oil Transportation

⊞ Guidance to Reading

The Russian geographical setting enables it to control the main hydrocarbon export markets of the central Asian countries. Russia makes a considerable investment in the oil and gas pipelines and exports them in marine terminals for an attractive economic performance. The Central Asian countries, which have been highly dependant on increased revenues that oil exports produced, promote energy cooperation with China, Iran and the others, control their energy resources and help to impact on the economic growth and sustainable development.

⊞ Text

The geographical setting of Russia enables it to control exit of **hydrocarbons** from the Central Asian countries to world markets. In addition, it has strong **commanding** positions (**compared to** those of the other Caspian countries) in **shipment** infrastructure, including a pipeline built to **bypass** Chechnya with a capacity of 5 million tons of oil per year, as well as the pipelines of the Caspian Pipeline Consortium and Atyrau – Samara. An **oil – transshipment point** in the city of Makhatchkala allows oil to be shipped both for export and to the domestic market using refineries in Volgograd, Samara and Saratov. In addition, Volgograd is where Europe's largest **inland navigation** company, YU-KOS's "**Volgotanker**", is based capable of shipping all oil produced during the **initial** development of the northern Caspian region.

For all the diversity of **projects** being **proposed**, only **the Caspian Pipeline Consortium (CPC)** has been **put in place thus far**. It has a 1,580 – kilometer pipeline with an initial **capacity** of 28 million tons per year. **What's more**, you need only to increase **pump** station capacities in order to reach its maximum **throughput** of 67 million tons per year (of this, 45 million tons for

Kazakhstani oil producers)—a project thought to be **implemented** in four phases. Work is **in progress** on the Atyrau pipeline to **link** Karachaganak and CPC—a project that will make it possible to increase oil supplies to 7 million tons in the **immediate** future and to 11 million tons **in the long run**. Furthermore, Russia is expanding cooperation with other projects **underway** in Kazakhstan, including the Atyrau – Samara pipeline project **aimed at** increasing the pipeline's capacity from 10 million tons to 15 million tons. In future, Kazakhstan will be able to export its crude (5 million tons) **via** the Baltic pipeline network that Russia new builds **heading for the Gulf of Finland**.

What the Chinese **leadership** sees as a top **priority** now is developing Xinjiang **deposits** and building a pipeline from Xinjiang to Shanghai. Faced with the **urgent** need to invest billions of dollars in the development of its domestic oil – and – gas infrastructure, China will hardly be able to **finance** the Northern Kazakhstan – China project in the **foreseeable** future. In addition, Beijing **is** currently **engaged in intensive negotiations** with Moscow over building oil – and – gas pipelines from Siberia to China. Currently, a project **involving** the construction of a pipeline from eastern Siberia to Beijing and further to the eastern coast is being agreed upon. Russia's YUKOS and **China's Sinopec** have signed an agreement over oil and petroleum products supplies to China: first by rail train (exports not exceeding 3 – 4 million tons per year) and in future via the Angarsk – China pipeline (20 million tons followed by 30 million tons in future). This pipeline will be shorter and, consequently, cheaper than the Kazakhstan one. This construction, once done **simultaneously** with two other Russian – Chinese projects (a gas pipeline from Kovyktinsky deposit and a power transmission line from Irkutsk), will reduce substantially construction costs, and the oil pipeline is thought to be **put into operation** as soon as 2005. Especially because YUKOS can use its own and outside funds to finance the designing and implementation of the project (in addition to YUKOS, LUKoil and Rosneft also **guaranteed** the supplies).

The Kazakhstan – Turkmenistan – Afghanistan – Pakistan pipeline project able to carry 50 million tons of oil per year and opening access to the Arabian Sea cannot be set **in motion** until the total **stabilization** of the situation in Afghanistan, which is hardly possible to expect in the near and, to all indications, in the not so distant future. The Afghanistan – Pakistan – oriented pipeline is important for the Central Asian nations **primarily** in political terms as it might **eliminate** a threat from the south. Besides, even if the situation in Afghanistan **normalizes** (or more precisely, if a central government is created **vested with** but limited powers outside Kabul, that is if the country **reverts** to a pre – Taliban political situation characterized by ethnic **decentralization** and **intestine strife** among the ruling **elites**) the success of the project would be still **doubtful**, because the start – up of the Caspian Pipeline Consortium has reduced the **demand** for **alternative** pipeline routes, **many a** factor pointing to Iran as a more **advantageous** route.

The Kazakhstan – Turkmenistan – Iran route has an attractive economic **performance**. Its capacity is 15 million tons to 25 million tons of oil per year, project costs are estimated at US $ 1.5 billion to US $ 2 billion and, in addition, it is the shortest route (1,650 – km long with a stretch of 200 kilometers **passing across** Kazakhstan) for Kazakhstan oil shipments to the terminals of the Persian Gulf. The project of oil supplies from Tengiz and Uzen across Turkmenistan and Iran is quite plausible and can be implemented in two or three phases. The first phase: after oil is delivered by **tankers** from Aktau to the Caspian ports of Iran it will be supplied to refineries in the north of Iran and further swapped in the Persian Gulf ports. The **aggregate** capacity of four Iranian refineries located in Teheran, Tebriz, Isfahan and Arak total are 810,000 barrels per day and are capable of **processing up to** 50 million tons per year. To put this project in place it would require a mere US $ 360 million investment in the infrastructure of Iran. Next, following the construction of the Uzen – Teheran pipeline oil can be **delivered** to the Iranian capital to be used by local refineries while Kazakhstan, **in turn**, will receive Iranian oil in the Persian Gulf on the same swap basis. The principal technical and organizational issues of this project involve technological **adjustment** of Iranian refineries for Kazakhstan's oil and **reverting** oil flows currently carried through Iranian pipelines from the Persian Gulf region to northern Kazakhstan's refineries.

Words and Expressions

transportation	运输;运输系统;运输工具
hydrocarbon	碳氢化合物
commanding	处于控制或支配地位的

shipment	装运,装船;运送,运输;发货
bypass	绕开,避开
inland	内地
navigation	航行;航海
initial	最初的
project	工程;计划
propose	建议;计划
capacity	能力;容量
pump	泵,抽水机
throughput	生产量,生产能力
implement	实施,执行;实现
link	连接
immediate	立即的;直接的;最接近的
underway	进行中的;起步的
via	取道,通过;经由
leadership	领导能力;领导阶层
priority	优先;优先权;优先次序;优先考虑的事
deposit	沉淀物,矿床
urgent	紧急的;急迫的
finance	提供资金,提供款项
foreseeable	可预知的;能预测的
intensive	加强的;集中的
negotiation	谈判;转让;顺利通过
involve	包含;牵涉;使陷于;潜心于
simultaneously	同时地
guarantee	保证;担保
stabilization	稳定;稳定化
primarily	首先;主要地,根本上
eliminate	消除;排除
normalize	使正常化;使规格化,使标准化
revert	回复;重提;返祖遗传;归还
decentralization	分散;非集权化;(人口、工业等的)疏散
intestine	内部的;国内的
strife	冲突;争吵;不和

elite	精英;精华;中坚分子
doubtful	可疑的;令人生疑的;疑心的;不能确定的
demand	需求;要求;需要
alternative	供选择的;选择性的;交替的
advantageous	有利的;有益的
performance	表现;绩效
tanker	油轮;运油飞机;油槽车
aggregate	集合的;合计的
process	加工;处理;对……起诉
deliver	传送
adjustment	调整,调节
revert	回复;恢复

Phrases and Expressions

compared to	与……相比较
put in place	到位;落实到位;正在实施
thus far	迄今;现在为止
what's more	而且,此外,加之,更多的是……
in progress	正在进行;在发展中
in the long run	从长期来看;从长远的角度说来
aim at	针对;瞄准;目的在于
head for	前往;出发;取向于,驶向
be engaged in	参与;从事于;忙于
put into operation	使生效;使运转,使开动
in addition to	除……之外
in motion	在开动中,在运转中
vest sb. / sth. with sth	授予某人/事物……
many a	许多
pass across	穿过
up to	多达
in turn	轮流,依次

Proper Names

oil – transshipment point	石油转运点

YUKOS	尤科斯(俄罗斯石油巨头)
Volgotanker	沃尔戈坦克(俄罗斯最大的航运公司)
CPC	里海管道财团
the Gulf of Finland	芬兰湾
China's Sinopec	中国石油化工集团公司

Language Focus

1. In addition, it has strong commanding positions (compared to those of the other Caspian countries) in shipment infrastructure, including a pipeline built to bypass Chechnya with a capacity of 5 million tons of oil per year, as well as the pipelines of the Caspian Pipeline Consortium and Atyrau – Samara.

(参考译文:另外,它在输油基础设施方面强有力的主导地位(与其他里海国家比较),包括绕过车臣修造的年输油量5百万吨的管道,以及里海管道财团的管道和阿特劳—萨马拉管道。)

本句中分词短语 built to bypass Chechnya 和介宾短语 with a capacity of 5 million tons of oil per year 都为后置定语,修饰 a pipeline;a pipeline... as well as the pipelines of... 为 including 的宾语。

2. The Kazakhstan – Turkmenistan – Afghanistan – Pakistan pipeline project able to carry 50 million tons of oil per year and opening access to the Arabian Sea cannot be set in motion until the total stabilization of the situation in Afghanistan, which is hardly possible to expect in the near and, to all indications, in the not so distant future.

(参考译文:每年能够输送石油5000万吨的哈萨克斯坦—土库曼斯坦—阿富汗—巴基斯坦管道项目和阿拉伯海的通道直到阿富汗的局势完全稳定才能启动,这种情况在稳定的近期以及不远的将来难以预测。)

本句中的名词性短语 The Kazakhstan – Turkmenistan – Afghanistan – Pakistan pipeline project 和 opening access to the Arabian Sea,为 and 连接的并列主语;able to carry 50 million tons of oil per year 这个形容词性的复合短语为后置定语;not... until 引导时间状语从句中,which 指代的是前面的句子,to all indications 为插入语。

3. ... if a central government is created vested with but limited powers outside Kabul, that is if the country reverts to a pre – Taliban political situation characterized by ethnic decentralization and intestine strife among the ruling elites.

(参考译文:或者更准确地说,如果授予成立的中央政府除喀布尔以外的既得却有限权力,也就是说,如果这个国家恢复到了前塔利班的政治局势,执政党精英们间的种族分散和内部冲突突出。)

本句中的分词短语 vested with but limited powers outside Kabul 和 characterized by... 都是后置定语,分别修饰 a central government 和 a pre – Taliban political situation。

4. ... many a factor pointing to Iran as a more advantageous route.

(参考译文:许多指向伊朗的因素都被视为更有利的路线。)

本句是省略句,完整的句子应为:(Any a pipeline route that has) many a factor pointing to Iran (could be) as a more advantageous route.

5. The principal technical and organizational issues of this project involve technological adjustment of Iranian refineries for Kazakhstan's oil and reverting oil flows currently carried through Iranian pipelines from the Persian Gulf region to northern Kazakhstan's refineries.

(参考译文:这个项目主要技术和组织方面的问题涉及为获取哈萨克斯坦石油伊朗炼油厂的技术调整;还涉及恢复从波斯湾地区北部经过伊朗抵达哈萨克斯坦炼油厂的石油管道运输。)

本句中谓语为 involve; Kazakhstan's oil 和 reverting oil flows 均为介词 for 的宾语,分词短语 currently carried through Iranian pipelines from... to... 为 reverting oil flows 的后置定语。

Reinforced Learning

Ⅰ. **Answer the following questions for a comprehension of the text.**

1. Why is Volgograd regarded as YUKOS's "Volgotanker"?

2. Why has only the Caspian Pipeline Consortium (CPC) been put in place thus far?

3. What does the agreement cover, between Russian and Chinese Sinopec over oil and petroleum products supplies to China?

4. In what respect, the Afghanistan – Pakistan – oriented pipeline is important for the Central Asian nations and why?

5. What is a pre – Taliban political situation characterized by?

Ⅱ. **Multiple choice: choose the correct one from the alternative answers to give the exact meaning of the words.**

1. It has strong commanding positions (compared to those of the other Cas-

pian countries) in shipment infrastructure.

    A. corresponding   B. leading

    C. advantageous   D. commercial

2. For all the diversity of projects being proposed, only the Caspian Pipeline Consortium (CPC) has been put in place thus far.

    A. differences   B. details   C. benefits   D. items

3. A project is thought to be implemented in four phases.

    A. organized   B. approved   C. carried out   D. financed

4. Russia is expanding cooperation with other projects underway.

    A. on the way   B. in the ground C. underground   D. in progress

5. Beijing is currently engaged in intensive negotiations with Moscow over building oil – and – gas pipelines from Siberia to China.

    A. cooperation   B. consultations   C. swaps   D. bargains

6. LUKoil and Rosneft also guaranteed the supplies.

    A. ensured   B. promoted   C. protected   D. guarded

7. The start – up of the Caspian Pipeline Consortium has reduced the demand for alternative pipeline routes.

    A. negative   B. relative   C. attractive   D. selective

8. The aggregate capacity of four Iranian refineries located in Teheran, Tebriz, Isfahan and Arak total are 810,000 barrels per day.

    A. productive   B. total   C. generating   D. carrying

9. To put this project in place it would require a mere US $ 360 million investment in the infrastructure of Iran.

    A. implement   B. draw up   C. build   D. start up

10. The principal technical and organizational issues of this project involve technological adjustment of Iranian refineries.

    A. analysis   B. communication

    C. correction   D. support

Ⅲ. Multiple choice: read the four suggested translations and choose the best answer.

1. You need only to increase pump station capacities in order to reach its maximum throughput of 67 million tons per year.

    A. 容量   B. 全部   C. 生产量   D. 吞吐率

2. China will hardly be able to <u>finance</u> the Northern Kazakhstan—China project in the foreseeable future.

    A. 批准   B. 承办   C. 提供资金   D. 实施

3. The Kazakhstan – Turkmenistan – Iran route has an attractive economic <u>performance</u>.

    A. 表现   B. 前景   C. 机遇   D. 环境

4. After oil is delivered by <u>tankers</u> from Aktau to the Caspian ports of Iran it will be supplied to refineries in the north of Iran and further swapped in the Persian Gulf ports.

    A. 输油线   B. 集装箱   C. 坦克   D. 油轮

5. Following the construction of the Uzen – Teheran pipeline oil can be <u>delivered</u> to the Iranian capital to be used by local refineries

    A. 探测   B. 提炼   C. 供应   D. 传送

IV. Put the following sentences into Chinese.

1. In addition, Volgograd is where Europe's largest inland navigation company, YUKOS's "Volgotanker", is based capable of shipping all oil produced during the initial development of the northern Caspian region.

2. In future, Kazakhstan will be able to export its crude (5 million tons) via the Baltic pipeline network that Russia new builds heading for the Gulf of Finland.

3. Currently, a project involving the construction of a pipeline from eastern Siberia to Beijing and further to the eastern coast is being agreed upon.

4. After oil is delivered by tankers from Aktau to the Caspian ports of Iran it will be supplied to refineries in the north of Iran and further swapped in the Persian Gulf ports.

5. Following the construction of the Uzen – Teheran pipeline oil can be delivered to the Iranian capital to be used by local refineries.

V. Put the following paragraphs into Chinese.

1. The Northern Kazakhstan—China route provides access (进入) for Caspian oil to Chinese and Asia – Pacific markets. It should be pointed out, though, that medium – term outlooks are not agreeable for China to start up the Northern Kazakhstan—China pipeline project. The project will not be plausible (似有理的) unless there are fairly high oil prices. Nor the recoupment (赔偿)

of the 3,000 – kilometer pipe with huge capital invested (at least US $ 3 billion) can be possible unless the pipeline carries an estimated 40 million tons per year. All Kazakhstan, for the moment, can invest in the project is but one – third of what is required. The volumes projected can be achieved only after Kazakhstan has substantially increased oil production in its western and central regions. The missing amount can be compensated by Caspian shelf deposits the development of which, once they are found to contain sufficiently large oil reserves, is still a matter of the very distant future.

2. Faced with the urgent need to invest billions of dollars in the development of its domestic oil – and – gas infrastructure, China will hardly be able to finance the Northern Kazakhstan – China project in the foreseeable future.

7.2   Pipelines in the Caspian Sea

Guidance to Reading

With the sharply increased geo – economic status, the oil and oil management in the Caspian Sea has been involved with many countries and regions in and out of the Caspian Sea. The pipelines that created huge monetary gains not only have a great and growing influence on nations bordering the Caspian Sea and the world economic situation, but also promote the energy and resource cooperation between Caspian Sea nations and the relevant countries and region in the world. The issues of pipelines intertwine inevitably with political as well as cultural and ethnic conflicts.

Text

In order for the oil to be transported to markets, pipelines have to be constructed. The cost of a single pipeline is estimated to be US $ 1.2 to US $ 3.3 billion according to the route chosen, and it is **probable** that more than one will be constructed in order to ensure that the flow of oil cannot be easily **restricted** by political pressures or **sabotage**. The countries across which the pipelines run will benefit both from the **transit fees** for the oil, and from increased political influence as a result of being able to control its movement.

The shortest and cheapest pipeline route is from Baku in Azerbaijan through Georgia to the Georgian port of Supsa on the Black Sea, and the Baku – Supsa pipeline was completed early in 1999 to carry Caspian oil. Georgia itself is not free of **conflict**, being still in dispute with the **breakaway** territory of Abkhazia in the north and having political problems which have led to **attempted assassinations** of Georgian president Eduard Shevardnadze. Russia has some **leverage** over Georgia because it has **troops** based in Georgia who act as **peacekeeper**s between Abkhazia and Georgia. The increased strategic importance of Georgia is also **indicated** by the US seeking to strengthen **bilateral** ties with it, for example, by giving it a grant of US $ 500 000 in 1996 to facilitate participation in NATO's partnership for Peace (PFP) defence cooperation programme.

The route strongly favoured for a further pipeline is from Baku to the Turkish **terminal** on the Mediterranean at Ceyhan. This is supported by Azerbaijan, the US, and Turkey, and would meet a Turkish and environmental **objective** of **reducing** the amount of oil to be shipped through the Bosphorous and its narrow straits. However, the US government cannot force **commercial** firms to follow a particular line of action that they consider to be **uneconomic**. While Richard Morningstar, President Clinton's special adviser on Caspian basin energy diplomacy, has said that the pipeline to Ceyhan is **viable**, as the president of Conoco oil pointed out **in response** at the March 3 hearing of the U. S. Senate Foreign Relations **Subcommittee** on International Economic Policy, there is a big difference between viable and attractive. After Turkey gave an **assurance** that the pipeline will be built for US $ 2. 4 billion, not US $ 3. 7 billion as previously cited, Azerbaijani President Haydar Aliyev expressed hopes that the pipeline would be **commenced** in 1999. Construction of the pipeline is now **due to** start in 2001 with completion being achieved in 2007 or 2008. However, certain issues such as finance and security are still under discussion. The 1999 earthquake in Turkey caused **concerns** over the potential risk to the pipeline from future **tremors**.

The **AIOC** and commercial firms involved would have **preferred** a route from Baku through Iran to Ceyhan because of the easier **terrain**. Such a possibility is **out of the question** because of the D'Amato legislation, which **outlaws** involvement by US and other companies with Iran **on the grounds that** Iran has been involved in state terrorism. This legislation was **consistent** with the interests of US oil companies when it meant keeping Iran out of the exploitation consortium. The pipeline to Ceyhan is expected to go through the area of northern Turkey where there is conflict between Turkish government forces and Kurdish **separatists**. It has been suggested that the leader of the rebel **Kurdish Workers' Party** (**PKK**), Abullah Ocalan, was **allowed** to be **captured** by the Turks in order to keep the Baku – Ceyhan pipeline prospect more **secure** by allowing Turkey to **put down** the PKK.

Although the US gave its approval for the **construction** of a pipeline running from Turkmenistan to Turkey through Iran which opened in December 1997, it was argued by US Secretary of State Madeleine Albright that this move was only to help Turkmenistan to **overcome** its financial difficulties. Turkmenistan has agreed to **conduct** a US – funded **feasibility** study on the construction of a possible oil and gas pipeline under the Caspian Sea to Azerbaijan. The US strongly favours such a pipeline route as it would allow Turkmen gas and oil exports to be independent of both Russia and Iran. The US ban has not stopped European companies becoming involved with Iran. For example, British explorer Monument Oil and Gas Plc has a **swap** arrangement with Iran **with respect to** Turkmen crude oil, whereby it sends its Caspian crude production to Iran's Neka **in exchange** for an equivalent **volume** of oil from the Gulf.

Although the Baku – Ceyhan pipeline was regarded as a "done deal" by US energy secretary Bill Richardson already **back** in November 1998, questions remain. It was estimated that the pipeline would have to carry at least one million barrels of oil a day to be viable, while the AIOC's production will **peak** at a **maximum** of 800, 000 barrels a day in about eight years' time, and the consortium is unsure there will be enough oil from other sources to make up the difference. Also, if the "Blue Stream" gas pipeline which Russian **Gasprom** and Italian **ENI** are planning to build under the Black Sea to Samsun, Turkey, and then Ankara, is completed first, this could result in the Baku – Ceyhan pipeline becoming uneconomic. The major merit of the Ceyhan pipeline from the point of view of the governments of the US, Turkey and Azerbaijan is that it would prevent both Russia and Iran from being able to affect or benefit from the exploitation of Azerbaijani oil. Shell and Enron had been in the running to lead the pipeline consortium, but while Shell has greater financial resources, Washington was able to provide Enron with more political backing than the Netherlands and the UK could provide for Shell.

While **neighboring** Armenia could be used as a pipeline route from Azerbaijan to Turkey, this has not so far been considered an acceptable prospect by Azerbaijan because of continued **hostility** to Armenia over its **occupation** of the **ethnic** Armenian enclave of Nagorno – Karabakh in Azerbaijan. The conflict arose as a result of religious and ethnic conflict between the Christian Armenian population in Nagorno – Karabakh and the Muslim Azeri one of the surrounding territory of Azerbaijan, and provides an example of the 'clash of **civilizations**' **ruling out** at least some economic options.

Words and Expressions

pipeline	管道;输油管
probable	很可能的
restrict	限制;约束;限定
sabotage	破坏;破坏活动
conflict	冲突,矛盾;斗争;争执
breakaway	分离
attempted	企图的,未遂的
assassination	暗杀,行刺
leverage	手段,影响力
troop	军队
peacekeeper	维和部队;(交战国之间的)停火执行者
indicate	表明;指出;预示;象征
bilateral	双边的;有两边的
terminal	末端;终点
objective	目的;目标
reduce	减少;降低
commercial	商业的;营利的;靠广告收入的
uneconomic	不经济的;浪费的
viable	可行的
subcommittee	小组委员会;委员会的附属委员会
assurance	保证;保险;确信;断言
commence	开始;着手
concern	关注;关心;关心的事
tremor	震颤;颤动
prefer	更喜欢;宁愿;提出;提升

terrain	地形,地势;领域;地带
outlaw	宣布……为非法
consistent	始终如一的;一致的;坚持的
separatist	分离主义者;独立派
allow	允许,容许,许可
capture	俘获,捕获
prospect	前途;预期;前景
secure	安全的;无虑的
construction	建设;建筑物
overcome	克服;胜过
conduct	管理;引导;表现
feasibility	可行性;可能性
swap	交换;交易
volume	量;大量
back	过去的,以前的
peak	使达到最高点
maximum	最大限度;最大量
neighboring	邻近的;附近的
hostility	敌意,战争行动
occupation	占有
ethnic	种族的;人种的
civilization	文明

Phrases and Expressions

transit fees	交通费,过境费
in response	作为回答
due to	预定;约定;预期
out of the question	不可能
on the grounds that	由于,因为
put down	镇压;记下;贬低;制止
with respect to	关于;至于
in exchange	作为交换
rule out	排除;取消

Proper Names

AIOC	阿塞拜疆国际营运公司
PKK	库尔德工人党
Gasprom	俄罗斯天然气公司
ENI	埃尼集团

Language Focus

1. ... and it is probable that more than one will be constructed in order to ensure that the flow of oil cannot be easily restricted by political pressures or sabotage.

（参考译文：为了不轻易受政治压力或破坏活动的影响，里海国家会建造多个石油管道以确保石油的流量。）

本句中 it 为形式主语，that 引导的是主语从句；在这个主语从句中包含又一个 that 引导的宾语从句。

2. Georgia itself is not free of conflict, being still in dispute with the breakaway territory of Abkhazia in the north and having political problems which have led to attempted assassinations of Georgian president Eduard She-vardnadze.

（参考译文：格鲁吉亚本身也是冲突不断，与北部分裂的阿布哈兹起争端以及政治上的问题导致格鲁吉亚总统谢瓦尔德纳泽险遭暗杀。）

本句中 and 连接并列的现在分词短语 being... 和 having... 为伴随状语，前者的 with 引导介宾短语为后置定语，修饰 dispute，后者的 which 引导的限定性定语从句，修饰 political problems。

3. The increased strategic importance of Georgia is also indicated by the US seeking to strengthen bilateral ties with it, for example, by giving it a grant of US ＄500,000 in 1996 to facilitate participation in NATO's partnership for Peace (PFP) defence cooperation programme.

（参考译文：美国谋求加强双边关系，表明格鲁吉亚猛增的战略重要性。例如，为推进参与北约和平伙伴关系防御合作计划的发展，美国于 1996 年援助格鲁吉亚 50 万美元。）

本句中的分词短语 seeking to... 为后置定语，修饰 the US；而随后的 NATO's partnership for Peace (PFP) 为 defence cooperation programme 的定语。

4. While Richard Morningstar, President Clinton's special adviser on Caspian basin energy diplomacy, has said that the pipeline to Ceyhan is viable, as the president of Conoco oil pointed out in response at the March 3 hearing of the U. S. Senate Foreign Relations Subcommittee on International Economic Policy, there is a big difference between viable and attractive.

（参考译文:克林顿总统里海盆地能源外交的特别顾问理查德·莫宁斯塔说,通往杰伊汉的管道是可行的,康菲石油总裁在3月3日美国参议院外交关系委员会国际经济政策听证会响应中指出,可行和可观是有很大差别的。）

Richard Morningstar 与 President Clinton's... 是同位语;as 引导的时间状语从句中,the U. S. Senate Foreign Relations Subcommittee on International Economic Policy 为 hearing of 的宾语,hearing of... 分词短语表时间关系,there is... 为 pointed out 的宾语从句。

5. The major merit of the Ceyhan pipeline from the point of view of the governments of the US, Turkey and Azerbaijan is that it would prevent both Russia and Iran from being able to affect or benefit from the exploitation of Azerbaijani oil.

（参考译文:从美国、土耳其和阿塞拜疆政府的角度看,杰伊汉管道的主要好处是它会阻止俄罗斯与伊朗能够影响阿塞拜疆石油开发或者阻止它们从阿塞拜疆石油开发中获益。）

本复合句的主干是:The major merit of the Ceyhan pipeline is that...;介宾短语 of the US, Turkey and Azerbaijan 为定语,修饰 the governments;that 引导的宾语从句中,基本结构为 prevent... from doing sth。

🔲 Reinforced Learning

Ⅰ. Answer the following questions for a comprehension of the text.

1. How much is a single pipeline in the Caspian Sea?

2. Why is Georgia under the influence of Russia?

3. Why was the leader of Kurdish Workers' Party (PKK), Abullah Ocalan captured?

4. Why did the US strongly favour the pipeline running from Turkmenistan to Turkey through Iran?

5. What were the causes of the conflict between Azerbaijan and Armenia?

II. Multiple choice: choose the correct one from the alternative answers to give the exact meaning of the words.

1. It is <u>probable</u> that more than one will be constructed in order to ensure that the flow of oil cannot be easily restricted by political pressures or sabotage.

    A. usable   B. advisable   C. likely   D. acceptable

2. Georgia itself is not free of <u>conflict</u>.

    A. disturbance B. trouble   C. difference D. diversity

3. The US government cannot force commercial firms to follow a particular line of action that they consider to be <u>uneconomic</u>.

    A. non – economical   B. ineffective

    C. inefficient   D. wasteful

4. Azerbaijani President Haydar Aliyev expressed hopes that the pipeline would be <u>commenced</u> in 1999.

    A. projected   B. built   C. completed D. begun

5. Construction of the pipeline is now <u>due to</u> start in 2001 with completion being achieved in 2007 or 2008.

    A. crucial to   B. arranged to   C. suitable to D. scheduled to

6. The 1999 earthquake in Turkey caused <u>concerns</u> over the potential risk to the pipeline from future tremors.

    A. harassment B. inconvenience C. attention   D. panic

7. Abullah Ocalan, was <u>allowed</u> to be captured by the Turks in order to keep the Baku – Ceyhan pipeline prospect more secure.

    A. prohibited B. permitted   C. alleged   D. accepted

8. This move was only to help Turkmenistan to <u>overcome</u> its financial difficulties.

    A. increase   B. solve   C. adjust   D. create

9. It sends its Caspian crude production to Iran's Neka in exchange for an equivalent <u>volume</u> of oil from the Gulf.

    A. amount   B. region   C. production D. profit

10. The AIOC's production will <u>peak</u> at a maximum of 800 000 barrels a day in about eight years' time.

    A. reach the highest point   B. reach the lowest point

    C. reach the middle point   D. not the above

Ⅲ. Multiple choice: read the four suggested translations and choose the best answer.

1. The countries across which the pipelines run will benefit both from the transit fees for the oil, and from increased political influence as a result of being able to control its movement.

    A. 转让费   B. 保管费   C. 过境费   D. 周转费

2. The AIOC and commercial firms involved would have preferred a route from Baku through Iran to Ceyhan because of the easier terrain.

    A. 广告的   B. 共同的   C. 开始的   D. 商业的

3. The US gave its approval for the construction of a pipeline running from Turkmenistan to Turkey through Iran.

    A. 经营   B. 运输   C. 建设   D. 建造物

4. Shell and Enron had been in the running to lead the pipeline consortium.

    A. 在奔跑   B. 参加比赛

    C. 在运转   D. 有实现的希望/机会

5. British explorer Monument Oil and Gas Plc has a swap arrangement with Iran with respect to Turkmen crude oil.

    A. 营销   B. 互惠   C. 交易   D. 妥协

Ⅳ. Put the following sentences into Chinese.

1. Russia has some leverage over Georgia because it has troops based in Georgia who act as peacekeepers between Abkhazia and Georgia.

2. The AIOC and commercial firms involved would have preferred a route from Baku through Iran to Ceyhan because of the easier terrain.

3. Such a possibility is out of the question because of the D'Amato legislation, which outlaws involvement by US and other companies with Iran on the grounds that Iran has been involved in state terrorism.

4. Turkmenistan has agreed to conduct a US – funded feasibility study on the construction of a possible oil and gas pipeline under the Caspian Sea to Azerbaijan.

5. Although the Baku – Ceyhan pipeline was regarded as a 'done deal' by US energy secretary Bill Richardson already back in November 1998, questions remain.

V. Put the following paragraphs into Chinese.

1. On the purely economic side, the longer the pipeline route, the less attractive it is to producers, other things being equal, inasmuch as（因为；鉴于）energy competes on a delivered – cost（交付成本）basis and transit fees（based upon distance）effectively lower the wellhead（井口）price received by producers. Because transit fees are a source of revenue to governments, politics as well as economics come into play in pipeline route selection. Built – in precautions to minimize environmental impacts, particularly in and around the Caspian Sea, also add to pipeline costs.

2. Aside from the purely economic and political motives of the West, there was also a sense of urgency held by western companies to intervene in the Caspian oil boom, especially once the full extent of the quantity of oil that could be extracted from the area was realized. Many of the world's oil reserves were steadily drying up. Therefore, the western world knew that in order to continue development and industry at its current rate, the tapping（开发，利用）of the Caspian oil reserves would be essential.

7.3　American Oil Pipeline Transportation

Guidance to Reading

Long distance, large diameter pipelines appeared as the new transportation way to deliver huge amounts of oil from producing regions to consuming regions for German disrupted American oil flow during World War II. Pipelines not only met the demand for oil, but stimulated the post – War economic boom, and changed the shape of the petroleum industry. Pipelines have been the irreplaceable core of the U. S. petroleum transportation system among PADDs.

Text

The **outbreak** of World War Ⅱ **engendered** a **watershed** event in petroleum transportation. Reflecting historical **demographic** and economic factors, the East Coast was the largest **consuming** region in the U. S. , but it **relied on** tanker shipments to supply its regional refineries and to move refined petroleum products from **the U. S. Gulf Coast**. With the involvement of the U. S. in the War, German **submarines** began sinking tankers along the Gulf and Atlantic

Coasts and in the **Caribbean**, thus **disrupting** the flow of oil. A joint industry – government effort found **alternative** transportation **in the form of** a technological breakthrough: long distance, large **diameter** pipelines. The new capability to transport large quantities of oil over long distances subsequently fueled the post – War economic boom, and changed the shape of the petroleum industry.

Pipelines are the **irreplaceable** core of the U. S. petroleum transportation system and hence the key to meeting petroleum demand. Without oil pipelines, petroleum products would not reach the millions of consumers in all fifty states.

Oil pipelines transport roughly two – thirds of the petroleum shipped in the United States. They **deliver** over 14 billion barrels (more than 600 billion gallons) of petroleum per year. Because many volumes are shipped more than once (as crude oil and then again as refined product, for instance), these **annual** pipeline shipments **are equal to** more than twice the actual U. S. **consumption** of oil.

Furthermore, oil pipeline shipments **account for** more than 17% of the **freight** moved nationally, but less than 2% of the national freight cost. The United States has the largest network of oil pipelines of any nation. All of Europe, for instance, has a pipeline network that is only 1/10 the size of the U. S. network.

The Oil Market Dictates Pipeline Flow from Region to Region

The oil market's infrastructure moves oil from the producing regions to the consuming regions, globally and regionally. These inter – regional oil flows in the U. S as follows:

• The Gulf Coast (**PADD** 3) is the largest supply area of the U. S., accounting for 55% of the nation's crude oil production and 47% of its refined product output. It is the largest oil supplier in **interregional trade**, accounting for 90% of the crude oil shipments and 80% of the refined petroleum production shipments among PADDs. Most of the crude oil goes to refineries in the Midwest, while most refined products go to the East Coast and, **to a lesser extent**, to the Midwest.

• The East Coast (PADD 1) has **virtually** no **indigenous** crude oil production, limited refining, and the highest regional, non – feedstock demand for refined products. Its refineries process **predominately** foreign crude oil. To meet regional demand, their output is **augmented** by refined product shipments from the Gulf Coast **as well as** imports from abroad. The East Coast receives more than 60% of the refined products shipped among regions and almost all of the refined product imported into the U. S.

• The Midwest (PADD 2) has significant regional crude oil production, but also processes crude oil from outside of the region: Canadian crude oil imported directly via pipeline, crude oil imported from other nations and then shipped to the Midwest via the Gulf Coast, and crude oil produced in the Gulf Coast region. These supplies from outside of the region – imports and domestic – account for 88% of its refinery input. Refined product output from regional refineries is also **supplement**ed with supplies from outside the region, primarily shipments from the Gulf Coast.

• **The Rocky Mountain Region** (PADD 4) has the lowest petroleum consumption, but has shown relatively rapid regional growth in recent years. It imports crude oil from Canada to augment local production for its refineries. Its distances are long, its **topography steep** and its infrastructure thin, however. Therefore, the inter – regional trade, while small in nationwide standards, is an important factor in keeping the region's supply and demand in balance.

• The West Coast (PADD 5) is **logistically** separate from the rest of the country. Its crude oil supply is dominated by production from **the Alaskan North Slope oil fields**, which now accounts for 55% of PADD 5 production, down from 65% when those fields were in peak production in the late 1980s. Essentially all of the rest of the region's production comes from California. Because of unique product quality requirements in California, the largest consuming state, essentially all of that state's refined product demand is met by output from the state's refineries.

Pipelines are the critical mode for moving oil between regions. In 2000, for instance, pipelines moved virtually all of the crude oil and about 70% of the products transported between PADDs. Pipelines from the Gulf Coast carry both domestic and imported crude oil to the Midwest, and refined product to the Midwest, the East Coast and, in much smaller volume, to the Rocky Mountain region. Pipelines also carry the Canadian crude oil supplies vital to the Midwest and the Rocky Mountain refineries. Supplying approximately 1 million barrels per day to these regions, Canada is the third largest foreign crude oil supplier to the U. S. , and accounts for about 25% and 30% respectively of the two regions' crude oil.

Pipelines are also irreplaceable in moving oil within the PADDs, from producing fields and coastal ports to refineries (crude oil and other refinery feedstocks) and from refineries and large redistribution centers to smaller regional supply centers, to airports, and even directly to large consumers (refined petroleum products). In reality, the oil market is constantly changing.

In the decades since large diameter, long distance pipelines have been available, they have developed into a key part of the thousands of movements and schedules and transactions that make up the oil market in the United States. Their ability to move large volumes long distances fueled the post – War economic boom, and shaped U. S. **demography** and development. In addition to moving the large volumes from producing regions to consuming regions, pipelines fill a critical role in moving smaller quantities of oil from market hubs to more distant consuming areas. Pipeline operations over the years have accommodated a greater number of unique products, carrying products that meet regional and seasonal environmental quality mandates. They are the only practical mode of transportation for most overland movements, and the cheapest. It is not surprising, therefore, that pipelines are by far the most important mode of transportation for oil in the United States.

🔲 Words and Expressions

outbreak	爆发,突然发生
engender	使产生;造成
watershed	分水岭;转折点
demographic	人口统计学的;人口学的
consuming	消费的;强烈的
submarine	潜水艇
disrupt	破坏;使瓦解;使分裂;使中断;使陷于混乱
alternative	供选择的;选择性的;交替的
diameter	直径
irreplaceable	不能替代的,不能调换的
deliver	交付;递送
annual	年度的;每年的
consumption	消费;消耗

freight	货运;运费
virtually	事实上,几乎;实质上
indigenous	本土的;国产的;固有的
predominately	占优势地;有影响力地;占绝大多数地
augment	增加;增大
supplement	补充,增补
topography	地势;地形学;地志
steep	陡峭的,急剧升降的
logistically	逻辑地
demography	人口统计学

Phrases and Expressions

rely on	依靠,依赖
in the form of	以……的形式
be equal to	相等,相当于;胜任;合适
account for	(数量上)占
to an extent	在一定程度上;到达……程度
as well as	也;和

Proper Names

the U. S. Gulf Coast	美国墨西哥湾沿岸
Caribbean	加勒比海
PADD	美国石油分区
interregional trade	区际贸易
The Rocky Mountain Region	落基山脉地区
the Alaskan North Slope oil fields	阿拉斯加北坡油田

Language Focus

1. Reflecting historical demographic and economic factors, the East Coast was the largest consuming region in the U. S. , but it relied on tanker shipments to supply its regional refineries and to move refined petroleum products from the U. S. Gulf Coast.

(参考译文:考虑历史、人口和经济因素,东海岸是美国最大的消费区域,但它依赖于油轮运输石油供应地方炼油厂,并从墨西哥湾沿岸运送成品油。)

本句是 but 连接的并列句,Reflecting... 是现在分词作原因状语,to supply... and to move... 是并列的不定式结构,为补语。

2. The new capability to transport large quantities of oil over long distances subsequently fueled the post – War economic boom, and changed the shape of the petroleum industry.

（参考译文:远距离运输大量石油的新能力促使美国战后经济繁荣,并且改变了石油工业态势。）

本句是简单句,主语是 The new capability,to transport... 是不定式作定语修饰主语,over long distances subsequently 是介词短语修饰主语,而谓语则由 fueled 和 changed 两个并列的动词充当。

3. In the decades since large diameter, long distance pipelines have been available, they have developed into a key part of the thousands of movements and schedules and transactions that make up the oil market in the United States.

（参考译文:自从大口径、长距离管道出现后,几十年来它们也已成为美国石油市场中无数运输、计划、交易的关键部分。）

本句是复合句,since... 引导句子修饰 In the decades,主句的主谓是 they have developed...,that 引导定语从句,修饰 movements and schedules and transactions。

⊞ Reinforced Learning

I. Answer the following questions for a comprehension of the text.

1. Why did the East Coast region rely on tanker shipments to supply its regional refineries and to move refined petroleum products in the U. S. ?

2. What conditions did oil pipelines transport in the United States?

3. In which part of the U. S. has the lowest petroleum consumption, but has shown relatively rapid regional growth in recent years?

4. What is critical for moving oil between regions?

5. What role did large diameter, long distance pipelines play in the U. S. ?

II. Multiple choice: choose the correct one from the alternative answers to give the exact meaning of the words.

1. To take an unnecessary action that will probably engender adverse effects.

    A. tender   B. create   C. cultivate   D. invent

2. Car companies have relied on cheap financing rates to maintain sales.

A. agree on   B. drew on   C. put on   D. depended on

3. They <u>deliver</u> over 14 billion barrels（more than 600 billion gallons）of petroleum per year.

A. transport   B. rescue   C. present   D. render

4. Direct criticism of leaders is still <u>virtually</u> taboo in China.

A. transparently B. actually   C. effectively   D. apparently

5. The best ways to <u>augment</u> brain function might not involve drugs or cell implants but lifestyle changes.

A. enhance   B. assist   C. motivate   D. incent

6. About 20 percent of airline revenues comes from air <u>freight</u>.

A. cargo   B. charge   C. expense   D. express

7. Since the <u>outbreak</u> of the financial crisis , our two countries have had good consultation and coordination.

A. burst   B. explosion   C. irruption   D. penetration

8. I wish all of departments have <u>irreplaceable</u> positions in our company.

A. placeable   B. unsubstitutable C. recognisable   D. misappropriated

9. The resources of some oil funds are <u>earmarked</u> for specific purposes.

A. donated   B. raised   C. designated   D. identifiable

10. The Furthermore , oil pipeline shipments <u>account</u> for more than 17% of the freight moved nationally , but less than 2% of the national freight cost.

A. up to   B. call for   C. allow for   D. take up

Ⅲ. Multiple choice：read the four suggested translations and choose the best answer.

1. The outbreak of World War Ⅱ engendered a <u>watershed event</u> in petroleum transportation.

A. 分水岭   B. 转折点   C. 分界点   D. 划时代

2. Furthermore , oil pipeline shipments account for more than 17% of the freight moved nationally , but less than 2% of the national <u>freight cost</u>.

A. 运费清单   B. 转租费用   C. 货运成本   D. 装货成本

3. Pipelines are the critical mode for moving oil between regions. In 2000 , for instance , pipelines moved virtually all of the crude oil and about 70% of the products transported between <u>PADDs</u>.

A. 美国石油分区   B. 美国石油体制

C. 美国石油分布   D. 美国石油状态

4. The Midwest（PADD 2）has significant regional crude oil production, but also <u>processes</u> crude oil from outside of the region.

    A. 作用   B. 加工   C. 过程   D. 处理

5 Pipeline operations over the years have <u>accommodated</u> a greater number of unique products, carrying products that meet regional and seasonal environmental quality mandates.

    A. 供应   B. 容纳   C. 调节   D. 适应

IV. Put the following sentences into Chinese.

1. Pipelines are the irreplaceable core of the U. S. petroleum transportation system and hence the key to meeting petroleum demand.

2. The oil market's infrastructure moves oil from the producing regions to the consuming regions, globally and regionally.

3. The East Coast（PADD 1）has virtually no indigenous crude oil production, limited refining, and the highest regional, non-feedstock demand for refined products.

4. Because of unique product quality requirements in California, the largest consuming state, essentially all of that state's refined product demand is met by output from the state's refineries.

5. It is not surprising, therefore, that pipelines are by far the most important mode of transportation for oil in the United States.

V. Put the following paragraphs into Chinese.

1. Logistics hubs（物流枢纽）allow the market to work, and pipelines allow hubs to work. By 2015, if all the rail expansion comes on time, China should solve the logistic bottleneck, at least in theory.

2. To understand the importance of pipeline transport, one must understand the role of logistics hubs. Logistics hubs serve as gateways（门户, 通道）for regional supply. They are characterized by interconnections（相互连接；彼此连络）among many pipelines and, often, other modes of transportation - such as tankers and barges, sometimes rail, and usually trucks, especially for local transport - that allow supply to move from system-to-system across counties, states, and regions in a hub-to-hub progression. These hubs are also characterized by their substantial storage capacity. The availability of storage and transportation options at these hubs enhances supply opportunities and increases supply flexibility, both essential ingredients for an efficient market.

Chinese Translation and Key to Exercises

第1章　石油与经济

1.1　自然资源财富和较差的经济发展

🔲 导语

"资源诅咒"文献侧重于这样一种趋势:自然资源丰富的国家却遭遇低经济增长和令人失望的发展结果。"荷兰病"理论,进一步强调需要把经济和政治的解释结合到资源出口分析中。尽管有共同的"荷兰病"经历,许多评论家认为,这种疾病对发达经济体的影响远远超过它对欠发达经济体的影响,影响效果因国家不同差异很大。

🔲 课文

"资源诅咒"文献最古老的分支侧重于这样一种趋势:自然资源丰富的国家却遭遇低经济增长和令人失望的发展结果。拉美经济学家汉斯·辛格和劳尔·普雷维什为最先提出这一问题的两位学者。他们认为,主要商品出口国长期以来贸易条件恶化。他们声称,世界市场上出口商品的价格相对于制成品的价格下降了,使商品出口国出现了支付和经济增长放缓之间的平衡问题。他们的论据得到了复杂的证明,一些研究说明贸易条件恶化,其他一些研究显示出贸易条件稳定。例如,卡丁顿和伟进行了统计分析,进而驳斥普雷维什—辛格假说。另一方面,萨普斯福德和巴拉苏布拉马尼安却发现了支持普雷维什—辛格假说的证据。然而,20世纪80年代以来,全球主要商品的贸易条件恶化了,更多共识产生了:至少在这段时间内,贸易条件恶化使许多国家出现了问题。尽管贸易条件恶化尚未影响到赤道几内亚的石油工业,然而,几内亚经济以石油生产为主体,以至于未来贸易条件恶化将对赤道几内亚经济造成毁灭性的影响。

经济学家认为,自然资源财富可能对经济有其他负面影响。有些人怀疑,商品市场的快速波动可能使依赖商品的经济体容易出现繁荣萧条周期,阻碍私人投资。在动荡的市场,如石油市场,可能是特别棘手的问题。然而,我们不得不等待石油价格下一次波动,看它是否会以任何有意义的方式影响赤道几内亚;但种种迹象表明,由于赤道几内亚 90% 的出口都来自石油,石油价格大幅度降低将摧毁该国的经济。自 1971 年以来,石油市场的极不稳定性表明,石油价格未来的波动是可能的,而且它们可能对未来的赤道几内亚很危险,除非该国的领导人可以采取有效的政策来抵御这些影响。

引起学术上关注的是以能源为主导发展的另一方面,它提出了蓬勃发展的部门和经济的其他部门之间最低限度的联系。到目前为止,这个问题一直极度困扰着赤道几内亚。由于石油工业所需的大多数投入来自国外,本土企业并没有从经济繁荣中获益,甚至服务行业主要依赖进口。从本质上讲,赤道几内亚的石油行业仍然是飞地,对经济的其他部门没什么影响。如果飞地经济正常地将资源租金投资在经济的其他部门以及基础设施和人力发展方面,它们可以创造其他部门的增长,改善卫生和教育服务的质量。从理论上说,相对于人均资源少的出口国家,赤道几内亚较高的人均石油收入应使这两项的选择更容易些。然而,像大多数石油生产国一样,赤道几内亚没在这方面采取行动,导致出现国家的基本经济问题:石油部门和非油部门之间缺乏联系。

最知名的和最好的研究"资源诅咒"文献的变异,"荷兰病"理论,进一步强调需要把经济和政治的解释并入资源出口分析中。20 世纪六七十年代石油发现影响了荷兰经济,"荷兰病"因而得名。新发现的石油带来出口热潮,但国内经济很快出现通货膨胀和制造业出口下降,导致低经济增长和失业率上升。20 世纪七八十年代的石油繁荣在尼日利亚、沙特阿拉伯和墨西哥等不同的国家都产生了类似的结果。当出口激增导致通货膨胀和随之而来的实际汇率上升,这看似矛盾的现象发生了。这使得国内油气田生产者不同于其他商品部门的生产者,竞争力较弱,利润较少。其他经济部门的衰落是"荷兰病"的症结所在。

科尔德和尼瑞的理论分析中找到了足够的论据支持"荷兰病"假说。其他研究从实证上证实了"荷兰病"对经济成果的影响。萨赫斯和沃纳历经十九年对 97 个国家综合统计研究表明,1971 年自然资源出口占国内生产总值比重高的国家,在 1971 年和 1989 年间出现了异常缓慢的增长。他们主要是通过"荷兰病"效应解释这种现象。案例研究也为"荷兰病"提供了充足的支持。例如,盖尔布记载了 6 例"荷兰病"的案例:阿尔及利亚、厄瓜多尔、印度尼西亚、尼日利亚、特立尼达和多巴哥、委内瑞拉。其中一个案例研究表明,20 世纪 80 年代的尼日利亚正是"荷兰病"的一个极端案例。1973—1974 年和 1979—1980 年的油价飙升为政府带来了石油暴利,但这笔意外之财和随之而来的支出增加刺激了通货膨胀和汇率上调,以及非矿业部门降幅90%。赤道几内亚的几内亚湾邻国加蓬,也遭受了"荷兰病"。尽管加蓬发展了繁荣的石油工业,其他经济部门,特别是农业已经崩溃,而不平等和贫困仍然存在。经济增长停滞,快速地耗尽该国的石油储备,让许多人担心不久后经济几乎全面崩溃,除非发现新的储量。

尽管有共同的"荷兰病"经历,许多评论家认为,这种疾病对发达经济体的影响远远超过它对欠发达经济体的影响,影响效果因国家不同差异很大。例如,本杰明等人指出,在喀麦隆,"荷兰病"影响了农业而不是制造业。罗斯进一步指出,周详的政策可以抵消大部分"荷兰病"效应。用特里·卡尔的话来说,"'荷兰病'不是自发的,影响的范围主要是决策在公共领域的结果。"此外,乔杜里也指出,各石油生产国的不同性质的部门战略和工业战略都是为了"掩盖'荷兰病'假定的相同结果"。伊拉克、马来西亚、伊朗和阿尔及利亚等一些国家,"通过启动产业化项目抵制对贸易投资的压力"。

Key to Exercises

Ⅰ.

1. The oldest branch of the resource curse literature emphasizes the tendency of natural resource abundant countries to suffer from low economic growth and disappointing development outcomes.

2. Future declines in the terms of trade would prove devastating to the Equato – Guinean economy.

3. Dutch Disease theory further highlights the need to integrate economic and political explanations into the analysis of resource exporters.

4. Sachs and Warner examination show that states with a high ratio of natural resource exports to GDP in 1971 had unusually slow growth rates between 1971 and 1989. They explain this phenomenon largely through a Dutch Disease effect.

5. Many critics have argued that this ailment affects developed economies far more than it affects under – developed ones.

Ⅱ. 1 ~ 5. BDDDA   6 ~ 10. CACBD

Ⅲ. 1 ~ 5. CDBAD

Ⅳ.

1. 他们认为,主要商品出口国长期以来贸易条件恶化。

2. 新发现的石油带来出口热潮,但国内经济很快出现通货膨胀和制造业出口下降,导致低经济增长和失业率上升。

3. 有些人怀疑,商品市场的快速波动可能使依赖商品的经济体容易出现繁荣萧条周期,阻碍私人投资。

4. 由于石油工业所需的大多数投入来自国外,本土企业并没有从经济繁荣中获益,甚至服务行业主要依赖进口。

5. 尽管有共同的"荷兰病"经历,许多评论家认为,这种疾病对发达经济体的影响远远超过它对欠发达经济体的影响,影响效果因国家不同差异很大。

V.

1. "荷兰病"是说明自然资源开发利用的增长与制造业跌幅之间明显关系的经济学概念。该机制说明自然资源收入(或流入的外国援助)的增加将使一个国家的货币与其他国家相比更加坚挺(表现在汇率方面),导致该国家其他出口对购买国而言越来越贵,进而使制造业竞争力较差。它通常是指自然资源的发现,也指"外汇大量流入导致的任何发展,包括自然资源价格、外国援助和外国直接投资等的急剧增长"。

2. 很难明确地说一个国家有"荷兰病",因为很难证明自然资源收入增加、实际汇率和下降滞后部门之间的关系。有许多事情可能会导致实际汇率升值。

1.2 非洲高油价和经济发展

🔲 导语

对于非洲中等石油净进口国家来说,由于石油价格翻倍导致累计五年生产损失了23%。然而,最近几年,非洲作为一个整体,一直得益于宏观经济管理。本课详细分析了非洲不同国家和地区所面临的机遇和挑战。

🔲 课文

高油价对非洲石油进口国的经济有着十分不利的影响,尤其是对那些有着沉重债务负担的石油进口国。高油价导致生产和消费减少,恶化国外净资产状况。对于中等石油进口国来说,在固定汇率制度中按照可应用模式计算,由于石油价格翻倍,致使累计五年的生产损失达23%。然而,通过政府干预,如采取生产率、货币政策和世界利率等各种冲击政策可以缓解经济衰退。

最近几年,非洲作为一个整体,一直得益于宏观经济管理,非洲国家政局稳定、政府执政水平有所提高,地区冲突有所缓解,加强了区域经济板块的合作,农业、矿产和石油产量增加。在金融危机之前,非洲许多国家的经济保持快速稳定地增长。在 1995 年至 2007 年期间,非洲地区的经济发展扭转了自 1975 年至 1985 年以来的崩溃局面,也彻底改变了从 1985 年至 1995 年的停滞状态。三十年来非洲经济首次与世界其他地区的经济以同样的速度增长。以下将阐述非洲主要国家和地区面临的挑战。

非洲的石油净进口国家

石油和天然气的高价格对非洲石油净进口国产生极大的影响。高物价是许多非洲国家发生骚乱和示威活动的原因(例如,莫桑比克,2008 年 2 月 5 日)。公众抗议的主要原因是柴油和汽油零售价的提高导致公共交通的成本上升了 50%。燃料零售价格上升导致生活成本普遍增加。预计依靠煤油照明和烹饪的贫困家庭的情形将更加糟糕。

由于极其缺乏建立稳定机制和价格平滑机制的资源,控制高油价是石油净进口国面临的主要挑战之一。大多数国家都选择了部分或完全通过国际油价来调节高油价,而非洲一些石油净出口国家则出台补贴政策。非洲国家在应对高油价问题上,所有这些机制已经证明效果不佳。

非洲石油财富的管理

在非洲的一些石油净出口国,石油和天然气开采已引发了重大的经济、社会、政治和环境问题。在大多数石油净出口国,石油财富并没有促进经济可持续发展。将石油财富转化为经济持续增长是石油净出口国面临的主要挑战。

富油国所面临的特殊挑战包括管理薄弱、问责制缺失、缺乏适当的预算和会计能力、石油和天然气石油净出口国缺乏透明度。这些问题导致投资的高度不确定性,而且在某些情况下,可能会激化社会矛盾。采掘业透明度行动计划(EITI)为解决透明度问题提供了机会。

公平分配石油收益是缓解富油国社会紧张局势的关键。例如,在尼日利亚,联邦政府把 13% 的石油收益分配给九个产油省,主要是为了减少冲突和促进地区发展。虽然这不可能完全满足尼日尔三角洲地区当地利益相关者的利益,却是朝着正确方向迈出的一步。

尼日利亚的石油财富管理:尼日尔三角洲地区面临的挑战

控制石油财富的斗争可以追溯到 20 世纪 60 年代。所有权是典型的产权问题:谁拥有尼日尔三角洲地区的石油资源?通过立法,特别是 1978 年最闻名的土地使用法,尼日利亚联邦政府获得了全国土地的所有权,包括土地上发现的矿物、矿石、石油和天然气资源。此法令引起了地方政府对石油的争夺,尼日尔三角洲的危机有三个相互关联的层面:经济(资源控制)、环境(石油开采对环境的负面影响)、社会(健康和人权问题)。

近年来,几个因素致使在控制资源方面的冲突激化:地方剥夺感增加,生态环境日益破坏,物质和社会基础设施的缺乏,贫穷的深化和对地方的忽视。解决这些问题的方法包括:地方参与制定该地区规划,赋权给地方,以及重建民众、石油公司和政府之间的信任。在实践中,还要采取几项举措:在政府和石油公司内部,努力或者继续努力启用原住民担任石油和天然气行业营运、管理的行政职位;签订与原住民维护和维修的合约;把油井设施分配给地方;让地方参与该地区项目的设计和实施;通过提供财政资源发展地方企业和培养员工技能;使他们积极参与该地区正在计划的各种项目。

此外,通过为特定项目创立分散信托基金来促进资产利用,也是尼日尔三角洲解决问题的关键,包括物质基础设施基金、社会基础设施和培训信托、环境修复信托和中小企业资金。这些信托基金由合作式管理机构负责,由联邦和地方代表共同管理。此方案将加强政府和地方的伙伴关系,激发不同基金之间的竞争,尤其为青年们创造就业机会。

利比亚面临挑战的反应

利比亚作为主要石油生产国,其石油基金提供了大量预算外支出资金。利比亚政府正准备推进财政改革方案。最近为金融机构设置公司治理标准的立法,推进了金融机构更好地管理及公共银行的操作更加独立。除此之外,面对公共部门就业和生产率下降,鼓励有资格的公务员转换企业家的活动,但迄今为止并没有产生预期的效果。

Key to Exercises

I.

1. For the median oil – importing country, the five – year cumulative output loss resulting from a doubling in the price of oil can be as large as 23 percent under a fixed exchange rate regime, as per the model applied.

2. Before the financial crisis, many African economies were moving towards fast and steady economic growth. Their performance over 1995—2007 reversed the collapses over 1975—1985 and the stagnations over 1985—1995. And, for the first time in three decades, African economies were growing at the same rate as the rest of the world economies.

3. Particular challenges faced by oil – rich countries include weak governance, low accountability, low capacity for proper budgeting and accounting,

and lack of transparency in the oil and gas industry.

4. In Nigeria, for example, the federal government passes 13 percent of oil revenues to the nine oil – producing states, primarily to reduce conflict and promote local development.

5. Ghana, Libyan and the Niger Delta.

Ⅱ. 1~5. CCADD   6~10. BBCCA

Ⅲ. 1~5. BDBCB

Ⅳ.

1. 高油价对非洲石油进口国的经济有着十分不利的影响,尤其是对那些有着沉重债务负担的石油进口国。

2. 最近几年,非洲作为一个整体,一直得益于宏观经济管理,非洲国家政局稳定、政府执政水平有所提高,地区冲突有所缓解,加强了区域经济板块的合作,农业、矿产和石油产量增加。

3. 在非洲的一些石油净出口国,石油和天然气开采已引发了重大的经济、社会、政治和环境问题。

4. 在尼日利亚,联邦政府把13%的石油收益分配给九个产油省,主要是为了减少冲突和促进地区发展。

5. 此外,通过为特定项目创立分散信托基金来促进资产利用,也是尼日尔三角洲解决问题的关键。

Ⅴ.

1. 2005年和2006年,撒哈拉以南非洲国家经济的平均增长率为5.4%。然而,由于面临包括高油价在内的冲击,对于非洲国家来说,一直保持经济持续高速增长是长期面临的挑战。应对高油价需要一整套措施,以最大限度地发挥其积极影响并减轻其负面影响。高油价对石油净进口国的负面影响则更加剧烈,但其负面影响可以通过政府措施或外援来缓解。

2. 在一个完全解除管制的市场里,产品上涨的价格完全转嫁给消费者。在国内价格及国际价格的定价模式中都试图模仿解除管制的市场模式。鉴于世界产品价格的波动,在政府希望采取措施控制价格的国家里,借鉴超过一个月的实际价格的均线可能是合理的。

1.3　亚太市场潜力

🔲 导语

在亚太地区,中国、韩国和日本是最主要的石油消费国。本课简要介绍了三国各自的石油来源和炼油能力,指出建立应急响应机制的重要性,以确保经济的发展。最后,提到在石油资源利用方面这三个国家与加拿大艾伯塔省的合作前景。

课文

亚太地区最大的原油市场是日本、韩国和中国。目前,这些国家都高度依赖中东进口的石油,其中主要是来自沙特阿拉伯的石油,来满足其能源需求。尽管能源需求日益增长并依赖外国进口能源,但由于缺乏成熟的应急响应体系如石油储备,这一地区更易受到供应缩减的冲击。其他影响亚洲石油进口的因素包括:领土纠纷、政治动荡、中东失业率上升、油轮运输原油的需求量增加及全球石油价格波动。加拿大政治稳定,因此,其有竞争力的油价越来越吸引渴望获得长期可靠能源供应的亚洲国家。

日本

2002 年,日本每日进口 400 万桶石油,其中 86.8% 来自中东,其余来自非洲(3.8%)、亚洲的其他国家主要是中国(7.5%),或其他来源,如俄罗斯(1.9%)。尽管日本把主要精力放在如天然气、煤炭、核能的可替代能源上,但原油进口量自 1995 年达到最高点后仅仅略微下降。中东仍然是其石油主要的供应地。例如,2004 年 2 月,中东提供的能源占日本原油进口的 92.6%。

日本有 33 家炼油厂,日消耗 470 万桶原油。由于越来越多地使用天然气和煤炭供电,日本炼油厂并没有得到充分利用(2002 年利用率为 81.4%),预计燃油需求将以每年约 1.4% 的幅度下降,到 2007 年,炼油厂的利用率预计会进一步下降。如果引进高浓度乙醇汽油的举措成功的话,燃油需求会进一步减少。

日本原油进口大致可分为中度或轻度含硫原油。然而,接近 95% 的日本蒸馏产能已配备脱硫机组,以达到日益严格的燃油含硫量规格。到 2004 年年底,汽油的硫含量必须从 100ppm 下降到 50ppm,到 2008 年,炼油厂必须生产无硫汽油(10ppm 以下)。到 2004 年年底,柴油的硫含量从当时值 500ppm 降低到 50ppm,2007 年后,炼油厂必须生产无硫柴油,到 2005 年,日本炼油厂将为指定地区自愿供应无硫汽油和柴油。

日本获得日本加拿大含油砂有限责任公司 Hangingstone SAGD 项目 75% 的所有权,由此可知,日本表示与艾伯塔省(加拿大的一个省)建立长期合作关系的兴趣。由于日本处理含硫原油的炼油能力和广泛脱硫能力过剩,加拿大的"Dilbit"或"Synbit"混合原料很容易满足日本的进口要求。然而,日本石油需求每年下降,这主要是因为日本政府努力减少对石油能源的依赖。虽然汽油需求有望增长,但燃油和柴油需求下降是石油需求减少的首要原因。因此,具有环烷基性质的艾伯塔的沥青对于日本炼油厂来说是不太理想的原料。

韩国

2002 年,韩国每日进口 210 万桶原油。其中 74.5% 的石油来自中东,其他两个最大的供应来源是印度尼西亚(5.5%)和刚果(2.7%),其余的供应来源包括加拿大(0.1%)。韩国共有 6 个炼油厂,日消耗量为 250 万桶。这些炼油厂的利用率几乎为 100%;而剩余产品用于出口。

假设工业和运输行业发展强劲,除了煤油,所有炼油产品预计都将增加,因此,韩国的石油需求预计将保持稳定。韩国燃料含硫规格没有日本那么严格,到 2006 年,汽油的硫含量由当时值 130ppm 下降到 50ppm,柴油的硫含量从 430ppm 下降到 30ppm。现今韩国仍与加拿大保持进口关系,预计柴油和锅炉给水的需求将增长,艾伯塔省沥青对于韩国炼油厂是一个很好的选择。

中国

与日本、韩国不同,中国拥有强大的国内石油行业,占主导地位的两大主要公司:中国石油天然气集团公司(中国石油),控制约三分之二的国内原油生产;中国石油化工集团公司(中国石化),控制国内一半以上的炼油。中国石油天然气股份有限公司的主要优势是其在中国石油——这家上市公司的保护之下,近海勘探和生产被授权给中国海洋石油总公司(中国海油),而该公司只占国内生产的 10%。

1993 年之前,中国是一个原油净出口国。此后,中国快速的经济增长带动对国外石油的依赖,石油进口每年增长约 5%。2004 年,石油进口预计将占中国石油总需求的 41%,这种趋势预计将持续到 2020 年,从 2000 年到 2020 年石油需求不断增加,可达 570 万桶/日。

与大多数其他亚太国家相比,中国不易受到中东石油出口波动的冲击。2002 年,中国进口原油总计 140 万桶/日,其中只有 49.5% 来自中东。然而,到 2003 年年底,进口量平均增长到 190 万桶/日,56% 来自中东。其他出口原油到中国的主要国家是安哥拉、苏丹、越南、印度尼西亚、马来西亚和俄罗斯。然而,为确保供应的多样性,中国从远至北海进口石油。中国也实施应急响应机制,建立六个储存点,其中大多数储存点设在主要的炼油或运输中心附近。到 2005 年,可存储 350 万桶原油,以满足 30 天的进口需求,而 2010 年,存储量可满足 50 天的进口需求。

由于国内生产原油,中国的原油进口少于日本和韩国。但是,如果经济像预计那样继续增长的话,中国将最终超过日、韩,成为亚太地区的主要石油进口国。鉴于市场不断扩大,对于艾伯塔省生产商来说,中国是一个有吸引力的出口市场。然而,中国重质原油炼油能力不足和脱硫装置的缺乏使得中国很难接受"Dilbit"或"Synbit"混合原料。另一方面,艾伯塔炼油厂不能提取合成原油产品,鉴于合成原油产品高柴油产量和低含硫量,因此,它将成为中国炼油厂的理想原料。

Key to Exercises

I.

1. The lack of a fully – developed emergency response system, such as an oil stockpile, territorial disputes, political turmoil, and increasing unemployment in the Middle East, as well as increasing demand for tankers to transport crude oil and global volatility of oil prices.

2. In 2002, Japan imported a total of 4.0 million b/d of crude oil, of which 86.8% of that was from the Middle East. The remaining imports were from Africa (3.8%), other Asian sources, primarily China (7.5%), and other sources such as Russia (1.9%).

3. 81.4% utilization ratio.

4. The existing import relationship with Canada, and the projected increase in demand for diesel and boiler feed, should make Alberta bitumen an attractive option for Korean refineries.

5. China has a strong domestic petroleum industry, dominated by three major companies: China National Petroleum Corporation (CNPC), National Petrochemical Corporation (SINOPEC), and China National Offshore Oil Corporation (CNOOC).

II. 1~5. DBCBB   6~10. ADBBD

III. 1~5. BCBBB

IV.

1. 亚太地区最大的原油市场是日本、韩国和中国。目前,这些国家都高度依赖中东进口的石油,其中主要是来自沙特阿拉伯的石油,来满足其能源需求。

2. 加拿大政治稳定,因此,其有竞争力的油价越来越吸引渴望获得长期可靠能源供应的亚洲国家。

3. 到 2005 年,日本炼油厂将为指定地区自愿供应无硫汽油和柴油。

4. 假设工业和运输行业发展强劲,除了煤油,所有炼油产品预计都将增加,因此,韩国的石油需求预计保持稳定。

5. 此后,中国快速的经济增长带动对国外石油的依赖,石油进口每年增长约 5%。

V.

1. 中国陆地上和海上的天然气产量迅速增长。由于其煤炭储量大,中国最近才开始利用新管道充分开采天然气储量,并在西部内陆及海上开采天然气盆地。

2. 从 1995 年到 2005 年之间,中国的石油消费量翻了一番,而同一时期世界石油需求增长了 20%。自 2003 年以来,中国的石油耗费已经超过日本,并在 1993 年成为石油净进口国。

1.4 墨西哥湾石油天然气工业对美国经济的影响

📖 导语

墨西哥湾不仅为美国经济发展提供了能源保障,而且海湾近海石油天然气工业推动了美国经济发展,拉动了国内生产总值,提供了就业机会并产生了各级政府的税收。墨西哥湾近海石油天然气工业活动使许多行业获益并蓬勃发展。

📖 课文

概要

对美国而言,近海油气工业无论对能源供应,还是对国内生产总值的贡献和创造的就业机会,都是具有重要意义的。2010 年,美国有 30% 以上的石油生产和 11% 的天然气生产在墨西哥海湾(GOM)。近海的油气生产对美国能源安全至关重要。此外,资本投资与油气工业的中间投入刺激了整个价值链,波及许多经济部门,创造了就业机会,促进了国内生产总值的增长,并且产生了各级政府的税收收入。油气产业活动,支持制造业和服务业的各种行业就业,包括石油和天然气机械、航空和海洋运输、法律和保险服务等。

对国家的影响

2008 年,墨西哥海湾近海工业的整体支出超过 285 亿元,创造了超过 308 亿元的国内生产总值。这一影响遍及全国,提供就业岗位超过 30.5 万个。约 9 万个工作岗位是与石油、天然气工业直接相关的(指直接为油气公司工作,或直接为油气工业的承包商工作),然而,有 22 万个却是间接相关的(指为石油公司提供商品和服务的工作,如元件制造、法律和金融服务等)和延伸的工作(指直接的和间接的就业收支所产生的经济领域内的工作岗位,如服务员、零售业工人、汽车制造商、服务供应商等)。

2009 年,产业资本的投资和运营开支某种程度上受到经济衰退的影响,降至 271 亿美元,相关的国内生产总值刚刚超过 293 亿美元。这种经济活动提供了约 28.5 万个工作岗位,其中,8 万个工作岗位直接与油气工业相关,20.5 万个是间接的和延伸的工作岗位。2010 年,资本投资和运营开支下降到较低的利率水平——242 亿美元。这主要是因为墨西哥湾的深水钻井暂停、后续缺乏深水钻井许可和由于减少浅水钻井的许可而相应地减缓了浅水钻井。尽管 2010 年有经济复苏的迹象,资本投资和运营开支的减少还是导致国内生产总值下降至 261 亿美元。致使与墨西哥湾近海油气工业相关的总就业水平下降到大约 24 万个工作岗位,其中 6 万个直接就业岗位,18 万个是间接的和延伸的工作岗位。2010 年较 2008 年就业水平整体下降了 21%,国内生产总值下降 15%。

对沿岸各州和地区的影响

墨西哥湾沿岸主要的四个州分别为得克萨斯、路易斯安那、密西西比和阿拉巴马(包括这些州的联邦水域),为油气生产区域,并取得了墨西哥湾近海油气工业的大部分支出。墨西哥湾油气工业的业务活动需要资本设备和中间投入的购买,而这几个州正处于业务活动绝大部分主要支出的位置。

整个墨西哥湾沿岸,工程与管理、设备制造、海上活动的支援、平台和上部的制造等活动相当普遍。由于主要投资和支出集中,墨西哥湾近海的油气工业对这些州的经济健康发展起着重要的作用。2010 年,这四个州的资本投资和运营支出总额为 175 亿美元,其中,阿拉巴马州为 27 亿美元,路易斯安那州为 73 亿美元,密西西比为 3 亿美元,得克萨斯州为 73 亿美元。2010 年与墨西哥湾近海油气活动相关这些州的国内生产总值刚好超过 191 亿美元,主要表现为:阿拉巴马州 26 亿美元,路易斯安那州 74 亿美元,密西西比州 2 亿美元,得克萨斯州 89 亿美元。

2010 年,由于墨西哥湾近海油气工业活动,墨西哥湾沿岸阿拉巴马、路易斯安那、密西西比和得克萨斯州各州,就业岗位达 17.5 万个,创造的直接就业岗位,约有 4.2 万个,间接的和延伸的就业岗位,约为 13.3 万个。由于墨西哥湾附近有许多油气工业的商品供应商和服务供应商,使得该地区的投资集中,为此沿岸这些州就业率最高。钻机员工和其他连续两个星期海上作业的员工为了交通便利,通常在邻近其陆上基地居住。

暂停期间,美国路易斯安那州中部大陆石油天然气协会声称,每一个闲置的钻井平台有 800～1400 个工作岗位存在风险。据该协会统计,每个平台每月这些工作可能造成超过 5 百万美元到 1 千万美元的工资损失,高峰期时多达 33 个钻机闲置。

2010 年,Quest 估计墨西哥湾近海油气工业活动,除沿岸各州外,能支持其他 36 个州的 6.5 万人就业。2010 年,由于墨西哥湾近海油气工业活动,基于这些州的总支出 67 亿美元,估计所创造的国内生产总值为 70 亿美元。主要提供制成品、零部件和服务行业的非墨西哥湾的各州,支出水平有望从 2010 年上升至 2013 年的 61%,达到 108 亿美元。这一支出的增长,预计使国内生产总值增长 61%,达 113 亿美元,就业人数增加 67%,提供就业岗位 10.5 万个。

对其他行业的影响

当许多领域受到墨西哥湾近海油气工业的经济影响时,某些行业所受的影响更大。由于墨西哥湾近海油气工业的投资和经营,其他行业最大的受益者是房地产及租赁行业。由于墨西哥湾近海油气工业的支持,该行业活动收益近 35 亿美元,提供超过 18500 个就业机会。

2010 年,获得大力支持的产业包括制造业,所创造的国内生产总值约 20 亿美元,并提供超过 2.3 万个就业机会,并且专业、科技服务业的国内生产总值达 12 亿美元,支持约 1.4 万人就业。墨西哥湾近海油气工业也支持房地产和建筑行业的就业。

2010 年,由于墨西哥湾近海油气工业活动所提供的间接和延伸工作岗位总计 180 万个,油气工业活动对其他部门产生的巨大影响,在整个经济领域内占较大份额。

Key to Exercises

I.

1. Because there was over 30 percent of the oil and 11 percent of the natural gas produced in the United States produced in the Gulf of Mexico (GOM) in 2010.

2. This was primarily due to the moratorium on drilling in the deepwater GOM and the subsequent lack of deepwater drilling permits issued and the associated slow down in drilling in the shallow water due to the decrease in permits issued.

3. The primary four states are Texas, Louisiana, Mississippi, and Alabama.

4. These states see the highest employment levels due to the concentration of spending in the region as many goods and services providers to the industry are located near to the Gulf coast.

5. The largest other industry beneficiary, due to the investment and operations of the offshore Gulf of Mexico oil and natural gas industry, was the real estate and rental and leasing industry.

Ⅱ. 1 ~ 5. DDBAD   6 ~ 10. BCADA

Ⅲ. 1 ~ 5. BCABC

Ⅳ.

1. 2010 年,资本投资和运营开支下降到较低的利率水平——242 亿美元。

2. 尽管 2010 年有经济复苏的迹象,资本投资和运营开支的减少还是导致国内生产总值下降至 261 亿美元。

3. 整个墨西哥湾沿岸,工程与管理、设备制造、海上活动的支援、平台和上部的制造等活动相当普遍。

4. 这一支出的增长,预计使国内生产总值增长 61%,达 113 亿美元,就业人数增加 67%,提供就业岗位 10.5 万个。

5. 油气工业活动对其他部门产生的巨大影响,在整个经济领域内占较大份额。

Ⅴ.

1. 深水地平线原油泄漏(也称为英国石油公司石油泄漏、墨西哥湾石油泄漏、英国石油公司石油灾难或马贡多油井井喷),2010 年发生在墨西哥湾,三个月来有增无减。这是石油工业历史上最大的海洋石油的意外泄漏。

2. 2011 年 1 月,白宫石油泄漏委员会就原油泄漏的原因发表了最终报告。他们指责英国石油公司和合作伙伴进行一系列削减成本的决议,缺乏一个确保油井安全的系统。他们还认为原油泄漏不是恶性企业和政府官员造成的孤立的事件,而是"它的根本原因是系统性的,如果业内和政府的政策没有重大改革,悲剧很可能会重演"。内部调查后,英国石油公司承认了导致墨西哥湾石油泄漏的错误。英国石油公司于 2010 年 6 月成立了一个 200 亿美元的基金用来补偿泄漏的受害者。到 2011 年 7 月,基金已经向 198475 个索赔者支付了 47 亿美元。基金已有近 100 万个诉讼要求,每周仍继续受理成千上万的诉讼要求。2011 年 9 月,美国政府发表了关于这次事故的最终调查报道。报告大体上指出,最主要的原因是水泥不合格,哈利伯顿、英国石油公司和越洋公司不同程度上应对这次事故负责任。

1.5 委内瑞拉以石油为基础的经济

导语

委内瑞拉是世界重要石油生产与出口国之一,还是发展潜力巨大的重要石油输出国。委内瑞拉不断拓展石油贸易多元化渠道,积极寻求进一步与南美洲地区其他国家的经济一体化。近几年来,美国对委内瑞拉石油的依赖性越来越大,委内瑞拉是美国最大的原油供应商。委内瑞拉国内生产总值、政府财政和国家外汇很大一部分都来自石油工业收入,石油工业是其国民经济的支柱产业。委内瑞拉国家石油公司(PDVSA)为最大的国有企业之一,已成为世界石油工业领域颇具影响的企业,极大地推动了委内瑞拉经济的发展。

课文

介绍

委内瑞拉探明的石油储量跻身世界十强。石油出口约占该国出口总收入的80%,约占中央政府收入的一半,并创造约三分之一的国内生产总值。近年来,世界石油价格的上涨已使委内瑞拉总统查韦斯扩大社会计划开支,加强与其他国家的商业关系,提升自己的国际形象。然而,委内瑞拉国家石油公司PDVSA的中期前景是令人质疑的,分析家道出了PDVSA的收益和国家的政治稳定之间的联系。分析家说,最近的全球金融危机和油价骤降使得PDVSA的金融风暴愈演愈烈。

查韦斯统治下的委内瑞拉经济

乌戈·查韦斯于1999年执政,自那时以来,委内瑞拉的经济一直以石油生产为中心。2006年,查韦斯宣布油田国有化,使得政府在这些项目中的股份从40%增加至60%。但是,政府官员认为,经济增长的努力并不仅仅集中于石油。委内瑞拉驻美国大使贝尔纳多·阿尔瓦雷斯·埃雷拉,在2006年外交事务的文章中写道,"2005年包括包括采矿业、制造业和农业在内的非石油部门增长10.6%,说明该国经济重要的多样化。"然而,即使这个国家朝多样化发展,"石油仍然占主导地位。"波莫纳学院拉丁美洲历史学教授米格尔·廷克·萨拉斯说。

PDVSA

委内瑞拉国有石油公司(PDVSA),监管油气勘探、生产和石油的炼制与出口。它是世界上第三大石油公司,仅次于沙特阿美公司和埃克森美孚公司。廷克·萨拉斯说,1976 年委内瑞拉石油国有化后,PDVSA 非常像"国中国","不受政府影响",兼为控制国家财富独立的实体。1980 年,PDVSA 收购了总部设在美国的炼油厂西铁古,目前,委内瑞拉国有石油公司是世界上最大的炼油厂之一。

PDVSA 的生产水平和财政状况

国际能源机构在一份研究委内瑞拉的超重原油产量的报告中指出,2005 年 PDVSA 的生产率为 320 万桶/日,但在 2006 年 9 月,生产率却下降到 255 万桶/日。目前,欧佩克、美国政府、国际能源机构一致认为,委内瑞拉的石油产量约 240 万桶/日。然而,委内瑞拉政府却声称,PDVSA 公司的产量约 330 万桶/日。

不管怎样,都有新的迹象表明 PDVSA 前景不容乐观。2008 年,委内瑞拉能源部公布未经审核的结果,证明 PDVSA 的利润较上年下降 35%。几个月后,公布审核后的数字,表明 2007 年利润增长 15%。然而,国际能源机构指出,2007 年 PDVSA 损失 79 亿美元,2008 年,大部分时间里油价非常高,这有助于掩盖一些公司的财务困境。自从他们开始急剧下降以来,尤其是 2008 年 10 月,当 PDVSA 失去向苏格兰皇家银行(CNBC)信贷的 50 亿美元后,它一直在努力维持其财政上的义务。公司从 2007 年未结账的 57 亿美元上升到 2008 年 1 月至 9 月的 79 亿美元,但分析家说,到目前为止,该公司不可能拖欠其债权人。然而,该公司可能需要严重减产,甚至可能出售资产。

委内瑞拉常规原油储量约为 780 亿桶,估计位于加拉加斯东南地区的奥里诺科河带区还有非常规的超重原油 2350 亿桶。据纽约时报报道,如果该地区的石油工业发展可以将焦油状超重原油变成更加适销对路的商品,则委内瑞拉的总储量颇具竞争力。然而,牛津分析指出,由于缺乏基础设施投资和正在进行的石油国有化,PDVSA 将努力适时地开发重油储备。石油行业专家建议,为了维持目前的生产水平,PDVSA 每年对其现有的油田至少需要投资 30 亿美元。

区域企业

委内瑞拉是南美洲的第三大市场,正在积极推进与该地区其他国家的经济一体化进程。2006 年 7 月,它成为南美贸易集团南方共同市场的成员,该共同市场的成员国有巴西、阿根廷、乌拉圭和巴拉圭。查韦斯推动建立被称为南方银行的区域发展银行。委内瑞拉最近的区域协定的要点包括:

阿根廷。委内瑞拉和阿根廷达成了协议,就基础设施的发展以及两国在油气勘探和开发方面联合建立投资银行。委内瑞拉还购买 35 亿美元的债券,以帮助阿根廷还清债务。

巴西。2008 年 5 月,巴西石油公司和 PDVSA 签署了一项协议,在巴西东北部建设炼油厂,预计需要投资 40.5 亿美元,巴西石油公司将持有该炼油厂 60% 的股份,由两国提供原油,预计每日可炼制汽油 20 万桶。

哥伦比亚。2007 年,委内瑞拉和哥伦比亚的天然气管道开通,这条天然气管道连接哥伦比亚北部的拉瓜希拉气田和委内瑞拉西部的帕拉瓜纳炼油基地。然而,在 2008 年 3 月的对峙中,查韦斯派遣军队到哥伦比亚边境,并暂时断绝外交关系,两国之间的紧张局势加剧。

玻利维亚。根据牛津分析,在 2006 年 1 月和 5 月委内瑞拉和玻利维亚签署协议,委内瑞拉以优惠价格供应柴油,并对玻利维亚的油气部门投资 15 亿美元,作为对玻利维亚的商品和劳务的交换。

厄瓜多尔。2008 年 2 月,委内瑞拉和厄瓜多尔同意合作,预计耗资 5.5 亿美元,在厄瓜多尔共建石油炼油厂。根据 2006 年 5 月签署的协议,委内瑞拉每天将以优惠价格帮助厄瓜多尔炼制 10 万桶原油。

古巴。根据古巴政府的统计,2007 年委内瑞拉和古巴之间的贸易额猛增至 70 亿美元(2006 年,贸易额为 17 亿美元)。委内瑞拉每天向古巴出售 10 万桶石油,折让高达 40%。在交流中,成千上万的委内瑞拉人前往古巴就医,古巴医生帮助对低收入的委内瑞拉人进行健康保健。

美国和委内瑞拉的石油关系

虽然委内瑞拉曾多次威胁要切断对美国的石油出口,但是分析家说,两国是相互依存的。根据美国能源资料协会统计,委内瑞拉每天向美国市场提供约 150 万桶原油和精炼石油产品,委内瑞拉的石油约占美国进口原油的 11%,这相当于委内瑞拉出口总额的 60%。PDVSA 或是通过与美国公司的合作或是通过 PDVSA 的美国子公司西铁古,在美国全资拥有 5 家炼油厂和部分拥有 4 座炼油厂。据美国政府问责办公室说,除罢工期间的异常外,委内瑞拉向美国出口的原油和精炼石油产品一直相对稳定。

世界银行的弗列佩斯·希维尔斯说:"委内瑞拉将继续是美国市场上不可或缺的重要角色。"他认为,在短期内,委内瑞拉对美国的供应做出重大转变将是非常困难的。不过,查韦斯为减轻委内瑞拉对美国的依赖日益致力于使他的石油客户多元化。美国政府问责办公室的报告中说,若委内瑞拉的石油在世界市场上突然消失,将会使世界石油价格上涨,并使美国经济增长减缓。

Key to Exercises

I.

1. They attribute it to the recent global financial crisis and sudden drop in oil prices.

2. In 2006, Chavez announced a nationalization of oil fields managed by foreign companies, which resulted in an increase of the government's shares in these projects from 40 percent to 60 percent.

3. Saudi Aramco, ExxonMobil and PDVSA.

4. Argentina, Brazil, Colombia, Bolivia, Ecuador and Cuba.

5. Because Chavez sent troops to the Colombian border and temporarily severed diplomatic ties.

II. 1~5. CADAD 6~10. BBCAB

III. 1~5. DBDBA

IV.

1. 国际能源机构在一份研究委内瑞拉的超重原油产量的报告中指出,2005 年 PDVSA 的生产率为 320 万桶/日,但在 2006 年 9 月生产率却下降到 255 万桶/日。

2. 如果该地区的石油工业发展可以将焦油状超重原油变成更加适销对路的商品,则委内瑞拉的总储量颇具竞争力。

3. 然而,牛津分析指出,由于缺乏基础设施投资和正在进行的石油国有化,PDVSA 将努力适时地开发重油储备。

4. 委内瑞拉是南美洲的第三大市场,正在积极推进与该地区其他国家的经济一体化进程。

5. 委内瑞拉和阿根廷达成了协议,就基础设施的发展以及两国在油气勘探和开发方面联合建立投资银行。

V.

1. 然而,在查韦斯领导下,该公司的授权急剧扩大。2002 年,查韦斯重新定义 PDVSA 的角色,包括政府的社会优先权。现在,PDVSA 关于社会事业须花费至少 10% 的年度投资预算,这笔钱是通过国家发展基金或 Fonden(2005 年成立的投资基金已不在政府预算内)发放的。总部设在华盛顿的政策分析中心美洲对话的主席彼得·哈基姆说,查韦斯逐步接管 PDVSA 给了他巨额资金去实现自己的政治和经济野心。

2. 就查韦斯对委内瑞拉的经济政策的影响,存在分歧。一些经济学家说,在查韦斯领导下,社会支出的巨大增长大大地减少了贫困人口,使失业率低于10%,是十年多来的最低水平;但其他经济学家则担心该国的高通胀水平。据国际货币基金组织预测,2008年的25.7%和2009年31%的通货膨胀率,已居世界国家之首。据媒体报道:该国已出现粮食短缺,如糖和牛奶。弗朗西斯科·罗德里格斯,这位前委内瑞拉国民大会首席经济分析师在《外交事务》2008年的一篇文章中提到,在查韦斯的任期内收入不平等增加了。

第2章 石油工业的现状

2.1 中东的石油产业

🔲 导语

中东国家与美国不同，其采矿权属于国家。石油公司必须与中东各政府谈判，获得许可或石油生产权，同时，中东国家也争夺石油公司的投资。石油公司合作和许可模式通常也限制中东各政府的影响力，本课以科威特和伊朗为例进行阐明。一个国家一个公司的优惠模式及共同参与许可模式是中东推行的主要模式。

🔲 课文

中东国家与其他许多国家一样，采矿权属于国家。石油公司必须与政府谈判，获得特许权或石油生产权，以换取生产每单位（桶或吨）石油的一次性付款、租金、和/或特许权使用权费。

在美国的大部分地区，采矿权伴随土地所有权，石油公司可以选择权利个体的"卖方"，在他们的土地上开采或生产石油。尽管作为"买方"的石油公司不止一个，但在现实中，卖家面对的市场集中，除非个人占有的土地非常大或占据着战略位置，否则卖家（对市场）没有影响力。这些结构特征揭示了为何与中东的各政府相比，美国的土地所有者在他们与石油公司的谈判中处于不利地位。今天确实如此，但过去并非总是如此。

第二次世界大战前，中东国家争夺石油公司投资的方式与得克萨斯或俄克拉荷马州的牧场主相似。大公司更害怕石油过剩而不是石油短缺。根据1928年的"红线协定"，三个最大石油公司——埃克森美孚、壳牌、英国石油公司（BP），和几个小的合作伙伴联合，通过了以下协议：除非所有的合作伙伴同意，在老牌奥斯曼帝国（统治下的地区）将不开采或开发新油田。

因为红线（即签协议）公司都不愿意做那些可能增加世界石油供应从而压低油价的事情，所以，被划分到红线以内的国家在寻找勘探新油田的公司上困难重重，而新油田可以增加国家收入。

石油公司伙伴和许可模式也限制中东各政府的影响力。政府不是解决几个公司在其领土的不同地区的竞争，而是每个政府普遍面对一个单一的经营公司,其往往是谈判桌对面的一个合资企业或合作伙伴。由于资本密集以及石油投资的高风险,在石油行业,合资企业很普遍。像海湾(公司)和英国石油公司这样的独立母公司建立其运营公司——科威特石油公司(KOC),并由这两家公司共同拥有。尽管两个独立的母公司都在科威特投资并从科威特获得石油利润,但他们在科威特的业务都是由一个公司即科威特石油公司开展。这种伙伴关系使大型跨国石油公司通过提供彼此的生产信息来更好地控制整个世界的石油供应。他们也不支持与合作伙伴之间为争取其他新的优惠的竞争,这为协调其全球运营提供了一种方法。

科威特选择哪家公司获得特许权将受到英国政府的限制,英国政府与科威特已签署条约,赋予英国最终权力,决定谁可以开发特威特石油。英国不允许科威特与非英公司签约,尽管埃米尔创办的公司至少有一个非英的合作伙伴。让步达成后,科威特的自主权实际上更受限。在与科威特石油公司(KOC)签订的合同条款里,科威特给予埃米尔90年的独家代理权,允许其在整个国家勘探及生产石油。在赋予科威特石油公司(KOC)特权期间,如果政府试图从其他公司获得更好的条件,那家公司将面临来自英国石油公司(BP)和海湾公司法律方面的挑战。甚至是来自本国政府更大的威胁,即英国和美国的干预。如果科威特尝试消除科威特石油公司(KOC)的特权地位,很可能要面临一种或两种不利的威胁。

这就是20世纪50年代初伊朗遇到的情况。总理穆罕默德·摩萨台统治的伊朗政府1951年将伊朗石油公司国有化。在中东国家,伊朗的特许权是少见的,因为只有英国石油公司一个母公司。当其持有的(资产)被国有化,英国石油公司获得了法庭的指令,禁止其他公司从伊朗政府购买石油。英国和美国害怕如此成功的国有化案例可能在其他中东石油出口国出现,于是英国和美国政府努力动摇并最终推翻了摩萨台政权。1953年,沙阿在短暂被逐后恢复了(政权),也恢复了外国石油公司对国有化伊朗的石油公司的管理。然而,伊朗政府没有恢复英国石油公司作为唯一所有者以前的地位,而是寻求"科威特解决方案"。沙阿邀请了非英(国家)参与伊朗国家石油公司(NIOC)。伊朗国家石油公司NIOC重组时,美国公司和法国国家石油公司——CFP得到了60%的股份,只剩下40%留给了英国石油公司(BP)。

中东大多数国家的一个国家一个公司的特许模式有助于该地区的石油边际供应商走向国际市场,也就是说,石油需要量的(消息)来源可以平衡全球供应和需求。在中东的某种特许形式下,这种平衡行为可能由所有大型公司参与完成,而大公司生产控股遍布全球。20世纪50年代伊朗危机的解决方案使得这种控制更加容易,因为伊朗国家石油公司(NIOC)的重组由中东地区的第一经营财团进行,该财团包括在第二次世界大战后期主导石油产业的"七姐妹"——大型石油公司中的每一个成员。

中东共同参与特许(模式)使石油公司可以分享信息。更重要的是,供应链管理是石油公司制衡东道国政府的杠杆。石油公司一旦决定总供给量,在不会轻易打击报复他们的国家,公司可以通过增加或减少承购调节生产。利比亚没有实行一个国家一个公司的特许模式,其石油勘探和开发比大多数海湾国家要晚得多。正如我们所看到的,这使利比亚政府带头攻击石油公司,从而引发了20世纪70年代的石油革命。

大型石油公司避免与其他公司在特权条款上进行竞争,目的是避免其他政府获得更优惠的条件。他们在其他方面如运输石油的价格或汽油等石油产品的价格也避免竞争。对于石油公司竞争的监管,在1928年另外的卡特尔协议——《作为协议》中有所概述。

《作为协议》表面上是全球性的,实际上在每个区域市场,此协议需要进行具体谈判,而不是在任何地方都严格遵循。有时大公司会挑战此协议,但最经常违反该协议的是一些小公司,似乎他们做什么都不可能影响卡特尔体制的整体价格结构。

Key to Exercises

I.

1. Under the "Red Line Agreement" of 1928, the three largest, Exxon, Shell, and BP, along with a few smaller partners, agreed that none of them would explore for or develop new oil in the old Ottoman Empire unless all the partners consented.

2. Joint ventures are common in the oil industry because of its capital intensity and because oil investments are highly risky.

3. The Iranian government, under Prime Minister Mohammad Mossadeq, nationalized Iran's oil in 1951. Iran's concession was unusual for the Middle East in that there was only one parent company, BP. When its holdings were nationalized, BP obtained court orders enjoining other companies from buying oil from the Iranian government. Afraid of the example that a successful nationalization might set for other Middle Eastern oil exporting states, the British and American governments worked to destabilize and eventually to overthrow the Mossadeq regime.

4. The one company – one country pattern of concessions through much of the Middle East helped to make the region the marginal supplier of oil to the international market, that is, the source of however much oil was needed to balance global supply and demand.

5. Joint participation in Middle Eastern concessions enabled oil companies to share information. Even more important for supply management was the leverage the companies could exercise against the host governments.

Ⅱ. 1 ~ 5. CBAAD   6 ~ 10. ACCBC

Ⅲ. 1 ~ 5. CBAAC

Ⅳ.

1. 根据 1928 年的"红线协定",三个最大石油公司——埃克森美孚、壳牌、英国石油公司(BP),和几个小的合作伙伴联合,通过了以下协议:除非所有的合作伙伴同意,在老牌奥斯曼帝国(统治下的地区)将不开采或开发新油田。

2. 他们也不支持与合作伙伴之间为争取其他新的优惠的竞争,这为协调其全球运营提供了一种方法。

3. 在中东国家,伊朗的特许权是少见的,因为只有英国石油公司一个母公司。

4. 利比亚没有实行一个国家一个公司的特许模式,其石油勘探和开发比大多数海湾国家要晚得多。

5. 大型石油公司避免与其他公司在特权条款上进行竞争,目的是避免其他政府获得更优惠的条件。

Ⅴ.

1. 中东是世界石油工业的地理"重心"。在该地区几乎每一个国家,无论是石油进口国还是石油输出国,石油对于外交政策和国内政治都是至关重要的。

2. 上游生产是指石油勘探,勘探含油区块、开发、建设油井和气体分离器等基础生产设施。下游生产是指运输,包括管道、油轮和铁路的运输;提炼业,即把原油加工成可用产品,如汽油及燃油;以及销售业,即汽油/汽油站及其他产品的销售。

2.2 非洲的石油炼制业

导语

非洲主要炼油中心位于南非、尼日利亚、埃及和阿尔及利亚。20 世纪 80

年代初,非洲许多炼油厂都面临着重大挑战,甚至一些非洲炼油厂被迫关闭。课文介绍了非洲四个国家的政府在发展炼油产业上的政策以及主要工程项目。

课文

下游行业包括炼油和零售业。炼油厂把原油转换成燃料产品、润滑油、沥青、化工原料及其他石油产品。非洲主要的炼油中心位于南非(4 个炼油厂和 3 个合成燃料厂)、尼日利亚(3 个炼油厂)、埃及(9 个炼油厂)、阿尔及利亚(4 个炼油厂)。最大的单一炼油厂是阿尔及利亚的斯基克达炼油厂(3 亿桶/日),最小的运营炼油厂位于马达加斯加的索利玛尔,其炼油能力为 1400 万桶/日。

由于全球炼油利润率低、本地市场小、经营成本高(由于规模小)及产量低,非洲许多炼油厂已被迫关闭。20 世纪 80 年代初,世界银行/国际货币基金组织坚持开放市场,仅存的炼油厂面临着重大挑战。虽然非洲装机容量高于目前的消费(需求),但非洲大陆仍严重缺乏精炼产品,需要通过进口来平衡其短缺。受精炼产品短缺,及经济利润最大化的吸引,炼油厂设在石油资源附近,尼日利亚、苏丹、乌干达和莫桑比克等国家正在计划建立新的炼油厂。

以尼日利亚炼油工业为例

尼日利亚石油及天然气下游行业有相当多的投资机会。政府的工作重点是解除行业管制,如批准私人建立炼油厂,取消下游产业的政府补贴,以及对现有炼油厂实行私有化。通过这些战略举措,至少有望满足国内需求。由于很多因素,包括管理不善和维护不善,现有的四个炼油厂的产量一直明显低于装机容量。

很多年来,解除对石油和天然气部门下游产业(石油精炼与销售)的管制一直受到关注。事实上,缺乏石油产品及逐步解除对石油产品价格的管制在尼日利亚已经引起激烈争论。政府决心鼓励私营企业参与和从事当地的石油与天然气行业,因而,批准私人建立炼油厂,解除石油产品价格管制,以提高国内的(炼油)能力。未来几年,随着新竞争者的加入,石油炼化部门和营销部门将进行整合。为国内和国际资金提供重要的投资机会。

全球环境能源的子公司,撒哈拉石油勘探公司,已承建在尼日利亚阿夸·伊博姆洲的埃基特日产量为 70000 桶的项目。

该炼油厂耗资大约 40 亿美元,意味着该项目在目前市场水平的现金流每年约为 1.5 亿美元。此计划提高了尼日利亚的炼油能力,在石油资源附近设厂也将为运营商节省可观的成本(如撒哈拉石油)。目前,全国有四家主要炼油厂标示能力为 438750 桶/日。

乌干达塔洛石油炼油厂计划

在决定建立一家投资数十亿美元的炼油厂之前,塔洛石油(公司)目前一直致力于寻找大量优质石油,并在乌干达阿尔贝蒂娜地堑已发现大量优质石油。

乌干达政府和塔洛石油已同意在初期方案中建立一家小型炼油厂,计划安装 100 兆瓦重燃油热电站。小型炼油厂(日产石油能力约 5000 万桶)将消耗塔洛公司 2 亿美元。

苏丹炼油能力提高一倍

由于已经达成了结束 21 年内战的协议,为了提高产量,在三年短期的投资计划中,苏丹计划炼油能力提高一倍。苏丹将在红海沿岸的苏丹港建立一家日产量为 10 万桶的新炼油厂,并提高现有两个炼油厂的生产能力。苏丹与印度石油和天然气公司、中国石化、马来西亚国家石油公司,及一家不为人知的土耳其公司进行谈判,建立新炼油厂。苏丹期望在未来的几年其原油产量大大增加,因此提高炼油能力是非常及时的。

莫桑比克批准建立新炼油厂

莫桑比克内阁已批准在北部的楠普拉省建设价值超过 13 亿美元的炼油厂,名为"艾尔物流有限公司纳卡拉"。该项目是由美国一家私营公司艾尔物流牵头,与一个莫桑比克和三个南非的投资者共同合作完成。该项目预期将创造约 450 个工作岗位,并为莫桑比克政府带来额外税收回报。该项目装机生产能力约为 10 万桶/日,大部分产品将出口到马拉维、津巴布韦和赞比亚。该项目还包括建设几个基础设施,以支持其主要生产,项目占地面积 838 公顷,位于纳卡拉港口地区,此港口也是莫桑比克最深且最繁忙的港口。

尽管对上述计划和远景进行了说明,但在过去三年里,包括 2007 年,全球炼油能力提高不大仍是事实。

尽管非常担心通货膨胀,建造成本价格上升,然而,莫桑比克仍计划大幅度增加炼油能力。像其他地方一样,非洲(世界各地)炼油能力增长缓慢有其他非经济原因:对地方及环境的担忧、更严格的环保法规及有效的地区规划,这些原因使得建立新炼油厂很难。

一些分析家认为,炼油能力是高油价的重要因素。因此,作为降低成品油产品成本的一种方法,在非洲提高炼油厂炼油能力是有意义的。然而,这需要在一个环保的方式下进行。

Key to Exercises

I.

1. Many African refineries have been forced to close because of low world-wide refining margins, small local markets, high operating costs (due to small size), and poor yields.

2. The government's focus is on deregulating the sector by licensing private refineries, eliminating government subsidies to the downstream sector, and privatizing existing ones.

3. The government's focus is on deregulating the sector by licensing private refineries, eliminating government subsidies to the downstream sector, and privatizing existing ones.

4. The project is spearheaded by a privately owned American company, Ayr Logistics, in partnership with one Mozambican and three South African investors, the district of the Nacala port, which is also home to Mozambique's deepest and busiest port.

5. Other non – economic reasons—in Africa for the slow growth in refining capacity (worldwide) are environmental and local concerns, more stringent environmental laws, and effective community organizing, which have made it very difficult to build new refineries. With an installed capacity of about 100000 bbl/d, most of the product will be exported to Malawi, Zimbabwe, and Zambia. The project also includes the construction of several infrastructures that will support the main activity of the project, which will be implemented over an area of 838 ha and will be situated in.

II. 1 ~ 5. DBCAB   6 ~ 10. DDBCD

III. 1 ~ 5. BCCCB

IV.

1. 下游行业包括炼油和零售业。炼油厂把原油转换成燃料产品、润滑油、沥青、化工原料及其他石油产品。

2. 虽然非洲装机容量高于目前的消费(需求),但非洲大陆仍严重缺乏精炼产品,需要通过进口来平衡其短缺。

3. 莫桑比克内阁已批准在北部的楠普拉省建设价值超过 13 亿美元的炼油厂。

4. 尽管对上述计划和远景进行了说明,但在过去三年里,包括 2007 年,全球炼油能力提高不大仍是事实。

5. 因此,作为降低成品油产品成本的一种方法,在非洲提高炼油厂炼油能力是有意义的。

Ⅴ.

1. 据彭博通讯社报道,莫桑比克内阁已批准在北部的楠普拉省建设炼油厂,价值超过 13 亿美元,名曰"艾尔物流有限公司纳卡拉"。这个项目也负责为纳卡拉社区提供人道主义援助和支持,由于大部分的土壤贫瘠、周期性的虫害,以及恶劣的天气,目前纳卡拉社区仍是贫困地区。

2. 非洲是日益重要的石油出口地,但由于对燃料需求的不断增长和炼油能力的不足,非洲是石油精炼产品的主要进口地。尼日利亚是世界第八大原油出口国,2003 年,其前总统奥卢塞贡·奥巴桑乔政府为私人投资者颁发 18 个许可证,允许建立炼油厂,但由于后来炼油厂没有建成,许多人被吊销许可。

2.3　澳大利亚石油概况

导语

为了保持澳大利亚石油工业的国际竞争力,西澳大利亚在上游和下游启动并运作了石油勘探开发项目,石油工业和其他资源行业促使西澳大利亚经济急剧增长。澳大利亚当前的石油开发主要集中在几大盆地,在其他许多尚未勘探的海区,油气储量颇为可观。

课文

自从 1953 年首次在距离西澳大利亚州首府珀斯 1070 千米的拉夫·兰芝发现石油后,石油和天然气就发展成为西澳大利亚州最宝贵的出口资源性产品。在过去的十年中,珀斯已成为澳大利亚的石油活动中心。西澳大利亚州是目前全国最大的石油生产地区,拥有澳大利亚约 57% 的石油,凝析油和天然气储量分别占澳大利亚 71% 和 78%。20 世纪 90 年代,石油工业是西澳大利亚增长最快的经济部门,珀斯吸引了国内外的公司。

20 世纪 80 年代以来,随着西北大陆架(NWS)项目的发展,石油产量激增。石油勘探仍主要集中在卡那封盆地北部的海岸。

在未来的几年中,正在规划的上游和下游的石油项目金额将超过 800 亿美元。在可预见的未来,产油量将激增。埃克斯茅斯次盆油田包括包含重油在内的未来的石油发展,为此会迅速下降。液化天然气(LNG)市场目前的繁荣支撑着液化天然气的发展,如戈尔贡、占茨佑和耶稣鱼公司,预计该行业在不久的将来将发展其他液化天然气项目。大多数石油和液化天然气的开发在未来十年都将投产。

为了增加政府收入、增加就业机会、促进区域发展和基础设施的发展,西澳大利亚人通过这些石油开发项目增加石油资源税并从中获益。这些项目对西澳大利亚州和国家都至关重要,因为它们提供更大程度的石油自给,以及额外的供应安全保障。

不过,也有挑战。石油生产和生产领域相关的特许权使用费快速下降。澳大利亚的主要生产盆地已经得到充分发展;为保持西澳大利亚的石油生产量,迫切需要促进和推动坎宁盆地的勘探活动,促进和鼓励勘探其他边远盆地。

澳大利亚需要增加其国内储备基地,尤其是液化石油气储备基地。根据澳大利亚农业资源经济局预计,除非有更多的行业努力以及在这方面政府的援助,否则澳大利亚自给自足的液态烃生产到 2020 年将由目前的 75%下降到 25%,这将对澳大利亚的国际收支和政府税收收入产生重大影响。

石油工业比以往任何时候发展迅猛,工业资源部的石油和特许权使用费司考虑到进行勘探活动的公司的优先事项,为最大限度地利用出现在西澳大利亚经济这个主要部门的潜在发展机会,该司努力按确定的日程表进行审批程序。

主要沉积盆地

澳大利亚有 7 个沉积盆地,面积估计有 210 万平方千米(包括大陆架),其中 5 个沉积盆地有碳氢化合物。经济生产只来自北卡那封盆地近海、珀斯盆地北部和陆上坎宁盆地。

西澳大利亚州是在世界上勘探最少的领土之一,近海每 3124 平方千米、陆上每 2647 平方千米才各有一口勘探井。西北大陆架井的密度为每 100 平方千米有一口井。这个庞大的资源地区,是世界上最有吸引力的一个勘探目标。在过去十年中,西澳大利亚州的勘探支出占澳大利亚总勘探支出的50% ~ 70%。

北卡那封盆地是澳大利亚西部最有生产力的盆地和过去 30 多年里勘探活动的热点地区。目前,98% 的油气生产来自北卡那封盆地,不久的将来,这个盆地与要投入生产的几个油气田,包括文森特、凡高、安吉尔和高贡等油气田很可能会大幅增产。

近海的珀斯盆地如同一个熟悉的球道,到目前为止,再次涉入的几家公司收益都不错。陆上有许多生产中的油气田,可近海却只有一个。相对而言,布劳斯盆地和波拿巴盆地都是未充分开发的。目前,尽管只有波拿巴盆地有一个生产的油气田,可在布劳斯盆地近海勘探活动却显著增加,人们相信,这些北方近海盆地有着丰富的油气储量。

生产和储备

由于西澳大利亚州石油、天然气资源和综合设施等多种因素,石油工业是 20 世纪 90 年代增长最快的经济部门。在过去十年中开发和生产的油田数量几乎增加了一倍。2007 年,有 68 个生产油田。同年有 7 个新油田——艾皮姆、多里克、爱斯达克、李、斯瑞坡、斯泰巴罗和西塞卡德投入生产。

2007 年 12 月底,西澳大利亚州液体和气体的石油生产总量估计分别为 28.6 亿桶和 37040 亿立方米(131 万亿标准立方英尺)。在 2007 年,液体石油和天然气日产量分别为 328000 桶和 8 千万立方米。至 2007 年 12 月 31 日,西澳大利亚州的油气田生产总额累计为原油 2.28 亿立方米(1435 百万桶)、凝析油 9250 万立方米(582 百万桶)、天然气 4480 亿立方米(15.8 万亿标准立方英尺)。

目前,该国的天然气和液态石油产量已超过维多利亚州的吉普斯兰盆地。

由于埃克斯茅斯次盆的重油田的开发,2008—2009 年是石油生产的高峰期,而后急剧下降。2010—2020 年,凝析气田凝析油的生产将在未来保持液态烃生产中发挥关键作用。因为凝析油主要来自液化天然气,所以凝析油产量下降速度可能要比石油产量下降速度慢得多。

Key to Exercises

I.

1. These petroleum development projects will benefit Western Australians through an increase in royalty revenue for the Government, new employment, regional development, and infrastructure development.

2. Australia's self-sufficiency in liquid hydrocarbon production will have a significant impact on Australia's balance of payments and on Government taxation revenue.

3. The Northern Carnarvon Basin is the most productive basin in Western Australia.

4. In 2007, seven new fields came on stream: Apium, Doric, Eskdale, Lee, Searipple, Stybarrow, and West Cycad.

5. A peak in oil production around 2008—2009 was mainly attributed to

the development of heavy oilfields in the Exmouth Sub – basin.

Ⅱ. 1 ~ 5. ABDBD　6 ~ 10. CAADD

Ⅲ. 1 ~ 5. CABDD

Ⅳ.

1. 20 世纪 80 年代以来,随着西北大陆架(NWS)项目的发展,石油产量激增。

2. 这些项目对西澳大利亚州和国家都至关重要,因为它们提供更大程度的石油自给,以及额外的供应安全保障。

3. 根据澳大利亚农业资源经济局预计,除非有更多的行业努力以及在这方面政府的援助,否则澳大利亚自给自足的液态烃生产到 2020 将由目前的 75% 下降到 25% 。

4. 在不久的将来,这个盆地与要投入生产的几个油气田,包括文森特、凡高、安吉尔和高贡等油气田很可能会大幅增产。

5. 由于西澳大利亚州石油、天然气资源和综合基础设施等多种因素,石油工业是 20 世纪 90 年代增长最快的经济部门。

Ⅴ.

1. 澳大利亚炼油工业对社会和工业的稳定是非常重要的。当地的炼油行业是供应和维护国家的社会及工业活动的关键。大多数炼油厂输出是用来供给运输部门,然而,农业产业化、重工业和一般家庭活动也依赖于本地生产的石油产品。如果澳大利亚炼油厂很长一段时间不能生产,对地区甚至国家的社会和经济稳定,将会造成很严重的后果。

2. 在未来 20 年中,上游石油工业面临着许多重大的挑战,如提高成品油价格和自给自足的能力,国内供给和需求之间的差距不断扩大,目前产油盆地的进一步发展需要加强陆上勘探,寻找新的边远盆地,澳大利亚的多元化消费,就目前油田和政府的监管制度改革推出一个更具竞争力的监管制度进而提高产量等。

第3章　石油工业的发展

3.1　里海石油与天然气的生产和前景

导语

里海作为世界重要能源供应地之一,目前油气产量高,探明储量大,还有大量的新增油气储量,使这一地区的油气生产前景广阔,必将突破现有的市场,提高自己在能源运输中对俄罗斯的话语权,开拓市场,并使东亚等国家成为其潜在的市场。

课文

目前的石油生产和探明储量

据英国石油公司和美国能源部的能源信息署(EIA)估计,目前里海地区是全球原油市场重要的供应商,但却不是主要的。2005年,里海地区包括液态天然气在内,日产量190万桶,占世界原油产量的2%。2005年,十三个非里海地区国家平均每个国家日产量超过190万桶。里海地区的石油产量较高,但苏联解体期间和随后的一段时间里,却蒙受损失。哈萨克斯坦产油量自20世纪90年代末以来迅速上升,2005年,在里海地区原油产量中哈萨克斯坦占67%,阿塞拜疆占22%。

根据英国石油公司公布的数据显示,里海地区已探明的石油储量为480亿桶。这大约相当于世界已探明石油总储量的4%,远高于英国石油公司提供的美国储量数据(290亿桶)。美国能源信息署对可采储量的估计表明,还有更大的生产潜力。

里海地区对世界天然气的供应远大于它对石油的供应。2005年,天然气年产3万亿立方英尺,占世界总产出的3%。天然气产量较高,但像石油一样,苏联解体期间和随后的一段时间里,却蒙受损失。土库曼斯坦是最大的天然气生产国,年产2万亿立方英尺,占该地区天然气产量的近2/3。

不像石油,该地区已探明的天然气储备占世界总量的比例高于天然气产量。很多情况下,本来想寻找石油的勘探却发现了天然气。2005年年底,英国石油公司公布了里海地区已探明天然气储量为257万亿立方英尺,占全球天然气总储量的4%。里海地区增加天然气生产所面临的障碍,有点类似于那些未来石油开发和生产所面临的挑战。

资源和生产前景

里海地区极可能有大量新的原油和天然气储备。这也得益于在那里拥有大量资产的许多石油公司的支持。大部分探明的石油储量尚未开发,但开发通常会有新发现,前景远大于原来估计。此外,许多地区尚未勘探。据估计,里海地区新增原油储量可能还有 1840 亿桶,这将是现有水平的近 5 倍。现探明的储量几乎相当于沙特阿拉伯的储量,约占世界总储量的 15%。

天然气探明储量相对石油来说要小得多,但潜在储量仍然非常大。估计该地区有新增天然气储量近 300 万亿立方英尺。若是如此,2010 年里海地区探明石油总储量将是现有水平的两倍多,远远超过现在沙特阿拉伯的天然气储量。按这样的预测,估计到 2010 年,里海地区天然气年产量将达 5.4 万亿立方英尺。里海地区大量的石油和天然气资源可与沙特阿拉伯相比,然而,也得承认,沙特阿拉伯的石油和天然气生产成本较低以及市场就近等许多优势。无论能源资源的数量还是生产成本,里海国家开发和销售石油与天然气的能力一定程度上取决于他们建立和保持与国际能源公司关系的能力。

现在和未来的市场

考虑到上述情况,未来的里海地区国家将成为石油和天然气出口大国。里海的石油和天然气现在有一些市场,而且拥有更多的潜在市场。这些包括一些试图满足经济体对能源需求的国家和那些希望减少对波斯湾能源依赖的国家。

几乎所有里海地区原油的北进和/或西行,都反映出苏联时期的规定和基础设施特征。炼油厂为运输网络中的一部分,原油大部分通过管道经俄罗斯销往欧洲市场。一些原油还要通过油轮穿过博斯普鲁斯海峡,经地中海进入西欧市场。通过管道向北和/或向西运输的天然气甚至比石油还多,主要通过俄罗斯和它的垄断管道系统——俄罗斯国家石油运输公司进行。这一点,再加上俄罗斯本身也生产石油和天然气,使俄罗斯有市场权力对通过其交通网络的里海能源征收过境费,并在某些情况下由俄罗斯决定征收的费用,如果有原油通过的话,俄罗斯还是愿意输送的。同时,以交付成本为基础的能源的竞争,反映出里海地区还要承受运输费用、井口的价格。

里海地区国家故而发展替代通过俄罗斯的路线——可能是路线的合作避免了里海地区原油抵达欧洲和其他市场的俄罗斯的长途运输,并在穿过俄罗斯的管道系统的过境费磋商中提供里海地区的影响力。此外,鉴于俄罗斯 2006 年 1 月初切断通过乌克兰的天然气供应管线,已经在寻求天然气来源多样化的西欧国家将更积极地寻找非俄罗斯的天然气,以减少将来切断管线所造成的影响。

里海地区能源资源对土耳其很有吸引力,里海地区与土耳其临近,并因为对通过领土的原油收取过境费,提供给土耳其一个抵消其能源进口的部分费用的机会。土耳其的能源消耗增长速度远远超过其经济产出,使其快速成为一个油气进口国,它已经是俄罗斯天然气进口大国。同时,土耳其和里海国家有着良好的关系。

东亚国家也是有潜在吸引力的市场。日本已经进口大量的天然气,印度和巴基斯坦的能源消耗正在迅速增长。也许最重要的是,就中国当前和潜在的经济规模,以及目前石油消费的激增而言,中国已探明石油与天然气的储量相对较少,这导致了油气的大量进口。例如,由哈萨克斯坦通向中国的石油管道,于2005年11月竣工并已开始输油;审议并通过哈萨克斯坦到中国的天然气管道的建设,不过,最近扩大或开发非中亚能源出口到上述那些地区可能会限制里海能源出口到这些地区的前景。这些发展中包括北非扩大天然气出口能力和埃及附近地区发现一个巨大的天然气田。

Key to Exercises

I.

1. Both of them estimate that the Caspian Sea region presently is a significant, but not major, supplier of crude oil to world markets.

2. Turkmenistan is the largest producer.

3. The considerable advantages of Saudi oil and gas are much lower costs of production and much easier market access.

4. That Caspian region crude oil goes north and/or west is mainly through Russia and its monopoly pipeline system — Transneft. Further on it, Russia itself produces oil and gas. Both of these entitle Russia to it.

5. Possibly a consortia of routes that would avoid long transits through Russia in reaching European and other markets and provide leverage in negotiating transit fees on shipments that do go through the Russian pipeline system.

II. 1 ~ 5. CBCAC   6 ~ 10. CADAB

III. 1 ~ 5. BCDAC

IV.

1. 根据英国石油公司公布的数据显示,里海地区已探明的石油储量为

480 亿桶。

2. 美国能源信息署对可采储量的估计表明,还有更大的生产潜力。

3. 大部分探明的石油储量尚未开发,但开发通常会有新发现,前景远大于原来估计。

4. 现探明的储量几乎相当于沙特阿拉伯的储量,约占世界总储量的 15%。

5. 这些包括一些试图满足经济体对能源需求的国家和那些希望减少对波斯湾能源依赖的国家。

V.

1. 里海是长 700 英里的中亚水域,沿岸国家有阿塞拜疆、伊朗、哈萨克斯坦、俄罗斯和土库曼斯坦。在五个国家中,只有伊朗是石油输出国组织的成员。1991 年苏联解体时,阿塞拜疆、哈萨克斯坦与土库曼斯坦获得了独立。里海地区历史上曾产出石油和天然气,但是人们认为,该地区具有产量较大的石油和天然气资源。

2. 此外,许多里海能源资源是海上的,需要特别的大型钻井设备。较偏远的地区非常有限的钻机生产能力使得钻井设备昂贵和后勤困难,阻碍了里海能源资源的发展。

3.2　俄罗斯石油和天然气面临的挑战

导语

俄罗斯可探测天然气储量比其他任何国家都多,已探明石油储量列(世界)十强。俄罗斯生产的原油近四分之三出口。因此在过去的五年里,能源出口是驱动俄罗斯经济增长的一个主要动力。然而,俄罗斯在维持及扩大生产和能源出口能力上面临很多困难。此外,俄罗斯政府已经通过多种方式控制国家能源供应。

课文

俄罗斯是世界能源市场的重要参与者。俄罗斯可探测天然气储量比其他任何国家都多,已探明石油储量列居(世界)十强。俄罗斯是世界最大的天然气出口国,第二大石油出口国,第三大能源消费国。

石油和天然气储量与产量

俄罗斯已探明的石油储量为 60 亿桶,大部分石油分布于西西伯利亚、乌拉尔山脉和中西伯利亚高原之间。丰富的地区资源使前苏联成为 20 世纪 80 年代世界上主要的石油生产国,1988 年日生产石油达 1250 万桶。俄罗斯约 25% 的石油储量和 6% 的天然气储量来自于该国远东地区位于日本北部的萨哈林岛。

　　1991 年苏联解体前,俄罗斯的石油产量已经开始下降,到 1997 年和 1998 年产量急剧下降到每天不到 600 万桶。国家下令激增产量,加速了大西西伯利亚油田的枯竭及苏联中央计划体系的崩溃。俄罗斯石油产量于 1999 年开始恢复。许多分析家将此归结于工业的私有化,私有化明确了生产动机,并把生产重点转向降低成本。世界石油价格的上涨,西方标准技术的应用,及老油田的振兴有助于提高产量。1998 年金融危机和随后卢布贬值的后继影响也是石油生产恢复的重要原因。据估算,2004 年俄罗斯石油产量约为 900 万桶/日,2005 年前几个月继续上升,但上升幅度不大。因为没有全面引入西方最现代化的石油和天然气的勘探、开发及生产技术,俄罗斯石油和天然气产量增长的潜力有限。

　　石油和天然气的出口与管道

　　俄罗斯生产的原油近四分之三出口,剩余石油在国内提炼,并出口部分精炼产品。2004 年,俄罗斯日产原油 670 万桶,其中三分之二出口到白俄罗斯、乌克兰、德国、波兰以及中欧及东欧的其他地区。出口石油中的三分之一运到海运港口,销往世界各地。最近,高油价使俄罗斯 40% 的出口石油通过更昂贵的铁路和内河驳船航线运输。俄罗斯精炼石油产品大部分出口到欧洲,其产品用于生产取暖燃油和柴油燃料。

　　由于俄罗斯石油产量强劲上扬和世界油价居高不下,在过去的五年里,能源出口是驱动俄罗斯经济增长的一个主要动力。这种经济增长类型使俄罗斯经济依赖于石油和天然气出口,并容易受到油价波动的冲击。平均每桶 1 美元的油价变化会同时导致俄罗斯政府 14 亿美元的收入变化。

　　在维持及扩大石油生产和能源出口能力方面,俄罗斯面临很多困难。俄罗斯的油气田日渐老化,现代西方能源技术尚未完全实施,国有垄断的俄罗斯国家石油运输公司控制的原油管道出口能力不足。此外,用于改善并扩大俄罗斯的石油和天然气生产与管道系统投资资金不足。

　　历史上,俄罗斯的天然气主要出口到东欧和前苏联国家。但是,20 世纪 80 年代中期,俄罗斯开始尝试出口多元化。现在,俄罗斯天然气工业股份公司已将出口转向土耳其、日本和其他亚洲国家,满足其不断增长的需求。如果俄罗斯天然气工业股份公司要实现增加欧洲销售的长期目标,就必须提高其产量,同时确保出口该地区路线更安全。

俄罗斯政府已经控制了国家能源供应。政府解散了之前的大型能源公司尤科斯,收购了其生产石油的主要子公司。尤科斯曾通过减少石油供应,控制了立陶宛大多数炼油厂,并以低价收购。俄罗斯尽全力控制能源供应的另一例证是敷设了计划好的新出口管道。例如,在联合王国(英国)的支持下,它已同意与德国在波罗的海海下直接建立天然气管道,为德国、最后为英国提供能源。俄罗斯继续保持与中亚国家的能源合作,中亚许多运输路线都来自欧洲国家俄罗斯。俄罗斯正在考虑(寻找)在东亚的石油管道的目的地,允许俄罗斯来决定石油销售对象。此外,俄罗斯试图切断对乌克兰的天然气供应,因为后者不同意支付大幅度增加的天然气费用。俄罗斯出口到欧洲的大部分天然气经由乌克兰,在欧洲其他国家抱怨后,俄罗斯恢复供应。

另外,很多人提议建设新的出口管道,或者扩大现有俄罗斯石油和天然气的出口管道。有些建议引起争议,虽然俄罗斯政府认识到有必要扩大其石油和天然气的出口能力,但俄罗斯政府资源不足。

对于美国的意义

美国也和俄罗斯一样,是重要的能源生产者和消费者,俄罗斯的能源发展趋势和政策通常会影响美国的能源市场和经济福利。俄罗斯能源产量的提高,以及向西或向东的能源出口可能会缓和大西洋与太平洋地区能源市场的供求情况。另一方面,前面提到的俄罗斯政府采取控制国家能源供应的举动可能造成石油供应减少的后果。可能同样重要的是,因为美国的石油和天然气设备及服务供应商努力提高其在俄罗斯的销售及投资,所以,俄罗斯石油和天然气工业的发展与美国存在潜在的联系。

与美国和俄罗斯的贸易相似,自苏联解体以来,美国加大了在俄罗斯的投资,特别是直接投资,但投资远远低于预期水平。即便如此,到2003年年底,美国是俄罗斯的第二大直接投资国,其投资主要集中在能源、交通、工程和运输方面。

然而,尽管美国认为,俄罗斯投资环境有所改善,但潜在的投资者抱怨俄罗斯不友好的投资环境,诸如缺乏知识产权保护、繁重的税收法、政府官僚效率低下等。

Key to Exercises

I.

1. Most of Russia's 60 billion barrels of proven oil reserves are located in Western Siberia, between the Ural Mountains and the Central Siberian Plateau.

2. Many analysts attribute this to privatization of the industry, which clarified incentives and shifted activity to less expensive production. Increases in

world oil prices, application of technology that was standard practice in the West, and rejuvenation of old oil fields helped boost output.

3. Russia's oil and gas fields are aging. Modern western energy technology has not been fully implemented. There is insufficient export capacity in the crude oil pipeline system controlled by Russia's state – owned pipeline monopoly, Transneft. And, there is insufficient investment capital for improving and expanding Russian oil and gas production and pipeline systems.

4. Historically, most of Russia's natural gas exports went to Eastern Europe and to customers in countries that previously were part of the Soviet Union.

5. For potential investors think the investment climate in Russia is inhospitable with respect to factors such as poor intellectual property rights protection, burden – some tax laws, and inefficient government bureaucracy.

Ⅱ. 1～5. CDCAA   6～10. CCBCC

Ⅲ. 1～5. BCBBD

Ⅳ.

1. 1991年苏联解体前,俄罗斯的石油产量已经开始下降,到1997年和1998年产量急剧下降到每天不到600万桶。

2. 因为没有全面引入西方最现代化的石油和天然气的勘探、开发及生产技术,俄罗斯石油和天然气产量的增长的潜力有限。

3. 由于俄罗斯石油产量强劲上扬和世界油价居高不下,在过去的五年里,能源出口是驱动俄罗斯经济增长的一个主要动力。

4. 历史上,俄罗斯的天然气主要出口到东欧和前苏联国家。

5. 美国也和俄罗斯一样,是重要的能源生产者和消费者,俄罗斯的能源发展趋势和政策通常会影响美国的能源市场和经济福利。

Ⅴ.

1. 由于东亚国家努力满足其日益增长的能源需求,同时减少对中东石油的依赖,因此中国、日本和韩国正在试图开发西伯利亚东部的未开发能源。中国和日本正忙于俄罗斯项目的招标战争,并争夺俄罗斯的石油管道路线。

2. 此外,作为欧洲国家天然气的主要供应商,俄罗斯有能力制定价格。例如,它可以保留供应,从而影响客户国家的政策。2003年,俄罗斯供应的天然气占斯洛伐克天然气消费量的100%,占保加利亚天然气消费量的97%,占捷克共和国天然气消费量的79%,占匈牙利天然气消费量的68%。

3.3　全球视角下的非洲石油和天然气资源地位

导语

　　众所周知,能源是经济增长和社会发展的重要保证,并对世界经济和政治产生重大影响。在全世界对能源的高需求和其他大洲石油储量有限的背景下,课文指出,非洲在全球能源使用方面将发挥着越来越重要的作用。此外,非洲石油生产国的政府也必须解决有关能源治理的一些难题和挑战。

课文

　　能源对于经济增长和社会发展是必不可少的。石油和天然气满足了全球三分之二的能源需求。人们普遍认为,人均能源消费量与经济发展水平和社会进步是密切相关的。值得注意的是,三种不可再生的化石燃料——石油、天然气、煤炭占据全球近90%的商业能源消耗。

　　全球能源消费的区域性结构显示,能源使用与占有存在巨大差异。尽管非洲人口占世界总人口的15%,但其能源消费量只占3%。更令人不可思议的是,非洲的能源生产份额约占全球的12%,且该比例呈上升趋势。

　　20世纪70年代末,世界能源市场发生了巨变,对世界经济与政治产生了深远的影响。主导国际能源油气的价格起伏不稳,并时而攀上峰顶,导致世界范围内的经济动荡就证明了这一点。自2000年以来,世界石油价格不断攀升,天然气价格随势而上。油价上升的原因包括以下几点:新兴经济体的需求日益增长,特别是中国和印度;主要产油国储备能力下降;一些重要的产油区产量达到极限,以及炼油能力提高不足。

　　西方世界持续高需求,加上新兴经济体,如中国、印度、巴西对能源的迫切需求,本世纪的前25年,全球能源消费量预计增长50%以上。到2025年,预计石油和天然气需求特别大,全球石油消费(需求)预计将增长57%。

　　即使对全世界的能源行业进行大量投资,石油和天然气行业生产并输送足够的能源来满足全球需求不大可能。

　　根据预测,"石油峰值"已经达到或将在未来几年内达到。

　　如果不策略地、积极地处理此难题,伴随能源价格的上涨,随之而来的能源短缺将给非洲的石油净进口国造成很大压力。

　　非洲拥有大量的化石资源和可再生能源。此外,它是世界上不断有大量的石油和天然气新发现的主要大陆。在过去的20年里,非洲的石油储量增长超过25%,天然气储量翻了一番。非洲的富油田及勘探前景使它成为全球石油生产和资源开采的重要参与者和重要目标。在可预见的未来,非洲大陆的石油产量将继续以平均每年6%的速度增长。非洲大部分的石油储量(和石油产量)来自利比亚、尼日利亚、阿尔及利亚、安哥拉、苏丹等国家,总计超过非洲石油储量的90%。非洲已探明天然气储量主要集中在四个国家——阿尔及利亚、埃及、利比亚和尼日利亚,占非洲大陆已探明储量的91.5%。尼日利亚未开发的天然气资源更成为该行业国际巨头理所当然的目标。此外,在坦桑尼亚发现大量天然气储量,在乌干达的阿尔贝蒂娜地堑和加纳西部发现可观的石油储量,在南非、莫桑比克和坦桑尼亚发现潜力可观的油田。

鉴于目前能源供应的不确定性,未来需求的主要驱动,消费国的政策(特别是关于核材料及其他石油和天然气的替代品),未来全球经济增长和技术发展,有必要明确建立非洲的(能源)地位,并制定确保未来充足(能源)供应的战略。由于高油价引起的能源危机,石油生产造成的环境影响,以及对以石油为原料的燃料和产品的可行性的日益担忧,致使人们实施发掘替代能源的举措。

获得石油和天然气资源的收益最大化

石油和天然气资源管理的一个关键问题是非洲的石油和天然气生产国政府从生产商收到租金份额不足。这可能源于多种原因,包括不提取最高租金的合同和制度;石油和天然气的最初政策旨在促进和吸引投资,并没有考虑发展的全球动力学和国家利益。石油和天然气的可持续发展要求利用资源的政策、原则和实践不妨碍后代受益。

非洲石油生产国的巨大挑战就是确保充足的、可靠的、环保的石油供应,且供应价格反映市场基本面。为了实现这一重要的目标,必须解决几个挑战:高波动的石油价格;国内外日益增长的石油需求;许多非洲国家对(石油)进口的日益依赖;最重要的是,非洲大陆石油和天然气资源的可持续管理。这些挑战的区域性及非洲净进口和净出口国家之间日益增长的依存性要求所有利益相关者加强伙伴关系,确保地区能源安全。

石油和天然气的可持续管理也面临这样的挑战,大笔能源收入往往取代更稳定的可持续的收入来源,致使现存的发展问题、透明度和问责制更加恶化。当公民直接向国家交税时,他们要求能源出口国政府的财政透明及实施问责制。因此,能源出口收入实际上割裂了人民和他们的政府之间的联系,这种联系也是公众利益和控制机制之间的联系。在石油资源丰富的非洲国家,政府治理指标,如政府效能、话语权和问责制、政治不稳定及暴力、法治原则、监管质量、控制腐败等相对比较薄弱。

尽管面临诸多问题和挑战,在合适的条件下,石油和天然气资源的繁荣可能成为(经济)增长和发展的重要催化剂。正确的体制和政策可以避免通常所说的"自然资源的诅咒"。这一点在非洲的一些国家已经得到证明,非洲国家有理由保持这种谨慎乐观的态度,原因就是一些国家已经从过去资源热潮中吸取教训,并将在未来继续坚持,使他们充分享受其自然资源财富益处的战略和政策。

Key to Exercises

Ⅰ.

1. Although Africa has about 15 percent of the world's population, it consumes only 3 percent of global commercial energy. The paradox is that Africa's share in global energy production is about 12 percent, and trending upwards.

2. Reasons for the rise in oil prices since 2000 include rising demand in emerging economies, especially in China and India, declining spare capacity in major producing countries, peaking of production in several important oil – producing areas, and lack of expansion in refinery capacity.

3. Considering the current uncertainties about energy supply, the key drivers of future demand, the policies of consumer countries (especially with respect to nuclear and other alternatives to oil and gas), and expected future global economic growth and technology development, there is need to clearly establish Africa's position and develop strategies for future supply adequacy.

4. A key concern regarding the governance of oil and gas resources is that the governments of African oil – and gas – producing countries receive an inadequate share of the large rents from production.

5. Natural resource export earnings actually sever important links between the people and their governments—links that are related to popular interests and control mechanisms.

Ⅱ. 1 ~ 5. CAADA   6 ~ 10. CAACC

Ⅲ. 1 ~ 5. CDBCC

Ⅳ.

1. 20 世纪 70 年代末,世界能源市场发生了巨变,对世界经济与政治产生了深远的影响。

2. 如果不策略地、积极地处理此难题,伴随能源价格的上涨,随之而来的能源短缺将给非洲的石油净进口国家造成很大压力。

3. 非洲的富油田及勘探前景使它成为全球石油生产和资源开采的重要参与者和重要目标。

4. 石油和天然气资源管理的一个关键问题是非洲的石油和天然气生产国政府从生产商收到租金份额不足。

5. 尽管面临诸多问题和挑战,在合适的条件下,石油和天然气资源的繁荣可能成为(经济)增长和发展的重要催化剂。

　V.

1. 非洲大陆有54个国家,2000年年中估计人口8.05亿。根据2008年能源调查统计,截至2007年年底,非洲已探明石油储量为1.17481亿桶,占世界石油储量的9.49%,2007年该地区平均日产1031.76万桶原油,占全球总产量的12.5%。

2. 非洲五国主导上游石油生产,总计占非洲大陆石油产量的85%,按照产量递减分别是尼日利亚、利比亚、阿尔及利亚、埃及和安哥拉。其他的石油生产国有加蓬、刚果、喀麦隆、突尼西亚、赤道几内亚、刚果民主共和国及科特迪瓦。非洲许多国家为了增加石油产量正在进行石油勘探。

第4章 石油,政治和经济

4.1 石油与中东地区的国际关系

🔲 导语

石油是影响中东国家和西方关系一个很重要的因素。本课探讨了几个西方国家包括美国、法国和意大利对中东地区的外交案例。这些国家一直变换其外交政策,旨在获得大量的廉价石油。另一方面,中东国家也试图利用石油资源来获得利益,甚至为了制裁西方国家,阿拉伯国家使用"石油武器",对支持以色列的西方国家实行石油禁运。

🔲 课文

石油是影响中东国家国际关系的一个非常重要的因素,涉及区域关系,或联盟国家之间的关系,也影响整个国际关系。国际关系是指发达国家和其他发展中国家的关系。

西方国家和阿拉伯石油

很明显,从大量的历史文献中可知,对石油的攫取是英国及随后的美国对中东地区态度变化的关键。我们已经注意到,中东地区国家制度的形成,以及其他重要国家在中东的政策几乎都与石油有着千丝万缕的联系。例如,伊拉克独立这一重要事件,最终是以服从伊拉克石油公司的利益达成,还有伊朗摩萨台政府的瓦解虽然不完全是,但最初却与其对盎格鲁—伊朗石油公司的国有化有关。同样,美国与沙特阿拉伯和伊朗过去结盟、将来也会继续结盟,虽然这种结盟在很多情况下存在问题,但源于石油这种结盟是不可避免的。后者(美国)接着在伊朗财团中纳入美国公司来发展自己,这使摩萨台的灭亡和穆罕默德·礼萨·巴列维国王的回归成为可能,并结束盎格鲁—伊朗公司的垄断,迫使它与其他几个公司,主要是美国公司一起控制(伊朗)(盎格鲁—伊朗公司更名为英国石油公司)。

其他国家的外交也取决于石油,虽然程度不大,只因为他们的资产少,所以他们更愿意重新洗牌而不是维持目前的秩序。于是,法国试图掌控阿尔及利亚,并尽可能保护在阿联酋的国际金融理财师的利益,除此之外,法国还尽量与"盎格鲁—撒克逊人"(即英国人的代名词)不同,他们强调与产油国之间的合作。其例证是法国 1972 年立即接受了伊拉克的国有化；1974 年拒绝成为在巴黎成立的国际能源机构会员国；并在后来的国际能源论坛上推出了一个"（建立）国际经济新秩序"的外交举措。最终，此举削弱了美国对伊朗的制裁。

意大利也积极建立一个国家能源石油公司，即埃尼集团，该公司是意大利对阿拉伯国家外交的主要推动者，致使意大利积极支持阿尔及利亚解放战争（1962 年，埃尼集团前总裁恩里科·马太的飞机坠毁，曾怀疑其炸弹是由法国特务机构安置），也支持穆罕默德·礼萨·巴列维国王在与摩萨台发生冲突时逃离伊朗，并与利比亚的关系密切。最近，埃尼集团无视美国对伊朗的禁运，并模仿法国，与伊拉克的萨达姆侯赛关系密切，但它没有得到多少回报。事实上，不管怎样，这些尝试都不是很成功；埃尼集团获得的最大好处是从苏联购买石油（此举使美国大怒），及在埃及的西奈半岛勘探石油。

石油也影响中东地区的外交，大多数情况下，在中东至少与石油相关的外交手段不能产生预期结果。最近几年，石油更频繁地被用来作为一种工具，而不是作为一个目标：从美国对伊朗和利比亚的禁运，以及联合国对伊拉克实施的禁运中得以见证。通常情况下，工业强国们为了追求政治特权，使其获得石油变得更加困难。他们不仅需要石油物丰价廉，而且政治上也要是正确的，有这样的感觉，石油来源国的政府还得对我们很友好。尽管没有任何经验能够证明，一个朋友（国家）生产的石油会更可靠或更便宜，但许多人似乎相信确实有（政治）优先或（政治）要求，并按照政治亲近程度将石油生产国划分等级。

中东石油出口国及国际关系

中东石油生产国自然地注意到石油对于大国的重要性，并尝试利用这一优势获得安全保证和先进的武器装备以应付内外挑战。应对内部挑战的保障是由美国总统吉米·卡特在伊朗提出的，他坚持基本人权和民主，接着任由巴列维政权倒台，大多数观察家至今认为其后果是灾难性的。

不太明显的一点是，事实上石油对石油生产国（中东）外交政策的影响并不那么显著。国际石油政策是由石油和能源部长来负责，通常此人被公认为一名技术人员，阿拉伯石油输出国家组织（欧佩克）或其他类似的论坛会讨论国际石油政策，但讨论的不过是人为设置狭隘的、技术层面的问题。唯一例外是在 1973 年会议上有人试图利用石油作为武器，此提议是短命的决定，而石油从来没有真正短缺过。

1973 年 10 月，以色列与其阿拉伯邻国之间爆发战争，阿拉伯石油输出国组织（欧佩克）宣布对美国和荷兰禁运。石油市场价格迅速上升，立即引起第一次"能源危机"。事实上,禁运是虚构的,直到1974年,中东石油生产一直稳步而快速地增长。由于油价上涨所引发的经济衰退和石油需求下降,致使次年中东石油产量下滑。实际上,石油从未作为武器使用过。然而,评论家仍然指出,欧佩克的决定是危险的先例,证明了海湾地区石油供应的不可靠性。

从刺激价格上涨的角度来看,此决定是成功的,但政治上是灾难性的失败,海湾地区的石油生产国至今仍感到后悔。事实上,认为海湾地区的石油供应不安全和不可靠的看法只是基于欧佩克的决定,自那时起,海湾产油国已经不止一次地证明他们能够提供所需的全部石油,甚至那些存在冲突的地区也是如此。

🔲 Key to Exercises

Ⅰ.

1. Oil is a very important factor in the international relations of the Middle Eastern states, both with respect to regional, or inter – Arab relations, and with respect to international relations at large—that is, relations with industrial and other developing countries.

2. Thus France attempted to hold on to Algeria, and did what was necessary to protect the interests of CFP (today's Total) in the UAE. Other examples of this are France's immediate acceptance of the Iraqi nationalization in 1972; refusal to become member of the IEA when it was established, in Paris, in 1974; promotion of diplomatic initiatives for a "new international economic order" and later for the International Energy Forum; finally, the active undermining of US sanctions against Iran.

3. Many industrial powers seem to believe that there is need to rank suppliers in accordance to political proximity, oil needs not only to be abundant and cheap, but also to come from a country whose government is friendly to them.

4. At the outbreak of war between Israel and its Arab neighbors in October 1973, the Organization of Arab Oil Exporting Countries (OAPEC) declared an embargo against the United States and the Netherlands. Prices increased rapidly on oil markets, precipitating the first "energy crises."

5. The guarantee against internal challenges was "lifted" from Iran by US President Jimmy Carter, who wanted to uphold basic human rights and democracy, and thus allowed the Pahlavi regime to collapse—with consequences that

most observers would consider quite disastrous, to this date.

II. 1~5. AACBD   6~10. DCBCB

III. 1~5. ACCCD

IV.

1. 我们已经注意到,中东地区国家制度的形成,以及其他重要国家在中东的政策几乎都与石油有着千丝万缕的联系。

2. 其他国家的外交也取决于石油,虽然程度不大,只因为他们的资产少,所以他们更愿意重新洗牌而不是维持目前的秩序。

3. 石油也影响中东地区的外交,大多数情况下,在中东至少与石油相关的外交手段不能产生预期结果。

4. 不太明显的一点是,事实上石油对石油生产国(中东)外交政策的影响并不那么显著。

5. 从刺激价格上涨的角度来看此决定是成功的,但政治上是灾难性的失败,海湾地区的石油生产国至今仍感到后悔。

V.

1. 战后结束了阿吉普恩里科·马泰对公司的管理,计划将其转换成一个国家垄断的公司,更名为埃尼公司。这个名字来源于公司最初的全名国家碳化氢公司的缩写。该公司于1953年2月10日由意大利政府批准成立,目的是集合国家所有的能源事宜于一身,落实国家能源战略。埃尼集团为意大利提供能源供应,并为国家的工业发展作出贡献。

2. 阿拉伯石油输出国组织是一个多国政府的组织,总部设在科威特,该组织负责协调阿拉伯产油国之间的能源政策,其主要目的是发展。

4.2   英美在中东的主要外交政策

导语

从历史的角度看,西方国家一直试图控制中东,以获得大量廉价的石油资源。第一次世界大战后,英法为了维护其利益试图分裂中东国家,以防止其成为独立强大的阿拉伯国家。随后美国成为世界霸主,在1957年,美国推出了适应中东外交的艾森豪威尔主义来抵制苏联的势力。

课文

第二次世界大战以来,美国是在中东起主导作用的世界强国。美国政策的每一次转变,每一次军事干预,中央情报局实施的每一个密谋的主要目标是:确保得到廉价而丰富的石油——世界上最重要的能源。尽管在中亚发现了新的石油储量,中东仍占世界已探明石油储量的三分之二,中东地区仍是最廉价的石油供应地。正如劳伦斯考伯关于科威特和胡萝卜的论述明确指出,不先理解"黑色黄金"在战略上和经济中的重要性,就不理解今天中东地区发生的一切。

美国一直依赖在伊朗、沙特阿拉伯、以色列的残暴专制的政权做不光彩的勾当。美国利用中央情报局煽动推翻"不友好"的政权。必要时,美国会直接干预,惩罚那些挑战其霸主地位的政府——如1991年的对伊战争。

奥斯曼帝国瓦解后,英国和法国在完全没有该地区人民参与的情况下,划分了中东新国家的界限。英国废弃了在第一次世界大战期间对各地方领导人做出的关于阿拉伯独立的所有承诺。在1919年的和平会议上,当战胜国坐下瓜分战利品时,他们心目中最重要的要求是保持该地区的分裂,以便更容易控制它。

私营石油公司积极推动他们的政府宣布放弃战时对阿拉伯人所有的承诺。因为石油商看得很清楚,关于石油开采权和特许权使用费的谈判,与中东地区一个强大的独立的阿拉伯国家相比,一群缺乏团结意识的对手会更容易对付。

英国控制了伊拉克、科威特和沙特阿拉伯。法国控制了叙利亚和黎巴嫩。当地的国王和酋长接手各自的国家,他们受英国的庇护得到了地位。科威特移交给萨巴赫家族。英国许诺哈希姆侯赛因国王建立阿拉伯联合共和国之后,授予他为约旦王。英国为伊本沙特阿拉伯命名——世界上唯一以其统治家族名字命名的国家。法国使黎巴嫩处于少数基督教群体掌握之中。

记者格伦弗兰克尔描述了英国高级专员柯利达爵士考克斯1922年在巴格达会议上如何解决伊拉克、科威特和沙特阿拉伯之间的边境问题。

经历了艰苦的五天的会议没有任何妥协迹象。于是,英国在巴格达的代表考克斯于1922年11月末一个夜晚,把谢赫·阿齐兹伊本沙特召见到帐下,很快他成为沙特阿拉伯的统治者,这些可以说明英国拆分战败奥斯曼帝国残余力量的事实。

伊拉克、沙特阿拉伯和科威特的现代边界是由大英帝国在人所共知的尤夸尔会议上确立的。

在此会议上有一个独特的例外。在1917年英国的"贝尔福宣言"中,英国承诺支持在巴勒斯坦建立一个"犹太民族家园"。英国将成为战后新型国家的保护国,支持犹太移民到巴勒斯坦,希望建立一个"阿拉伯世界的安全战略前哨"。尽管亚瑟·贝尔福勋爵是反犹太主义者,但他和英国统治阶级其他成员认识到建立一个殖民定居地前哨的价值,殖民地定居者依赖英国的支持,可能成为英国在该地区利益的忠实保护者。然而,前哨的价值并未充分显现出来,直到1948年以色列成立后的几年后,美国从中充分获益。

第二次世界大战之后,在中东地区,美国迅速成为头号强国。在此期间,美国的政策主要集中在中东地区国家不受民族主义政权的控制。他们在伊朗第一次感觉到这种威胁,获得民众广泛支持的穆罕默德摩萨台民选成为伊朗总统,对英国独资的盎格鲁—伊朗石油公司实行国有化。中情局克米特罗斯福策划政变,摩萨台被推翻,由伊朗国王取而代之。伊朗国王获得了美国的大量帮助和臭名昭著的野蛮秘密警察组织萨瓦克(伊朗国家安全情报组织)的支持。

具有讽刺意味的是,在美国中央情报局的默许下,1952年埃及发生了政变,民族主义军官贾迈勒·阿卜杜纳赛尔上台,美国担心埃及可能成为一个泛阿拉伯民主运动的中心。在遏制苏联的冷战时期,美国在中东的利益受到压制,然而很明显,任何政权试图摆脱美国的控制,无论其是否与苏联有联系,都被认为是一种威胁。在1957年,艾森豪威尔主义宣称,美国"准备使用武装力量协助"任何一个中东国家,"要求援助,反对来自受国际共产主义控制的任何国家的武装侵略"。

艾森豪威尔主义反映了华盛顿对纳赛尔转向东欧获得武器的愤怒。美国拒绝装备埃及,除非它同意加入美国发起的巴格达条约,此条约是以美国主导的一个地区安全协议。艾森豪威尔主义很快就经受考验,因为该地区一系列事态发展似乎预示着一个民族主义浪潮的到来。在约旦,侯赛因国王面临新当选亲纳赛尔议会的威胁。1958年,埃及和叙利亚联合组成阿拉伯联合共和国。在黎巴嫩,阿拉伯穆斯林民族主义者领导了一场斗争,反对卡米尔夏蒙为首的少数基督教政权。对美国来说,更重要的是,同年伊拉克民族主义者的军事政变推翻了亲英独裁者努里·赛义德。在中东地区,这一事件被视为对美国威信的严重打击,并威胁到美国的石油利益。

美国政府担心伊拉克新政权可能重申科威特的历史索赔,科威特是由英国批准建立的小国,为了防止大国(伊拉克)控制并成为当时海湾地区最大的产油区。美国国务卿约翰·福斯特·杜勒斯街、参谋长联席会议主席南桑·特维宁和中央情报局局长艾伦·杜勒斯在一次紧急会议上达成的一份备忘录宣称,如果美国不干预,"美国将失去影响力","根基"就会受到"威胁",美国的信誉将受到"整个世界的质疑",美国也担心民族主义会威胁其在科威特和伊拉克利润丰厚的石油利益。

黎巴嫩夏蒙担心其失去权力,因此根据艾森豪威尔主义要求美国援助。目标是对付伊拉克,美国抓住了这个机会并宣布了核警报。当伊拉克新政权宣布保证"履行其义务",美国撤出部队。

Key to Exercises

I .

1. The world's most important energy resource—oil.

2. For the oilmen of Britain saw only too well that oil concessions and royalties would be easier to negotiate with a series of rival Arab states lacking any sense of unity, than with a powerful independent Arab state in the Middle East.

3. The 1917 Balfour Declaration had committed Britain to supporting the formation of a "national home for the Jewish people" in Palestine.

4. In 1957 Eisenhower Doctrine declared that the United States was "prepared to use armed forces to assist" any Middle Eastern country "requesting assistance against armed aggression from any country controlled by international communism. "

5. U. S. officials feared that the new Iraqi regime might reassert its historical claim on Kuwait.

II . 1 ~ 5. CBACC   6 ~ 10. BDADC

III. 1 ~ 5. CCBAC

IV.

1. 美国政策的每一次转变,每一次军事干预,中央情报局实施的每一个密谋的主要目标是:确保得到廉价而丰富的石油——世界上最重要的能源。

2. 奥斯曼帝国瓦解后,英国和法国在完全没有该地区人民参与的情况下,划分了中东新国家的界限。

3. 第二次世界大战之后,在中东地区,美国迅速成为头号强国。

4. 在遏制苏联的冷战时期,美国在中东的利益受到压制,然而很明显,任何政权试图摆脱美国的控制,无论其是否与苏联有联系,都被认为是一种威胁。

5. 在中东地区,这一事件被视为对美国威信的严重打击,并威胁到美国的石油利益。

V.

1. 艾森豪威尔主义这一术语,是总统德怀特·戴维·艾森豪威尔于1957 年 1 月 5 日在"向国会提出关于中东的特别咨文"的讲话中提出。按照艾森豪威尔主义,如果中东的国家受到另外一个国家的武装侵略威胁时,它可以要求美国提供以经济和军事援助。

2. 贝尔福宣称支持在巴勒斯坦建立一个犹太家园,但保证不伤害巴勒斯坦非犹太民族的权力。盟军作战的其他国家支持该声明。

4.3 中国石油需求和亚太地区石油地缘政治

导语

随着中国经济的高速发展,中国对石油的需求增加显著,并有可能进一步增加。因此,大量进口石油是满足需求增长的解决方法。另一方面,中国试图多元化其石油供应和运输路线,可能会导致与日本和其他亚洲国家产生严重冲突。尽管存在与最重要的邻邦(日本、韩国、印度)发生冲突的危险,但也可以加强合作,协调地利用资源。

课文

国际能源事务领域一位著名专家曾说过:"中国能源需求的快速增长对全球商品市场和商品价格产生了重大影响,在中国,日益增长的能源需求造成了新的能源危机和能源紧张。事实上,中国政府选择以何种方式处理其能源紧张将不仅影响中国经济,而且影响全球经济。现今,中国的能源需求具有全球意义,在中国为了进口俄罗斯石油与日本的竞争中得以见证。在未来20年,美国、中国和日本最终将争夺中东原油。中国十分依赖进口国外石油,因此中国在中东将发挥越来越重要的作用,在中亚、西非及世界上可以满足中国日益增长的能源需求的其他地区也将如此"。

中国能源:需求极大

近年来,中国经济增长强劲,导致其石油消费量显著增加。例如,1995年到2005年之间,石油需求翻了一番,达到680万桶/日。2003年以来,中国石油消耗已超过日本,同年成为世界第二大石油消费国。2004年,中国消耗660万桶/日,虽只是美国消费的三分之一(2050万桶/日),但仍比上年增长16%。

1993以来,中国成为石油净进口国,因此,中国大大增加了对外采购。2004年,石油总进口(原油和石油产品)上升到340万桶/日,占国家(石油)消费的一半以上。2000年,进口仅190万桶/日,相当于消费总量的38%。

预计,中国未来几十年石油需求将全方位强劲增长,最重要的是,石油进口将大幅增加。到2020年,消费量可能达到1200万桶/日,到2030年,可达到1600万桶/日,进口增加更为迅速,2020年进口达700万桶/日,2030年达到1100万桶/日。总之,根据绝大多数的预测,接下来25年,中国原油消耗可能翻一番,石油进口将是目前的三倍。接下来20年,中国石油消耗可能平均每年会增加约4.5%,预计是西方发达国家石油消耗增长的四倍以上。

石油消费和石油进口的增长由几个因素造成:与1980年到2004年期间GDP增长率为9.5%相比,未来二三十年每年约6%~7%的GDP高增长率。其他重要因素包括能源密集型工业产业的发展,中国车辆数目急剧增加(从2004年两千万辆增至2020年一亿三千万辆),及减少相对低效及污染极大的煤能源使用的需求。

如果中国的石油进口量从现今的400万桶/日增加到2020年的700万桶/日,到2025年的800万桶/日,2030年至110万桶/日,这种增长速度将影响全球原油的利用率和价格。中国已经在积极寻求本国以外的石油(和天然气),在未来几年里这种探求无疑将加速,将影响并改变亚太地区及世界各地的石油和能源地缘政治。

中国不断增长的石油需求深刻地改变了国际特别是亚太地区的能源地缘政治。最近石油消费的增长,及预测石油进口的增加(尤其是来自中东),导致中国领导人极其关注国家的能源安全。他们以多种不同方式回应。特别是他们通过寻找新的供应来源,控制采购和运输通道,极力地促进国内生产,下决心提高石油进口的安全性和可靠性。这已经造成与美国和其他石油消费大国,如日本、印度以及与其他亚太国家的紧张局势,并可能导致进一步的争端。然而,加强大东亚经济体之间的合作(中国、日本和韩国)也是一种可能。

中国和亚太地区石油地缘政治:中国因素

因为中国日益关注美国在中东的霸权(预计到2025年,中国70%的石油进口来源于中东——是目前比例的两倍),因此,地缘政治的影响将尤为激烈,中国也十分关注脆弱的石油运输,石油运输大部分要通过霍尔木兹海峡和马六甲海峡由海路到达中国。尤其是,中国计划使其石油供应多元化,从俄罗斯、中亚、西非和拉丁美洲进口更多的石油,并尽一切可能确保原油进口运输通道的安全。

中国努力控制和提高石油供应,将对亚洲及世界各地的能源地缘政治产生重要影响。中国也将成为国际能源地缘政治中一个重要和活跃的力量。中国与产油国的能源贸易将使中国在这些国家中产生更大的经济、政治和军事影响。而中国在其东部和南海的领土要求,可能会导致与一些邻国的冲突。例如,建设俄罗斯和中亚的石油和天然气管道有可能和日本产生冲突。在陆地和海洋上寻找替代马六甲海峡(即现在的四分之三的中国石油进口的线路)的(运输)要塞,导致与泰国、缅甸和印度尼西亚保持战略友好关系。在印度洋和中国南海通道的海军护航可能会导致与印度、越南和美国的紧张局势。此外,不惜代价地增加国内生产已经并将继续导致中国在领土争端问题上采取坚定立场,包括对中国东海(尤其是钓鱼岛及其附属岛屿,日本称其为尖阁列岛)、中国南海(尤其是南沙群岛)的主权。在这个问题上的强硬立场可能导致与日本和其他东亚国家的紧张局势。

然而,尽管因为石油竞争,亚太地区地缘政治紧张局势确实有加剧的趋势,但该地区务实的国家就能源问题有可能达成加强合作的协议。最终会有一天,中国、日本、韩国甚至印度将分享共同利益,也就是他们都希望减少对中东石油的依赖及增加天然气的消费比例。

关于石油消费和石油进口问题,亚太地区是正在走向一个日益竞争的时代,还是相反走向一个更密切的能源合作时代,下结论还为时尚早。无论如何,在未来几年,是合作还是竞争,很大程度上取决于中国的战略决策。

Key to Exercises

I.

1. In 2004, China consumed 6.6 million bbl/d, still only a third of US consumption (20.5 million bbl/d), but nonetheless a 16% increase over the previous year.

2. In short, according to the vast majority of forecasts, China could more than double its consumption of crude and treble its oil imports over the next quarter of a century. China could increase its oil consumption by an average of about 4.5% a year over the next two decades, more than quadrupling the consumption increases forecast for developed western countries.

3. This rise in consumption and in oil imports will be the result of several factors, including rapid GDP growth of about 6% – 7% a year over the next two or three decades, energy – intensive industrial sector and the need to reduce the relative weight in energy consumption of inefficient and extremely polluting coal.

4. The construction of oil and gas pipelines from Russian and central Asia could also lead to conflict with Japan, and China take a firmer stance on territorial issues, including its sovereignty in the East China Sea (especially the Diaoyu islands, known as the Senkaku islands to the Japanese).

5. It is still early to determine whether the Asia Pacific region is headed towards an era of increasing rivalries or, on the contrary, towards an era of greater cooperation on energy issues, particularly those involving the consumption and importation of oil.

Ⅱ. 1 ~ 5. BADCA　6 ~ 10. CDCAB

Ⅲ. 1 ~ 5. BDCCA

Ⅳ.

1. 中国不断增长的石油需求深刻地改变了国际特别是亚太地区的能源地缘政治。

2. 未来20年,中国在中东将发挥越来越重要的作用,因为中国非常依赖进口国外石油,如中亚、西非和在世界上可以满足中国日益增长的能源需求的其他地区。

3. 事实上,北京选择以何种方式处理其能源紧张不仅影响中国经济,而且影响全球经济。

4. 尤其是,中国计划多元化其石油供应,从俄罗斯、中亚、西非和拉丁美洲进口更多的石油,并尽一切可能确保原油进口的运输通道的安全。

5. 中国努力控制和提高石油供应,将对亚洲及世界各地的能源地缘政治将产生重要影响。

Ⅴ.

1. 增加能源产量是远远不够的,尽管中国煤炭和天然气能够自给自足,但石油却难以实现自给自足。虽然在中国煤炭供应占能源消耗近70%,但近年来石油消费的相对比重显著增加,尽管其比重远低于其他亚洲国家。

2. 20世纪90年代中后期,一项研究指出,中国日益增长的石油需求和不断增长的原油进口具有战略意义,特别是关于中国与中东、中亚、俄罗斯和东亚的其他国家的关系方面。

第5章 石油监管

5.1 石油生产国的财政规则和财政责任立法

导语

在石油生产国,财政规则和财政责任立法限制整体的财政政策,因此,它们起着很重要的作用。一般说来,石油生产国适当的财政规则的设计比其他国家更具挑战性,虽然石油生产国的财政规则和财政责任立法的经验相对有限,但越来越多的国家开始实施财政规则和财政责任立法。

课文

在宏观经济背景下,财政规则定义为旨在长期拟定财政政策的设计和实施的体制机制。它们往往被载入宪法或法律,如财政责任法。有些国家选择非正式的财政准则。不同国家的财政规则和财政责任立法设计差异很大,其中主要的差异在于,以量化指标为标准数值规则之间的差异,这一差异指导绩效并以绩效为基准(如财政平衡或债务);以及因为程序规则建立透明度、适用范围和问责制的要求不同。

石油生产国财政规则和财政责任立法的应用

在石油生产国,财政规则和财政责任立法经常神圣地记载着要求降低财政政策的顺周期性和(或)要求促进长期储蓄和可持续发展的目标。虽然石油基金是比较常见的,财政规则和财政责任立法却有更重要的作用,因为它们的目的是约束整体的财政政策。

石油生产国适当的财政规则设计比其他国家更具挑战性。这归因于石油收入的特点:高度的不稳定性和不确定性以及对非再生资源的依赖。因此,在其他国家经常使用的财政规则在石油生产国的适用性令人质疑。例如,或以特定的整体为目标、或以主要的结余为目标、或以特定的占国内生产总值的负债比率为目标的规则,可能会是高度顺周期的,因为它们会使油价波动,进而影响开支和非油平衡。

石油生产国的财政规则和财政责任立法过去的经验相对有限,但越来越多的国家开始实施财政规则和财政责任立法。只有少数石油生产国有财政责任立法。20 世纪 90 年代初,艾伯塔省是最早和较全面的一个。2002

年,厄瓜多尔推出财政责任立法,但主要侧重于数值财政规则。1999年,委内瑞拉通过有机预算法,朝着改善财政政策和问责制迈出了一步。2006年墨西哥也通过了财政责任立法。从设置数值财政规则或准则的国家情况来看,目标通常置于非油平衡(挪威和东帝汶)、整体平衡(艾伯塔省和墨西哥)、支出(赤道几内亚)或几个财政变量(厄瓜多尔)。

挪威和艾伯塔省采取了不同的体制框架,虽然面临着挑战,但在管理财政政策方面都较为成功。挪威实施了相对灵活的框架,使用非石油赤字作为锚,艾伯塔省则推出全面的财政责任立法。这两种情况有共同之处:强有力的机构和就主张财政纪律方面达成广泛的共识。

(1)根据挪威2001年推出的财政准则,中央政府的结构性非石油赤字不得超过石油基金总金融资产的4%,非石油赤字相当于基金积累金融资产预期的长远回报的真实收益率。准则允许反周期财政政策的偏差和对石油基金价值的冲击,准则被视为一种工具,这种工具有助于建立财政政策的长期基准,削减开支的压力,并使预算免受石油价格波动的影响。尽管油价上涨时挪威一直保持适度的支出增长,框架允许一定程度的顺周期性,高油价导致大量金融资产的积累,这反过来又可能导致非石油赤字上升。此外,到目前为止尚不符合财政准则,随着时间的推移,这可能会减少财政准则的信誉和加大支出压力。

(2)继20世纪80年代末的财政状况恶化,艾伯塔省在20世纪90年代初进行了重大的财政调整。整个省通过了全面财政责任立法(1993—1995年)加强财政政策,防止未来出现赤字,到2025年消除省级债务。随着时间的推移,财政责任立法规则已收紧,需要每年平衡预算(自1999年以来)和无净债务(自2005年以来)。考虑到投资支出造成的不断上涨的公众压力,以及如何避免过度扩张的财政政策,近年来财政责任立法的重点已经转移到如何更好地管理额外的石油收入,这在一定程度上反映了艾伯塔省整体收支平衡框架的重点:形成顺周期政策。

其他石油生产国的经验,主要是财政规则方面的,强调有效和持久的规则实施中的困难——主要是因为设计问题和政治经济因素。特别是,财政政策问题已主要集中在短期约束,导致过于僵化难以适应经济波动和缺乏强有力的政治支持。最近油价上涨,减少了流动性紧缩,使一些国家难以控制政府支出压力。

某些情况下,财政规则或框架已随着时间的推移而减弱或被忽视。特别是:

(1)2002年,厄瓜多尔推出了财政责任立法,其中包括三个财政规则,分别侧重中央政府的非油平衡、主要开支的实质增长和公共债务占 GDP 比例。立法旨在帮助改善财政状况,管理较高的石油收入,减少支出的顺周期性。然而,财政结果往往与赤字和支出规则背道而驰。公共债务比率的约束得到了满足,部分是因为近年来石油价格大幅度的上升(名义国内生产总值的相应增加)。最后,当流动性约束减弱,不断增长的政治和社会压力导致在2005 年修订财政责任立法并放宽对支出的约束。

(2)根据目前的开支不应超过非油收入的支出规则,近年来,赤道几内亚却一直反其道而行之。这个规则被重新解释为一个中期目标,以及与非油收入相比,开支大幅增长且增长过快。鉴于近年来赤道几内亚石油行业迅速扩大(超过国内生产总值的 80%),规则不再为财政政策提供现实的基准。

(3)1999 年,委内瑞拉通过公共财政的有机法律,旨在加强财政政策和减少支出的波动性。法律侧重于改进预算过程,包括使用多年的框架,并推行为了当前平衡、开支增长和公共债务的财政规则。然而,该法的实施已被推迟,而支出仍与石油收入密切相关。此外,预算机构质量已经恶化,部分是因为预算外资金的分散和准财政活动的扩散。

Key to Exercises

I.

1. In OPCs, fiscal rules and FRL often enshrine a desire to reduce the procyclicality of fiscal policy and/or to promote long – term savings and sustainability objectives. Fiscal rules and FRL can have a more critical role due to their constraint on overall fiscal policy.

2. While Norway implemented a relatively flexible framework, using the non – oil deficit as an anchor, Alberta introduced comprehensive FRL.

3. The focus in recent years has shifted to how best to manage the additional oil revenues, given rising public pressures for investment spending, and how to avoid an excessively expansionary fiscal policy.

4. Ecuador introduced FRL in 2002, which included three fiscal rules focused on the central government's non – oil balance, primary expenditure growth in real terms, and the public debt ratio to GDP. The legislation was intended to help improve the fiscal position, manage higher oil revenues, and reduce the procyclicality of expenditures.

5. a proliferation of extra budgetary funds and quasi – fiscal activities.

Ⅱ.1~5. BBCDC 6~10. ACBAB

Ⅲ.1~5. CACDB

Ⅳ.

1. 在石油生产国,财政规则和财政责任立法经常神圣地记载着要求降低财政政策的顺周期性和(或)要求促进长期储蓄和可持续发展的目标。

2. 准则允许反周期财政政策的偏差和对石油基金价值的冲击,准则被视为一种工具,这种工具有助于建立财政政策的长期基准,削减开支的压力,并使预算免受石油价格波动的影响。

3. 立法旨在帮助改善财政状况,管理较高的石油收入,减少支出的顺周期性。

4. 鉴于近年来赤道几内亚石油行业迅速扩大(超过国内生产总值的80%),规则不再为财政政策提供现实的基准。

5. 此外,预算机构质量已经恶化,部分是因为预算外资金的分散和准财政活动的扩散。

Ⅴ.

1. 首府埃德蒙顿(Edmonton)位于艾伯塔省的地理中心,是加拿大最靠近北面的大城市,同时也是加拿大北方资源开发的大门和补给中心。由于接近加拿大最大的油田,加拿大西部的炼油厂大多聚集此地。艾伯塔省是加拿大常规原油、合成原油、天然气和天然气产品最大的生产地。

2. 财政规则,引起了越来越多的关注,许多国家都采取了一些规则。目前的财政政策规则设计和实施相当多样。而盎格鲁撒克逊国家,主要侧重透明度;欧洲大陆(经济货币同盟稳定与增长公约,瑞士的建议)和新兴市场经济体则依靠一套性能指标的数值参考值(目标、限制)进行设计和实施财政政策规则。

5.2　中东石油生产和石油政策

🔲 导语

中东石油生产对于世界能源供应发挥着至关重要的作用。本课文介绍了四个主要海湾产油国的产油史及其产油的兴衰经历。由于阿拉伯和以色列的民族紧张关系是影响产油国和其他大国石油外交的一个关键因素。因此,中东国家有必要调整与世界其他各国的关系,特别是加强与新兴亚洲经济体的紧密联系,来促进在该地区石油工业的发展。

课文

中东在国际石油行业中起着独特的作用。中东五个海湾产油国拥有世界已探明石油储量的 65% 。如果石油是一个竞争性的行业,迄今为止中东生产的石油是最廉价的,并几乎独占世界石油市场。然而,石油不是竞争性的行业,中东在全球石油产量中占据的份额一直不大,远低于其在全球储备中所占的份额。多年来,伊拉克的石油产量尤其如此,原因是伊拉克与世界其他地区关系紧张。

伊朗是海湾地区第一个输出石油的国家,直到 1950 年,伊朗一直以出口位居第一而骄傲。同年,控制伊朗全部石油生产的盎格鲁—伊朗公司和伊朗国民政府总理穆罕默德·摩萨台之间发生了争论。随后,盎格鲁·伊朗公司国有化,所有的国际石油企业抵制伊朗石油;伊朗石油产量暴跌,到1952 年和 1953 年其产量几乎为零,直到推翻摩萨台的政变发生及伊朗联盟形成后,生产才得以恢复,而盎格鲁—伊朗公司的产量减少到 40% 。

伊拉克于 1928 年开始生产石油,因为伊拉克石油公司(IPC)和伊拉克政府之间持续争论,其产量保持较低水平。沙特阿拉伯于 1938 年开始生产,战争期间产量受到限制,1945 年后产量才突飞猛进。科威特于 1946 年才开始生产,但产量增长速度非常迅速,并在 1953 年超过沙特阿拉伯的产量。这三个国家——伊拉克、沙特阿拉伯和科威特产量的迅速增加,弥补了 1951 年伊朗的产量暴跌;沙特阿拉伯和科威特的产量依然很高,而伊拉克的产量减少。1973 年,科威特的产量达到最高值——300 万桶/日,此后产量下降。伊拉克入侵后到 1991 年时,产量减少到几乎为零,此后产量恢复。伊朗产量在1974 年达到了高峰,并在 1979 年伊斯兰革命后急剧下降。1980 年两伊战争爆发后,其产量继续下降,1988 年战争结束后恢复生产。两伊战争之前,伊拉克产量在 1979 年达到高峰。战争的最后阶段恢复生产,1990 年入侵科威特时生产再次崩溃。伊拉克在联合国"石油换食品"计划中恢复生产,当(西方)联盟侵略及占领伊拉克后,2003 年其生产再次崩溃。1980 年,沙特阿拉伯的产量达到顶峰,弥补了伊朗和伊拉克石油减产的损失。此后,其产量主要受到欧佩克配额的限制。

谈到中东,石油问题是不可回避的。它影响了中东地区与世界其他国家,尤其是与几个强国的关系。尽管以美国为首的势力仍一再否认他们侵略伊拉克,其目的是解放石油行业及确保其在中东的石油利益。从企业的角度来看,美国和英国的主要能源与工程公司是借此巨大机遇获得益处,并凭此进入伊拉克市场。随着联合国解除对伊拉克的制裁——允许投资,石油利益很可能发挥了重要作用。在这一问题上,法国威胁联合国,否决美国为首的战争,这与法国石油公司道达尔在伊拉克股份总额最多的事实相关。开采伊拉克油田对俄罗斯和中国的公司也具有重大意义。因为投资分布不均匀,解除对伊制裁的政策影响了区域关系,相反,高度集中的投资使富油国和贫油国之间形成非常鲜明的两极分化。此政策对阿拉伯国家的国内政治产生了影响,在没有石油租金的情况下,阿拉伯国家稳定的政权也不可能存活到21世纪。

通常情况下,产油国外交一直努力追求的目标与其作为重要石油出口国的地位毫不相关,而是促进伊斯兰教或反对以色列的斗争、泛阿拉伯主义、形式稍微温和的泛非主义或纯粹的军事扩张。事实上,使石油生产国深陷困境的大多数问题应归咎于他们不明智的外交政策。即使在海湾国家,其中有比伊拉克冒险行为更为有害的事件,利比亚(洛克比空难)、阿尔及利亚(仍然与摩洛哥在撒哈拉沙漠的南部发生的第三世界遗产冲突),海湾国家一直承担着支持阿拉法特、阿富汗圣战者和随处可见的伊斯兰倾向所造成的后果。即使尼日利亚、委内瑞拉和其他国家想证明,没有一项伟大的事业,石油可能造成灾难,但挪威的一个优势是不想赞助"伟大的事业"。

值得注意的是,在国际关系中,石油输出国对于石油投入的关注甚少。虽然欧佩克成员国会面讨论石油生产和石油价格问题,但另一方面,用于形成完整的、系统的石油外交政策的资源不足。2000年以来,阿拉伯海湾主要产油国的外交趋于多元化,尤其致力于与最重要的客户进行对话,并向他们保证石油供应的可靠性,特别是与海湾地区增长最快的石油市场——亚洲新兴经济体形成日益密切的联系。沙特阿拉伯还大大增加了关于石油事务的公共外交,如其在国际论坛上频繁地演讲。

▯ Key to Exercises

Ⅰ.

1. Iran was the first country in the Gulf to become an oil exporter, and kept the pride of first place until 1950. Due to the nationalization of Anglo – Iranian, all international oil companies boycotted Iranian oil; production collapsed to almost nothing in 1952 and 1953. And Iranian production reached a peak in 1974, and declined precipitously after the revolution in 1979. It continued to decline after the onset of the Iran – Iraq War in 1980 but recovered after the war ended in 1988.

2. From a corporate point of view, major US and UK energy and engineering companies will benefit from great opportunities and leverage to access the

Iraq market.

3. In this respect, the French threat of UN veto against the US – led war has been linked to that fact the French oil company Total had the highest stake in Iraq.

4. Mostly, the diplomacy of the oil – producing countries has been busy pursuing objectivesis, be it the promotion of Islam or the fight against Israel, pan – Arabism, or some milder form of pan – Africanism, or sheer military expansionism.

5. Since 2000 the major Arab Gulf producers have considerably diversified their diplomatic initiative, notably engaging in dialogue with their most important clients to reassure them about the reliability of supplies. In particular, closer ties have been shaped with some of the emerging Asian economies, which are the most rapidly growing markets for Gulf oil.

Ⅱ. 1 ~ 5. BACDC   6 ~ 10. BABDC

Ⅲ. 1 ~ 5. CDCDD

Ⅳ.

1. 然而,石油不是竞争性的行业,中东在全球石油产量中占据的份额一直不大,远低于其在全球储备中所占的份额。

2. 同年,控制伊朗全部石油生产的盎格鲁—伊朗公司和伊朗国民政府总理穆罕默德摩萨台之间发生了争论。

3. 尽管以美国为首的势力仍一再否认他们侵略伊拉克,其目的是解放石油行业及确保其在中东的石油利益。

4. 开采伊拉克油田对俄罗斯和中国的公司也具有重大意义。

5. 值得注意的是,在国际关系中,石油输出国对于石油投入的关注甚少。

Ⅴ.

1. 1988 年 12 月 21 日,一架在美国注册的波音 747 飞机,泛美航空公司的 103 航班,从伦敦的希思罗机场起飞,在飞往纽约肯尼迪机场的途中,被隐藏在一件行李中的简易爆炸装置摧毁,爆炸发生在飞机的货舱。这次爆炸导致 259 名乘客和机上机组成员全部死亡,其中包括 189 名美国人以及 11 名苏格兰洛克比镇的居民。

2. 欧佩克(石油输出国组织)是一个国际政府组织,由阿尔及利亚、安哥拉、厄瓜多尔、伊朗、伊拉克、科威特、利比亚、尼日利亚、卡塔尔、沙特阿拉伯、阿拉伯联合酋长国和委内瑞拉这 12 个石油生产国组成。自 1965 年以来,欧佩克的总部一直设在维也纳,其成员国的石油部长定期会晤,被认为是世界上最有影响力的组织之一。

5.3 解决里海石油和石油管理问题的法律依据

导语

国际法院(ICJ)和联合国(UN)适当的援助,可以缓解里海地区的石油和石油管理方面的问题,使得里海的石油能够供应世界。在正常情况下,国际法院和国际海洋法法庭的仲裁将基于《联合国海洋法公约》缔结两个国家间的协议。《帝汶沟条约》和《帝汶海条约》使帝汶地区紧张的石油问题得以缓解,推动了相关国家和地区的经济发展。

课文

里海地区拥有大量的石油储备,适量出口可以帮助世界上的很多国家。妨碍石油出口的主要问题是里海的法律地位,以及有石油管道的国家和地区因石油和环保问题而导致的政治不稳定因素。阿塞拜疆、伊朗、哈萨克斯坦、俄罗斯和土库曼斯坦——与里海相邻的五个国家就水域划分有分歧,这是该地区动荡的一个原因。此外,当前和未来石油管道的周边水域也存在各种各样的问题。美国反恐战争已经对阿富汗地区造成了严重破坏,印度和巴基斯坦经常就克什米尔地区的边界问题纷争迭起,土耳其声称博斯普鲁斯海峡中的环境问题将会妨碍该地区已增加的石油出口。国际法院(ICJ)和联合国(UN)适当介入,能够缓解这些问题,让里海地区的石油能为世界所用。

石油和石油管理方面的问题已经提交国际法院,如喀麦隆和尼日利亚之间关于巴卡西半岛石油所有权的争端。国际法院的裁决倾向于喀麦隆,联合国考虑到国际法院不能解决的区域问题后做出了有助于执行法院的裁决。联合国裁决这宗案件所依据的法律条文是治理国际水道的《联合国海洋法公约》。国际法院关心的另一个石油管理问题是东帝汶和澳大利亚对帝汶沟大多数领土归属权的争端。尽管法院还没有介入,法院可能会调用《联合国海洋法公约》,将该地区大部分石油的归属权判给东帝汶。此外,这一裁决将会废除先前两国之间(印度尼西亚和澳大利亚)签署的条约:不再分别拥有争端中边界的归属权。这些案件的判例可应用到里海地区。然而,由于许多国家介入,里海地区的情况更为复杂,而国际法院的判决和联合国对执行这项判决的援助,将带来该地区急需的稳定。

1989 年,印度尼西亚和澳大利亚签署了《帝汶沟条约》,其中规定:澳大利亚和印度尼西亚将共同开发在东帝汶内的帝汶沟,以换取澳大利亚承认东帝汶作为印度尼西亚的一部分。帝汶沟位于东帝汶和澳大利亚之间,是印度洋的一部分。帝汶沟分为三个区域:一个由印度尼西亚和澳大利亚共同开发,一个主要由印度尼西亚开发,另一个主要由澳大利亚开发。1999年,东帝汶宣布从印度尼西亚独立出来,在联合国部队的帮助下(大部分来自澳大利亚),东帝汶才能抵抗住印度尼西亚的反对。东帝汶的独立得到国际的正式承认,东帝汶与澳大利亚协商《帝汶海条约》,这只是《帝汶沟条约》的修订版。根据《帝汶海条约》,以前为《帝汶沟条约》所划定的三个区域将保持不变,东帝汶将获得合作开发区域百分之九十的石油收益。名义上,该协议看起来倾向东帝汶;而实际上,该条约对东帝汶不太有利。这样的安排,与澳大利亚给予东帝汶的外援相比,东帝汶在石油收入方面对澳大利亚将作出更多让步。此外,东帝汶希望在这个石油丰富的边界地区按《联合国海洋法公约》来决议,这将使东帝汶在该地区占有较大的石油份额。尽管《帝汶海条约》有缺憾,新近独立的政府为了振兴经济,于 2002 年 5 月还是签署了这一条约。

正常情况下,国际法院和国际海洋法法庭的仲裁基于《联合国海洋法公约》缔结两个国家间的协议。

联合国秘书长科菲·安南设立了一个委员会,缔结双方的可行性协议。联合国任命特别代表乌尔德·阿卜杜拉主持委员会并监督协议,采取措施确保可行性协议能让当地政府和国家元首定期会晤,讨论边界问题和建立信心的措施。

该委员会将考虑相关两国之间的态度和他们在该地区的利益。这些情况都强调国际法院和联合国协调各派达成合作协议的重要性,尤其是关于石油方面的合作协议。国际法院可以客观地基于案情进行裁决案件;联合国根据地区的态度拟出细则贯彻这一裁决。这是划分里海地区石油最好的方法。

Key to Exercises

I.

1. Azerbaijan, Iran, Kazakhstan, Russia and Turkmenistan —the five countries border the Sea.

2. Similar issues over oil and oil management should be brought before the ICJ, an ICJ decision and UN help to tackle the issues.

3. In 1989, Indonesia and Australia signed the Timor Gap Treaty, which stipulated that Australia and Indonesia would jointly develop the oil fields within the Timor Gap in return for Australian recognition of East Timor as a part of Indonesia.

4. Despite these shortcomings of the Timor Sea Treaty, the newly independent government of East Timor signed the treaty in May 2002 in an effort to jump – start the young economy.

5. Based on the UNCLOS.

Ⅱ. 1 ~ 5. CDDDA 6 ~ 10. CCADB

Ⅲ. 1 ~ 5. BDCBA

Ⅳ.

1. 此外,当前和未来石油管道的周边水域也存在各种各样的问题。

2. 国际法院(ICJ)和联合国(UN)适当介入,能够缓解这些问题,让里海地区的石油能为世界所用。

3. 尽管法院还没有介入,法院可能会调用《联合国海洋法公约》,将该地区大部分石油的归属权判给东帝汶。

4. 然而,由于许多国家介入,里海地区的情况更为复杂,而国际法院的判决和联合国对执行这项判决的援助,将带来该地区急需的稳定。

5. 东帝汶的独立得到国际的正式承认,东帝汶与澳大利亚协商《帝汶海条约》,这只是《帝汶沟条约》的修订版。

Ⅴ.

1. 国际法院与联合国还没有介入这场争端,因为东帝汶尚未请求国际援助,相反,东帝汶正在等待澳大利亚批准该条约。然而,如果国际法院要介入,预计国际法院将会援用《国际海洋法公约》和规则支持东帝汶。这将解除印度尼西亚和澳大利亚签署的两国不再共享帝汶沟的《帝汶沟条约》,因为东帝汶已经宣布从印度尼西亚独立出来。

2. 另一项国际石油争端是延伸到非洲的几内亚湾的巴卡西半岛。这一地区位于尼日利亚和喀麦隆的边界,两国都声称具有这块石油丰富的土地的所有权,尽管事实上主要是尼日利亚人居住在此。

第6章 石油基金

6.1 石油基金

导语

石油出口国为利用庞大且不断增长的石油收入纷纷成立了石油基金。在基金运营过程中,大多数基金侧重稳定和储备目标;许多石油基金对资源的储备和撤出有相对严格的操作规则。对于刚性积累规则,一些国家石油基金资源使用的规定也被用于缓和它的影响。

课文

21世纪初,石油价格飞涨,使财富发生了历史性转变,从消费地区转移到主要石油出口国。近年来,许多石油出口国设立了石油基金,以利用其庞大且不断增长的石油收入。

石油基金的基本框架可以概括如下:

(1)石油基金首要的政策目标包括宏观经济稳定(鉴于石油收入的不稳定性和不可预测平滑政府支出);金融储蓄(代际公平);提高石油收入管理和财政政策管理的透明度。

(2)一般石油基金的经营目标是根据平滑石油收入的预算而制定的,将部分收入存入基金,并提供石油现金流和金融资产总额变化的信息。操作规则包括资源的积累和撤出的具体规则、资产管理原则和治理、透明度和问责制的规定。

近期出现了石油基金激增的现象。有21个产油国已设立石油基金,其中16个产油国的石油基金于1995年后创建。2005—2006年,2个基金被取消。10个基金侧重稳定,8个基金兼有稳定和储备目标。

新的石油基金主要侧重于稳定目标,而近期油价上升进而强调了储备目标,并在某些情况下,加强了资产管理。20世纪70年代初以来,石油价格实际降到了最低点,1999—2000年创建的几个基金包括把增加预算石油收入的稳定作为一个重要目标。然而,由于石油价格上涨,如今国家更专注于长期的储备目标。例如,俄罗斯现正考虑建立单独的储备基金。特立尼达和多巴哥已经起草了立法,建立储备和稳定基金。此外,近年来产油量大的一些国家(例如,阿塞拜疆、乍得、厄瓜多尔)建立了基金,有助于加强额外石油收入的管理。

从运营角度看,基金的表现集中在操作规则、一体化的预算、资产负债管理和透明度。

许多石油基金对资源的储备和撤出有相对严格的操作规则。

(1)许多石油稳定基金有储备和(或)退出规则;或有价格的储备和(或)退出规则;或有收入的储备和(或)退出规则(例如,阿尔及利亚、伊朗、利比亚、墨西哥、俄罗斯、特立尼达和多巴哥、委内瑞拉)。

(2)大多数储备基金是收入分成基金,预先确定部分或总石油收入存入基金中(例如,赤道几内亚的下一代基金、加蓬和科威特)。

(3)相比之下,只有少数是融资基金,基金的运作直接与非石油预算赤字相联系(挪威和东帝汶)。

创建有硬性规定的基金主要根据这样的期望,从预算中删除"高"的石油收入,将有助于缓和和(或)使支出更加稳定,并作为一种减少政策的自由裁量权的手段。然而,严格的操作规则可能不符合实际的财政政策(如果政府没有流动性约束)。适当的和财政上、政治上可持续的操作规则日趋复杂,是由确定石油价格变动的永久性和临时性成分的困难和政治经济因素所导致。此外,强调石油基金资产总值不应减少对评估政府整体财务状况的关注。

一些国家已经改变、绕过或消除刚性积累规则。在刚性规定的操作中,经常出现紧张局势,特别是重大外部变化的情况,政策重点的转移或增加开支的压力,或者更广泛的资产负债管理目标也能导致紧张局势的出现。20世纪80年代和90年代,在阿拉斯加、艾伯塔省、阿曼、巴布亚新几内亚和其他国家的资金操作规则发生了变化,在某些情况下还多次发生变化。一些国家针对近期国际油价的持续上涨已向上调整控制石油基金储备和取消石油基金的参考油价,或改变收入基数(例如,哈萨克斯坦、俄罗斯、特立尼达和多巴哥)。2002年,墨西哥立法授权减少石油基金。委内瑞拉自其稳定基金创建以来,已经几次改变了其操作规则,且长时间暂停运作。加蓬尚未完全遵守规定,未将石油收入的一部分存入下一代基金。乍得、厄瓜多尔、巴布亚新几内亚发现它们在基金操作上或政治上不可行,就取消了石油基金。

石油基金资源使用的规定也用于缓和刚性积累规则的影响。在一些国家,规则允许从石油基金到预算的全权转让(例如,巴林和利比亚)。在阿尔及利亚,石油基金的储备和撤出规则基于保守的参考油价进行,即每桶19美元,当局与此同时发行债务为预算进行融资,这为当时的石油基金负责(债务支付的高利率和体现政府成本的石油基金资产的回报二者之间的差价）。

一些石油基金的资源是专款专用的。一些专款专用的规定出于政治经济方面的考虑,例如,创建支持石油基金的选区（如阿拉斯加）,使得更容易抵制因使用石油收入不当随之而来的政治压力,或为特定目的优先考虑使用资源,像扶贫或债务服务（例如,阿塞拜疆、乍得和厄瓜多尔）。专款专用,原则上,有助于限制政府重新分配开支不当的自由裁量权。然而,它造成资源置于分配预算过程外,并且减少了灵活性,使流动性管理复杂化,影响政府支出的效率。没有流动性的约束,石油基金专款专用的影响也是不确定的,因为资源是可替代的。

Key to Exercises

I.

1. In recent years many of these exporters have set up oil funds to utilize their massive and growing oil revenues.

2. There is a period of the lowest oil price levels in real terms since the early 1970s.

3. Financing funds are linked directly to the budget's non – oil deficit, such as Norway and Timor – Leste.

4. The introduction of funds with rigid rules has been mostly based on the expectation that removing "high" oil revenues from the budget would help moderate and/or make expenditures more stable, and as a means of reducing policy discretion.

5. Mexico's legislature authorized the depletion of the oil fund in 2002.

II. 1 ~ 5. CDBDC   6 ~ 10. DBCDC

III. 1 ~ 5. ADDBA

IV.

1. 21 世纪初石油价格飞涨,使财富发生了历史性转变,从消费地区转移到主要石油出口国。

2. 从运营角度看,基金的表现集中在操作规则、一体化的预算、资产负债管理和透明度。

3. 委内瑞拉自其稳定基金创建以来,已经几次改变了其操作规则,且长时间暂停运作。

4. 加蓬尚未完全遵守规定,未将石油收入的一部分存入下一代基金。

5. 石油基金资源使用的规定也用于缓和刚性积累规则的影响。

V.

1. 为了加强整合资产和负债管理的财政政策的协调并提高公共开支的效率,从而将石油基金与预算有机地结合,通过确保基金作为政府的账户,而不是一个独立的机构运作得到了最好的实现。

2. 只要石油基金与政府其他金融业务很好地融合,就可以在资产管理中发挥有益的作用。管理石油基金的资源,应考虑到主要风险,中、长期地支持政府的整体资产负债管理的策略。这需要清晰、全面、透明的投资和风险管理框架的发展。宏观经济的稳定、竞争力和流动性,说明海外石油基金资源的可取性。

6.2　石油基金的预算系统整合与资产管理

🔲 导语

石油基金的评估通常基于国家案例的定性分析,从基金运作的角度来看,基金的表现具体体现在预算系统整合、资产管理和其他方面。

🔲 课文

预算系统的整合

石油基金的操作可以根据其如何帮助(或抑制)满足基本目的预算制度进行评估。除了专款专用和透明度,石油基金的经验指向几个关键问题:

(1)预算外支出的权力。这可能会导致决策分裂、控制支出下降和资源配置效率降低。大约有一半的石油基金有权在国内消费或者投资预算系统外的资产。例如,在阿塞拜疆和哈萨克斯坦,根据总统的指示,石油基金可进行预算外的支出。利比亚石油基金也为大量的预算外支出融资。在伊朗和科威特,石油基金可投资或借给预算过程外的国内私营经济体。

(2)创建"卓越岛屿"。当公共财政管理系统被看成是脆弱的,在许多发展中国家,有时认为建立一个有单独程序和单独控制的基金所带来的收益比预算更好。然而,几乎没有确切的证据支持创建这样的"卓越岛屿"。此外,也必须考虑到这种做法对一个国家公共财政管理体制的发展所造成的潜在的负面影响。

(3)现金管理。一些国家已经经历了与刚性石油基金规则和现金管理分散相关的资产负债困难。鉴于对机构能力和治理与善加利用石油资源目标的关注,乍得设立了独立的现金管理系统,支持多个预算和石油基金的复杂安排,并设立了专项财政收入。该国的主要经营预算支出的压力,导致拖欠和借贷成本高,而石油基金则累积了低收益资产。2006 年年初,政府废除了石油基金来缓解对其经营预算的流动性约束。1999—2000 年,委内瑞拉依然是预算赤字,政府只会把存款放入对高昂的融资有追索权的石油基金(由法律规定)。2000 年年末,该石油基金的运作暂时中止。厄瓜多尔尽管持有大笔存款,但大量的专项石油收入(包括石油基金)和现金分散导致国内欠款积聚。

融资基金与预算过程相结合。这些基金使财政政策和金融资产积累明确地联系起来,提出可替代性问题。它们不会企图通过动用预算中的一些资源来"惩戒"支出——基金的流入与流出取决于石油收入和体现非石油财政的立场决策。基金的创建与要求提高透明度、促进公众的跨时约束意识是分不开的。

(1)石油基金首要的政策目标包括宏观经济稳定(鉴于石油收入的不稳定性和不可预测平滑政府支出);金融储蓄(代际公平);提高石油收入管理和财政政策管理的透明度。

(2)挪威的石油基金形式上是在中央银行的政府存款账户上,从石油活动中和将非石油赤字的融资纳入预算中获得中央政府净收入。该石油基金无权支出,支出的决策和财政政策的立场都在预算过程中规定。此外,基金的支配有着严格的透明度和问责制的规定。

(3)东帝汶的石油基金按照挪威基金设计。东帝汶的石油基金全部纳入中央政府的预算,具有较高标准的透明度和问责制监管。

很多国家已经或正努力更好地整合他们的石油基金与预算系统。这反映了财政控制中的潜在损失意识日益增强和公众支出效率意识日益增强,如关于统一的支出政策、以同样的预算标准批准和执行支出,以及加强资产/负债管理的效率的公共支出效率。例如,自 2005 年以来,阿塞拜疆报道提交国会的石油基金运作年度预算报告(虽然议会不会批准石油基金的预算)。利比亚政府已经表示有意消除利用石油基金为预算外开支融资的做法。为了更好地与预算结合,哈萨克斯坦石油基金的规则最近被修订。艾伯塔根据石油基金不尽如人意的表现,停止最初的储备基金预算外运作。阿尔及利亚当局正努力实施石油资金规则,增加与预算的结合和将现有石油基金转换成融资基金。

资产管理

近年来,石油基金的财政平衡大幅度扩大。对一些国家(例如,阿塞拜疆、乍得和伊朗)进行观察后发现,基金积累原则的刚性规定一定程度上造成了储蓄和债务共存;一些国家极力地减少债务(例如,阿尔及利亚、科威特、利比亚和俄罗斯);一些国家显然试图避免因更快地偿还国内债务而对国内流动性造成的影响(例如,挪威),或试图发行债务来发展国内债券市场。

调查的石油基金中只有少数有清晰的、广泛的、透明的投资策略。特别是:

(1)为了缓和本国货币升值造成的恐慌,建立石油基金的国家普遍倾向把基金资产转向国外。在某些情况下,一些国家的政府把他们在中央银行的存款(例如,几乎所有的非洲和西半球国家、阿尔及利亚、哈萨克斯坦和俄罗斯),作为政府的投资。科威特和阿曼的基金有一些国内的投资,而伊朗允许将多达外汇贷款金额的50%的石油资金投入到国内私营部门。

(2)石油基金持有资产回报率不同,但一般较低。这十年中最初几年比较活跃的基金平均实际回报率低于2%(例如,阿拉斯加、艾伯塔省和阿塞拜疆)。这部分是因为这十年初国际资本市场回报率的急剧下滑。中非经济与货币共同体国家,包括那些有石油基金的国家,都关注他们在区域中央银行中非国家银行的存款报酬。少数国家,尽管政府仍然可以间接从中央银行股利发放中取得收入,但中央银行石油基金却无利息。

🔲 Key to Exercises

Ⅰ.

1. The critical issues concerning oil funds include extra – budgetary spending authority, creation of "islands of excellence" and cash management, in addition to earmarking and transparency.

2. The abolishment of the oil fund aimed at easing liquidity constraints on its operating budget.

3. It is characterized by its design along the lines of Norway's fund, the integration into the central government budget and management with a high standard of transparency and accountability.

4. It is mainly to allay fears about appreciation of the domestic currency.

5. Average real returns were below 2 percent in relatively active funds.

Ⅱ.1~5. ACBDD　6~10. CDDBB

Ⅲ.1~5. BBCDA

Ⅳ.

1. 石油基金的操作可以根据其如何帮助(或抑制)满足基本目的预算制

度进行评估。

2. 此外,也必须考虑到这种做法对一个国家公共财政管理体制的发展所造成的潜在的负面影响。

3. 一些国家已经经历了与刚性石油基金规则和现金管理分散相关的资产负债困难。

4. 2006 年年初,政府废除了石油基金来缓解对其经营预算的流动性约束。

5. 艾伯塔根据石油基金不尽如人意的表现,停止最初的储备基金预算外运作。

V.

1. 主权财富基金资产的绝对规模——就连其中规模最小的东帝汶石油基金的资产总量也在 10 亿美元以上,和它们的增长速度——而东帝汶基金的成立时间只有 3 年——意味着那些负责管理主权基金的机构不得不寻找外部帮助。

2. 石油生产国的石油基金的透明度和问责制的做法大不相同。石油基金的监督采用几种不同的形式,特别是关于遵守规定:政府和国家石油公司规定的存款和退出规则、基金账目的审计、投资决策遵照商定的框架与否,以及披露信息的标准。披露石油基金的资产和投资的方式往往反映出公共部门透明度的一贯倾向。

6.3　挪威石油基金

导语

挪威政府全球养老基金是世界上规模最大、增长最快的主权财富基金之一,作为其他主权财富基金的范例,有许多堪称典范的特征,在许多方面都被认为是国际标准的典范做法。挪威政府全球养老基金有助于为主权财富基金设计一套成功的自愿原则,既有助于主权财富基金所在的国家,以加强其国内政策框架和机构,并促进他们的宏观经济利益和金融利益,又有助于缓解接受主权财富基金投资的国家的担忧和促进一个开放的国际货币金融体系。

课文

最近更名为"政府全球养老基金"的挪威石油基金,往往被视为模范的主权财富基金(SWF)。

　　它独特地将基金定位为新的一套自愿性原则的模式和潜在的重要出资方,专为主权财富基金而制定。

　　由于主权财富基金在全球金融市场的不断增长,为此受到越来越严格的审查。他们的总资产目前估计约为 3 万亿美元。专家预计,他们的资产将迅速增加,在未来 5 ~ 10 年将达 10 万亿美元以上。

　　主权财富基金日益增长的重要性和积极的投资策略预计将影响国际金融市场的结构和资产定价。一方面,他们的长期规划、无资产负债比率和对即将撤出的资金不索赔的情况,可以帮助稳定国际金融市场,提高市场的流动性和抑制资产价格的波动。

　　另一方面,其庞大的规模、快速的增幅、投资策略突然改变的可能性,再加上在某些情况下,围绕着其投资的目的还存在缺乏透明度和不确定性的问题,都可能会增加市场的不确定性,从而加剧动荡。

自愿行为准则

　　鉴于对主权财富基金的关注,国际货币基金组织被赋予一个新的任务:促进这些基金的一套自愿原则的发展。这套原则包括公共治理、透明度和问责制等问题。为此,在 2008 年 4 月底,成立一个主权财富基金国际工作小组开始按照这套原则进行工作。

　　这套新原则应有助于主权财富基金所在的国家来强化国内政策框架和机构,并促进他们的宏观经济利益和金融利益。这套新原则,也将有助于缓解接受主权财富基金投资的国家的担忧和促进一个开放的国际货币金融体系。

挪威的经验

　　挪威政府全球养老基金(GPF)有许多堪称典范的特征,可作为其他主权财富基金的范例。GPF 是世界上规模最大、增长最快的主权财富基金之一,2007 年年底,资产总额为 3730 亿美元,将近挪威国内生产总值的 100%。但除了规模,挪威 GPF 主要以其特征而闻名,在许多方面被视为国际标准的典范做法:

　　(1)GPF 的明确目标是支持政府储蓄,促进资源的代际转移。该基金有利于政府对石油收入的长期管理。鉴于挪威预期的人口老龄化问题,它用于公共养老金支出的前期投资。

　　(2)GPF 作为财政政策工具,加上财政方针,旨在限制政府开支。基金的资本来自石油活动的收入。基金开支是为非石油财政赤字融资的财政预算的转移。2001 年推出财政方针,呼吁对非石油的结构性中央财政赤字进行限制,约为 GPF 资产的 4%。因为 4% 是预计的长期实质回报率,这样相当于保存基金的本金只支出它的收益(类似于养老基金)。

(3)基金充分纳入财政预算。该基金的净分配作为综合预算编制过程的一部分,这个过程使财政预算和国家石油收入使用的实际盈余透明化。

(4)它奉行高度透明的投资策略。财政部——基金的所有者——定期报告管理框架、该基金的目标、投资策略和业绩以及道德准则。中央银行——基金业务经理——发布基金管理的季度和年度报告,包括所有投资绩效和年度清单。公布股东大会上基金表决的详细信息。

(5)资产专门投资于国外。这一战略,确保风险分散和良好的经济效益。此外,它有助于防止非石油经济受到石油工业的冲击,如它可以对汇率施压(所谓的"荷兰病"效应)。GPF 在全球超过 7000 多家公司持有少量股份(2007 年年底,平均拥有的股份为 0.6%,最多时达 5%)。

(6)它的高回报、中等风险的投资策略一直以来很成功。目前,该基金正在调整其投资组合,适应新的战略基准,将其资金 60% 投资于股票,40%投资于固定收益类产品。GPF 有计划地逐步进入房地产,提高风险收益权衡。在过去十年中投资策略正常的年均收益是 4.3%。

(7)其资产管理受一套道德准则的制约。这些准则,由财政部基于联合国和经济合作与发展组织制定的国际公认的原则设立。利用这两个政策工具,提高基金的道德承诺。首先,当与基金的经济利益一致时,鉴于强化良好的、负责的行为,尊重人权和环境,该基金在投资的企业行使所有权。再者,财政部决定回避个别公司的基金投资,这种投资行为造成了无法接受的风险,使基金成为极不道德活动的同谋。

挪威的作用

挪威 GPF 提出的一些要素有助于为主权财富基金设计一套成功的自愿原则。挪威基金的财政政策工具的作用可长期地引导那些拥有不可再生资源的国家以可持续的方式管理他们的政策。

高度透明的、有竞争力的和成功的 GPF 资产管理策略——市场采购价格下降到调整投资组合——可以作为一个开放战略的范例,不仅能产生金融效益,而且能提高市场流动性和财政资源的分配;并且是稳定影响的行为。其道德准则的经验,进一步证明,致力于共同利益不一定与高回报相对立。

鉴于他们管理 GPF 的经验,挪威当局已公开支持国际货币基金组织对主权财富基金的工作,并坚决给予外国投资者与本国投资者相同的待遇。他们认为主权财富基金的投资活动,和其他投资者的活动一样不必受限,尤其是,与对冲基金相比,主权财富基金破坏市场尚未被证明。挪威也警告,限制主权财富基金与石油相关的投资可能会减少石油开采,这可能会对石油市场造成不稳定的影响。

Key to Exercises

Ⅰ.

1. SWFs have been receiving increased scrutiny due to their growing presence in global financial markets.

2. On the one hand, their long horizons, lack of leverage, and absence of claims for imminent withdrawal of funds could help stabilize international financial markets by enhancing market liquidity and dampening asset price volatility. On the other hand, their sheer size, rapid growth, and potential to abruptly change investment strategies, coupled with—in some cases—a lack of transparency and uncertainty surrounding the purpose of their investments, could exacerbate market uncertainty and thus increase volatility.

3. It largely works on the set of principles.

4. Currently, the fund is adjusting its portfolio to its new strategic benchmark of 60 percent of assets in equities and 40 percent in fixed income.

5. The fund's role as a fiscal policy tool could guide those countries with nonrenewable resources in managing their policies in a sustainable way over the long run.

Ⅱ. 1~5. ACBDC 6~10. CAADB

Ⅲ. 1~5. DCBBA

Ⅳ.

1. 主权财富基金日益增长的重要性和积极的投资策略预计将影响国际金融市场的结构和资产定价。

2. 但除了规模,挪威 GPF 主要以其特征而闻名,在许多方面被视为国际标准的典范做法。

3. GPF 作为财政政策工具,加上财政方针,旨在限制政府开支。

4. 基金开支为财政预算向非石油财政赤字提供资金的转移。

5. 其道德准则的经验,进一步证明,致力于共同利益不一定与高回报相对立。

Ⅴ.

1. 政府养老基金成立于2006年,由两部分组成:"政府全球养老金",这是一个石油基金的延续;"政府挪威养老金",以前作为国家保险计划基金。

政府全球养老金的收入,包括来自石油活动的政府的总收入,以及基金的投资回报。财政部负责基金的管理。政府全球养老金的运营管理委托给挪威银行,政府挪威养老金的运营管理委托给国家保险计划基金,管理按照财政部规定的法规进行。

2. 近几年来,随着新兴经济体主权基金的迅猛发展,西方国家试图通过行政和立法等手段对其进行干预,使主权基金的投资活动遭遇金融保护主义壁垒,形成主权财富基金在投资活动中面临的某些困境,导致主权基金的一些投资活动不能顺利进行,甚至无法进行。

第7章　石油运输

7.1　中亚的石油运输问题

🔲 导语

　　俄罗斯的地理环境使它控制着中亚国家的碳氢化合物出口市场,为了可观的经济效益,铺设油气管道和利用海上终端站出口油气,俄罗斯都进行大量投资。对高度依赖石油出口收入的中亚国家而言,通过加大与中国、伊朗等国家的能源合作,加大对自身能源的话语权,有利于实现经济增长及可持续发展。

🔲 课文

　　俄罗斯的地理环境使它控制着中亚国家的碳氢化合物出口市场。另外,它在输油基础设施方面强有力的主导地位(与其他里海国家比较),包括绕过车臣修造的年输油量5百万吨的管道,以及里海管道财团的管道和阿特劳—萨马拉管道。在马哈奇卡拉市的石油转运点既能进行石油出口,又可让伏尔加格勒、萨马拉、萨拉托夫炼油厂的油进入国内市场。此外,伏尔加格勒是欧洲最大的内陆航运公司尤科斯的"沃尔戈坦克"所在地,尤科斯承运着里海北部地区初步发展过程中所有生产的石油。

　　由于石油管道拟议规划的不同,迄今只有里海管道财团(CPC)已到位。其管道长1580千米,初始运力为每年2800多万吨石油,更重要的是,达到其每年最大吞吐量6700万吨(当中,哈萨克斯坦的石油产量为4500万吨),只需要增加泵站容量。预计项目分四个阶段实施,连接卡拉恰干纳克和中国石油的阿特劳管道正在施工,工程项目使石油供应近期将达700万吨,最终可达1100万吨。此外,俄罗斯正在扩大在卡拉恰干纳克进行中的其他项目合作,其中包括将输油量从1000万吨扩大到1500万吨的哈萨克斯坦阿特劳—萨马拉管道项目。今后,哈萨克斯坦将能够通过俄罗斯新建的波罗的海管道网络向芬兰湾出口原油(500万吨)。

　　中国领导层认为,现在的首要任务是开发新疆矿藏和建立从新疆到上海的输送管道。由于中国国内油气基础设施发展迫切需要投资数十亿美元,中国将难以在可预见的未来为哈萨克斯坦北部—中国项目提供资金。

目前,中国和俄罗斯加紧谈判从西伯利亚到中国的油气管道建设。当前工程项目分为:从西伯利亚东部到北京的管道建造;就更远地到达东部沿海地区的管道问题正在达成共识。俄罗斯尤科斯和中国石化已经签署了一项关于石油和石油产品供应到中国的协议:首先通过火车(出口不超过每年3~4百万吨),今后通过安加尔斯克—中国管道(2000万吨,将来3000万吨)。这条管线不会很长,因此,比哈萨克斯坦管道费用要便宜得多。这项工程,一旦与其他两个中俄项目(起始于Kovyktinsky天然气冷凝物沉积区的天然气管道和伊尔库茨克州的电力传输线)同时进行,将大大地降低施工成本,预计输油管道最快会在2005年开始运行。特别是由于尤科斯能使用它自己的和外部资金资助项目设计和实施(除尤科斯外,卢克石油和俄罗斯石油公司也保证了供应)。

每年能够输送石油5000万吨的哈萨克斯坦—土库曼斯坦—阿富汗—巴基斯坦管道项目和阿拉伯海的通道直到阿富汗的局势完全稳定才能启动,这种情况近期难以预测,种种迹象表明应在不远的将来。对中亚各国而言,阿富汗—巴基斯坦管道是很重要的,尤其在政治方面,因为它可能会消除来自南方(印度)的威胁。此外,即使阿富汗局势正常化(或者更准确地说,如果授予成立的中央政府除喀布尔以外的既得却有限权力,也就是说,如果这个国家恢复到了前塔利班的政治局势,执政党精英间的种族分散和内部冲突突出)项目的成功也始终让人质疑,因为启动里海管道财团已降低了替代管道线路的需求,许多指向伊朗的因素都被视为更有利的路线。

哈萨克斯坦—土库曼斯坦—伊朗管道路线的经济效益很客观。管道年输油量1500万~2500万吨,工程成本估计在15亿美元到20亿美元之间,除此之外,抵达波斯湾的哈萨克斯坦石油装运码头是最短的路线(全长1650千米,有200千米穿过哈萨克斯坦)。从田吉兹和乌津出发跨土库曼斯坦与伊朗的石油供应工程相当合理,分两个或三个阶段进行。第一阶段:油轮将油从阿克套运到伊朗的里海港口,供应伊朗北部的炼油厂,进而在波斯湾港口进行交易。设在德黑兰、大布里士、伊斯法罕、阿拉克总的四个伊朗炼油厂日产油810000桶,年产量多达5000万吨。若要实施这一项目,它仅需要投资3.6亿美元到伊朗的基础设施。乌津—德黑兰管道建完后,石油可以输送到伊朗首都,供地方炼油厂使用,然而反过来,哈萨克斯坦,将收到相同的交易基础上的波斯湾的伊朗石油。这个项目主要技术和组织方面的问题涉及为获取哈萨克斯坦石油伊朗炼油厂的技术调整;还涉及恢复从波斯湾地区北部经过伊朗抵达哈萨克斯坦炼油厂的石油管道运输。

Key to Exercises

Ⅰ.

1. Because it is capable of shipping all oil produced during the initial development of the northern Caspian region.

2. For all the diversity of projects being proposed.

3. First by rail train (exports not exceeding 3 – 4 million tons per year) and in future via the Angarsk – China pipeline (20 million tons followed by 30 million tons in future).

4. Primarily in political terms as it might eliminate a threat from the south.

5. By ethnic decentralization and intestine strife among the ruling elites.

Ⅱ. 1 ~ 5. BACDB　6 ~ 10. ADBAC

Ⅲ. 1 ~ 5. CCADD

Ⅳ.

1. 此外,伏尔加格勒是欧洲最大的内陆航运公司尤科斯的"沃尔戈坦克"所在地,尤科斯承运着里海北部地区初步发展过程中所有生产的石油。

2. 今后,哈萨克斯坦将能够通过俄罗斯新建的波罗的海管道网络向芬兰湾出口原油(500 万吨)。

3. 当前工程项目分为:从西伯利亚东部到北京的管道建造;就更远地到达东部沿海地区的管道问题正在达成共识。

4. 油轮将油从阿克套运到伊朗的里海港口,供应伊朗北部的炼油厂,进而在波斯湾港口进行交易。

5. 乌津—德黑兰管道建完后,石油可以输送到伊朗首都供地方炼油厂使用。

Ⅴ.

1. 哈萨克斯坦北部—中国管线将里海的石油输送到中国和亚太地区。应该指出,虽然如此,启动哈萨克斯坦北部—中国的管道工程项目对中国而言中期前景不容乐观。除非石油价格较高,不然该项目是行不通的;除非管道年输送约 4000 万吨,否则巨额资本投资的 3000 千米管道的追偿(至少 30 亿美元)也不可能。目前所有哈萨克斯坦对该项目的投资仅占该项目所需资金的 1/3。哈萨克斯坦大量增加在其西部和中部地区的石油产量,才能达到预计的容量。一旦被探测出含有大量的石油储备,减少量可由里海大陆架沉积的矿藏来补偿,可那还是很遥远的事。

2. 中国面临迫切需要投资数十亿美元来发展其国内的油气基础设施,

因此,中国在可预见的未来仍然很难资助北哈萨克斯坦—中国这一项目。

7.2 里海的石油管道

导语

随着里海地缘经济地位陡升,里海地区石油和石油管理方面的问题,与里海以及世界部分国家和地区有着千丝万缕的联系。能产生巨大经济利益的里海地区的石油管道既对里海地区经济形势以及世界经济形势、各国和里海国家能源合作产生了一定影响,也与政治、文化、种族冲突等问题不可避免地交织在一起。

课文

为了将石油投放到市场,必须修建管道。根据选择的路线,单个管道的成本大约为 1.2 亿美元到 33 亿美元不等,为了不轻易受政治压力或破坏活动的影响,里海国家会建造多个石油管道以确保石油的流量。管道经过的国家通过控制石油的输送收取石油过境费和施加政治影响而获利。

路途最短和最经济实惠的管线是从阿塞拜疆的巴库穿过格鲁吉亚到黑海格鲁吉亚的港口苏普萨,巴库—苏普萨管线早在 1999 年年初竣工,输送里海的石油。格鲁吉亚本身也是冲突不断,与北部分裂的阿布哈兹起争端以及政治上的问题导致格鲁吉亚总统谢瓦尔德纳泽险遭暗杀。俄罗斯在格鲁吉亚有支防止阿布哈兹和格鲁吉亚交战的维和部队,为此,它在格鲁吉亚有一定的影响力。美国谋求加强双边关系,表明格鲁吉亚猛增的战略重要性。例如,为推进参与北约和平伙伴关系防御合作计划的发展,美国于 1996 年援助格鲁吉亚 50 万美元。

备受青睐的石油管线是从巴库到土耳其地中海沿岸的杰伊汉。这是由阿塞拜疆、美国和土耳其支持的,满足了减少通过博斯普鲁斯海峡石油的土耳其目标及环境目标。然而,美国政府无法迫使商业公司去从事他们认为不赚钱的一些特殊活动。克林顿总统里海盆地能源外交的特别顾问理查德·莫宁斯塔说,通往杰伊汉的管道是可行的,康菲石油总裁在 3 月 3 日美国参议院外交关系委员会国际经济政策听证会响应中指出,可行和可观是有很大差别的。当土耳其保证将建设耗资 24 亿美元的管道,不是过去提到的 37 亿美元时,阿塞拜疆总统海达尔·阿利耶夫希望该石油管道于 1999 年开始动工。管道建设预计始于 2001 年,2007 年或 2008 年竣工。但是,某些金融问题和安全问题仍在协商。1999 年,土耳其地震引起人们关注未来地震对管道所造成的潜在风险。

由于地形地势的原因,阿塞拜疆国际营运公司和相关的商业公司倾向于从巴库出发通过伊朗到达杰伊汉的路线。但这是不可能的,由于伊朗已经卷入恐怖主义,为此达马托立法宣布与伊朗有关的美国和其他公司的介入都属非法。当它意味着伊朗被挡在财团外时,这项法案符合美国石油公司的利益。到达杰伊汉的石油管道预计要经过北部的土耳其政府军和库尔德分离主义分子冲突的地区。有人提议,为了保证巴库—杰伊汉石油管道的安全,应允许土耳其人抓捕叛军库尔德工人党(PKK)领导人阿卜杜拉·奥贾兰,允许土耳其镇压库尔德工人党。

尽管美国批准了1997年12月建造从土库曼斯坦通过伊朗到达土耳其的石油管道,国务卿奥尔布莱特认为,此举只是帮助土库曼斯坦克服其财务困难。土库曼斯坦已经同意进行美国资助的从里海到阿塞拜疆的石油天然气管道建设项目的可行性研究。因为这样的管道路线让土库曼斯坦油气出口独立于俄罗斯和伊朗,所以备受美国青睐。美国禁令没有停止欧洲公司与伊朗的密切联系。例如,英国勘探者丰碑石油天然气有限公司就土库曼斯坦原油与伊朗有一个贸易协定,借此将里海原油生产转移到伊朗内卡进行以换取等量的海湾石油。

尽管巴库—杰伊汉管道是早在1998年11月美国能源部长比尔·理查森以前达成的协议,可问题依然存在。据估计,这个管道将每天至少输送100万桶石油是可行的,而阿塞拜疆国际营运公司的生产峰值在八年间日产多达80万桶,该财团也不确定其他产油区是否有足够的石油弥补差额。同样,如果俄罗斯天然气公司和意大利埃尼集团计划建造的黑海到萨姆松、土耳其和安卡拉的"蓝溪"天然气管道率先竣工,这可能会导致巴库—杰伊汉管道无利可图。从美国、土耳其和阿塞拜疆政府的角度看,杰伊汉管道的主要好处是它会阻止俄罗斯与伊朗能够影响阿塞拜疆石油开发或者阻止它们从阿塞拜疆石油开发中获益。壳牌和安然一直领导石油管道财团,但是壳牌有更多的金融资源,华盛顿能够提供安然比荷兰更多的政治支持而英国可以提供壳牌支持。

而邻国亚美尼亚本可以成为从阿塞拜疆到土耳其的管线,到目前为止,阿塞拜疆还是无法认可,因为就亚美尼亚占领了阿塞拜疆境内的纳戈尔诺—卡拉巴赫的亚美尼亚族的飞地事件,一直以来阿塞拜疆对亚美尼亚都有敌意。纳戈尔诺—卡拉巴赫的亚美尼亚基督教徒与阿塞拜疆周边领土的阿塞拜疆穆斯林发生的宗教和种族冲突,提供了一个至少排除一些经济因素的"文明冲突"的示例。

Key to Exercises

Ⅰ.

1. A single pipeline is estimated to be US $ 1.2 to US $ 3.3 billion according to the route chosen.

2. Russia has some leverage over Georgia because it has troops based in Georgia who act as peacekeepers between Abkhazia and Georgia.

3. To keep the Baku – Ceyhan pipeline prospect more secure.

4. Armenian occupation of the ethnic Armenian enclave of Nagorno – Karabakh in Azerbaijan.

5. They were the religious and ethnic conflicts.

Ⅱ. 1 ~ 5. CADDD   6 ~ 10. CBBAA

Ⅲ. 1 ~ 5. BCBCC

Ⅳ.

1. 俄罗斯在格鲁吉亚有防止阿布哈兹和格鲁吉亚交战的维和部队,为此,它在格鲁吉亚有一定的影响力。

2. 由于地形地势的原因,阿塞拜疆国际营运公司和相关的商业公司倾向于从巴库出发通过伊朗到达杰伊汉的路线。

3. 但这是不可能的,由于伊朗已经卷入恐怖主义,为此达马托立法宣布与伊朗有关的美国和其他公司的介入都属非法。

4. 土库曼斯坦已经同意进行美国资助的从里海到阿塞拜疆的石油天然气管道建设项目的可行性研究。

5. 尽管巴库—杰伊汉管道是早在1998年11月美国能源部长比尔·理查森以前达成的协议,可问题依然存在。

Ⅴ.

1. 在经济方面,其他条件都相同的情况下,管道沿线越长,对生产者而言越缺少吸引力,因为基于交付成本基数的能源竞争和过境费(基于距离)能有效降低生产者收取的井口费用。由于交通费用是各国政府收入的来源,政治和经济因素都介入了管道线路的选择。内置的预防措施可尽量减少环境影响,特别是里海海下和周边,这也增加了管道的成本。

2. 除了西方纯粹的经济和政治动机外,尤其是意识到可以从这个地区获得大量的石油,西方公司也迫切地想干预到里海地区的石油繁荣。世界上的许多石油储备都在不断枯竭,因此,西方国家知道,为了能以目前的速度继续发展和推动工业,开发里海的石油储备将至关重要。

7.3 美国的石油管道运输

导语

第二次世界大战中,由于德国中断美国的石油运输,为满足石油需求,于是出现了长距离、大口径的管道运输这种新型石油运输方式,将石油从生产区域输送到消费区域。管道运输不仅满足了石油需求,而且促使战后经济繁荣,改变了石油工业的发展态势。管道运输是美国石油分区间石油运输系统不可替代的核心。

课文

第二次世界大战爆发成了石油运输过程中的一个转折点。考虑历史、人口和经济因素,东海岸是美国最大的消费区域,但它依赖于油轮运输石油供应地方炼油厂,并从墨西哥湾沿岸运送成品油。因为第二次世界大战中美国的参战,德国潜艇开始击沉墨西哥湾、大西洋海岸和加勒比海的油轮,从而中断石油运输。企业和政府共同努力找到了可替代的石油运输方式:远距离、大口径的管道,取得了技术上的突破。远距离运输大量石油的新能力促使美国战后经济繁荣,并且改变了石油工业态势。

管道是美国石油运输系统中不可替代的核心,因此是满足石油需求的关键。没有石油管线,石油产品不会送达 50 个州数百万消费者手中。

管道输油周转量约占石油总周转量的三分之二。它们每年运输的石油超过 140 亿桶(超过 6000 亿加仑),因为不止一次大量地运输(如原油,又如成品油)。每年,这些管道输油量是美国实际石油消费量的 2 倍以上。

此外,石油管道的运输量超过全国范围内货运量的 17%,却低于全国货运成本 2%,美国有通往各国的最大的石油管道网络。例如,欧洲所有的石油管道网络仅有美国规模的 1/10。

石油市场决定管道流经区域

无论是全球还是各地区,石油市场的基础设施都是将石油从生产区域输送到消费区域。美国的跨区域流动情况如下:

(1)墨西哥湾沿岸(美国石油分区第三区)是美国原油供应量最大的区,占国家原油产量的 55% 和精炼产品输出的 47%。在美国所有石油分区中,作为区域贸易中最大的石油供应区,占原油总运输量的 90% 和成品油总运输量的 80%。虽然大多数成品油输送到东海岸,较少的输送到中西部地区,但该区大部分原油进入中西部的炼油厂。

（2）东海岸（美国石油分区第一区）几乎没有原油生产，提炼能力有限，对成品油的非原料需求却是区域中最高的。其炼油厂大量处理的是外国原油。为了满足区域需求，东海岸炼油厂既增加了从墨西哥湾沿岸输出的成品油，又增加了从国外的进口。东海岸接收了分区间60%以上的成品油和几乎所有进口到美国的成品油。

（3）中西部（美国石油分区第二区）有重大的区域性原油生产，并加工区域外的原油：直接通过管道进口加拿大和其他国家的原油，通过墨西哥湾沿岸进口并运到中西部地区；墨西哥湾沿岸地区本身也产原油。区域外的原油供应——进口和国产，占精炼投入的88%。区外的石油供应增加了本区炼油厂的成品油输出，这部分供应主要来自墨西哥湾沿岸。

（4）落基山脉地区（美国石油分区第四区）石油消费最低，但近年来，区域的石油消费增长较快。从加拿大进口原油来扩大本区炼油厂生产，但是其（管线）距离很长，山势陡峭，基础设施薄弱。因此，在美国国内，本区的区际贸易较少，这也是保持该地区供应和需求平衡的重要因素。

（5）西海岸（美国石油分区第五区）逻辑上独立于其他地区。其原油供应主要来自阿拉斯加北坡油田，现在占美国石油分区第五区生产量的55%，在20世纪80年代末的生产高峰时达65%。该地区石油生产的其余部分基本上来自加利福尼亚州。由于石油消费最大的加利福尼亚州独特的产品质量要求，加利福尼亚州基本上所有成品油的需求都通过本州炼油厂的输出来满足。

管道是地区间运输石油的关键模式。例如，2000年，管道几乎运输了美国石油分区所有的原油和约70%的石油产品。墨西哥湾沿岸的管道将国产与进口原油输送到中西部，成品油输送到中西部、东海岸，极少的成品油输送到落基山地区。对中西部地区和落基山炼油厂至关重要的，是管道输送的加拿大供应的原油。加拿大是美国第三大原油供应国，每日向这些地区供应大约1百万桶，分别占这两个地区原油供应的约25%和30%。

管道是石油分区间石油运输中无可替代的，从生产领域和沿海港口到炼油厂（原油和其他炼油厂原料），以及从炼油厂和大型再分配中心到规模较小的区域供应中心、机场，甚至直接到大型消费者（成品油）。在现实中，石油市场正在不断变化。

自从大口径、长距离管道出现后，几十年来它们也已成为美国石油市场中无数运输、计划、交易的关键部分。他们大容量、远距离的石油输送能力促使美国战后经济繁荣，人口和发展发生了重大变化。除从生产地区向消费地区运输大量的石油外，管道将较少量的石油从交易中心输送到偏远的消费地区，也起了关键性的作用。多年来的管道运行输送了大量独特的产品,携带着满足地区要求和季节要求、符合环境质量要求的产品。他们是绝大多数陆路运输唯一可行的和最便宜的运输方式。因此,管道是美国石油运输最为重要的运输方式并不奇怪。

Key to Exercises

I.

1. With the involvement of the U. S. in the War, German submarines began sinking tankers along the Gulf and Atlantic Coasts and in the Caribbean, thus disrupting the flow of oil.

2. Pipelines are the irreplaceable core of the U. S. petroleum transportation system and hence the key to meeting petroleum demand.

3. The Rocky Mountain Region (PADD 4).

4. Pipelines are the critical mode for moving oil between regions.

5. They have developed into a key part of the thousands of movements and schedules and transactions that make up the oil market in the United States. Their ability to move large volumes long distances fueled the post – War economic boom, and shaped U. S. demography and development. In addition to moving the large volumes from producing regions to consuming regions, pipelines fill a critical role in moving smaller quantities of oil from market hubs to more distant consuming areas.

II. 1 ~ 5. BDABA   6 ~ 10. AABCD

III. 1 ~ 5. BCADB

IV.

1. 管道是美国石油运输系统中不可替代的核心,因此是满足石油需求的关键。

2. 无论是全球还是各地区,石油市场的基础设施都是将石油从生产区域输送到消费区域。

3. 东海岸(美国石油分区第一区)几乎没有原油生产,提炼能力有限,对成品油的非原料需求却是区域中最高的。

4. 由于石油消费最大的加利福尼亚州独特的产品质量要求,加利福尼亚州基本所有成品油的需求都通过本州炼油厂的输出来满足。

5. 因此,管道是美国石油运输最为重要的运输方式并不奇怪。

V.

1. 物流枢纽让市场来工作,管道让枢纽来工作。到 2015 年,如果所有铁路扩张如期完成,中国应该能够解决物流瓶颈,至少在理论上可以解决。

2. 了解管道运输的重要性,必须了解物流枢纽的作用。物流枢纽作为区域供应的通道。他们的特点是许多管道的互连,往往还有其他运输方式,如油轮和驳船,有时是铁轨,通常是卡车,尤其是当地的交通——让供应从一个系统到另一个系统,跨越县、州和地区相连的一个又一个枢纽。这些枢纽还有一个特点是其巨大的存储容量。存储量和运输方式的选择增加了供应的机会并提高了供应的灵活性,它们是一个有效市场的两个要素。

References

[1] Bernard A Gelb. The Caspian Sea Region and Energy Resources[M]. New York: Novinka Books,2004

[2] Brendun Mcsherry. The Political Economy of Oil in Equatorial Guinea[J]. Africa Studies Quarterly,2006,8(3)

[3] Cesar J Alvarez, Stephanie Hanson. "Venezuela's Oil – Based Economy" Council on Foreign Relations, 2009

[4] Cheryl J Trench. How Pipelines Make the Oil Market Work – Their Networks, Operation and Regulation [Technical memorandums]. http://www. pipeline101. com/reports/Notes. pdf

[5] C J Laureshen, D Du Plessis, C M Xu and K H Chung. Asian – Pacific Markets – A New Strategy for Alberta Oil[R]. Canadian international oil conference, 2004 (17)

[6] Delia Velculescu. "Norway's Oil Fund Shows the Way for Wealth Funds" IMF Survey Magazine. http://www. imf. org/external/pubs/ft/survey/so/2008/pol070908a. htm

[7] Gawdat Bahgat. Oil Funds: Perils and Opportunities[J]. Middle Eastern Studies, 2009 , 45(2). http://www. tandfonline. com/doi/abs/10. 1080/00263200802697399#preview

[8] Gene Whitney, Carl E Behrens. Energy: Natural Gas: The Production and Use of Natural Gas, Natural Gas Imports and Exports, EPAct project Liquefied Natural Gas (LNG) Import Terminals and Infrastructure security. [M]. The Capitol Net Inc, 2010

[9] Giacomo Luciani. Oil and political economy in the international relations of the Middle East. http://www. princeton. edu/ ~ gluciani/pdfs/Chapter% 20in% 20Fawcett. pdf

[10] Gulmira Kurganbayeva. Energy Potential of Central Asian Countries:Oil – and Ges Complex. http://unpan1. un. org/intradoc/groups/public/documents/APCITY/UNPAN020529. pdf

[11] IMF Fiscal Affairs Department. The Role of Fiscal Institutions in Managing the Oil Revenue Boom. http://www. imf. org/external/np/pp/2007/eng/030507. pdf

[12] Jennifer Buonanno. Caspian Sea Oil Management. http://www. stanford. edu/class/e297a/Caspian% 20Sea% 20Oil% 20Management. pdf

[13] Mary Ann Tétreault. The Political Economy of Middle Eastern Oil[A]// Understanding the Contemporary Middle East. 3rd ed. Lynne Rienner Pulishers, 2008

[14] Pablo Bustelo. Oil China and Oil in the Asian Pacific Region: Rising Demand for Oil [J]. New England Journal of Public Policy, 1998,21(2)

[15] Paul D'Amato. U. S. Intervention in the Middle East: Blood for Oil[J]. International Socialist Review Issue 15, December 2000 – January 2001

[16] Quest Offshore Resources, Inc. United States Gulf of Mexico Oil and Natural Gas Industry Economic Impact Analysis The Economic Impacts of GOM Oil and Natural Gas Development on the U. S. Economy[Z]. American Petroleum Institute, 2011,06. http://www. api. org/policy – and – issues/policy – items/jobs/gulf – of – mexico – analysis

[17] Theo Thomas, Paulo A Medas, Rolando Ossowski, Mauricio Villafuerte. Managing the Oil Revenue Boom: The Role of Fiscal Institutions[M]. Washington DC: International Monetary Fund, 2008

[18] Tina Hunter. Legal Regulatory Framework for the Sustainable Extraction of Australian Offshore Petroleum Resources [D]. Dissertation for the degree philosophiae doctor (PhD) at the University of Bergen, 2010,08